SELF-STARVATION

COMMENTARY

"The author writes with enthusiasm and authority. Her style is personal, often anecdotal and sometimes long-winded, but the English translation is good and very readable...This is an important book and I recommend it warmly to those who wish to learn about anorexia nervosa and especially to gain insight into the psychodynamics of these patients, and their families."

Edward Stonehill

"This outstanding book expounds the message that therapy must focus on the emotional life of an entire family rather than on one member who has been labeled the patient. I strongly recommend it for all health care providers who will be treating this complex disorder and especially for those who provide family therapy."

Bette Gillman, M.S.W.

SELF-STARVATION

*From Individual to Family Therapy in
the Treatment of Anorexia Nervosa*

MARA SELVINI PALAZZOLI

Translated by Arnold Pomerans

NEW YORK • JASON ARONSON • LONDON

To my mother Italia Palazzoli

Psychiatric and Psychological Clinic Library, Milan
directed at the time of the original publication by
Gaetano Benedetti and Pier Francesco Galli

Contents

Preface to the American Edition

As one who in 1967 embarked upon the adventure of making the conceptual leap from a model based on energy to one based on information—and therefore on the feedback mechanism—I almost naturally view even my own book, four years after its original appearance in English, as an input (however modest) introduced into the total system, with the goal of drawing up a balance of the outputs (just in case there have been any!).

In the time since the London edition has been sold out, some very interesting feedbacks have reached me, both from anorexics themselves and from fellow professionals. The first group has reacted in an absolutely univocal manner: unlimited confirmation, as reflected in this passage from one of many letters: "a veteran anorexic myself...indeed, you have stripped me naked and exposed my every secret!" From many countries requests for obviously impossible family treatments have reached me. One family arriving from the other side of the world even went so far as to come to my office without an appointment!

The second group, that of my colleagues, expressed itself, verbally or by letters or reviews, in a radically antinomic manner. Some, enthusiastic about my intrapsychic considerations, deplored my subsequent desertion of that perspective; others congratulated me for exactly the opposite reason. These antinomic reactions express the crisis and conflict of models which at present characterize the entire field of the human sciences.

An interesting phenomenon has been noticed in Italy. In this country of mine, although the greatly revised London edition, with its new Part Four devoted to family therapy, has not been published in Italian (according to my wishes, as I was terrified at the prospect of an "assault" by an astronomical number of anorexic families), the response of the families is at present unanimous, in contrast to the silence of most of the academic world. One can only conclude that the layman, unhampered by any vested interests, is more open to the systemic model. I want to point out that this response comes not only from families of anorexics—who notoriously possess the greatest power to drive their families into treatment—but also from families presenting different types of identified patients. We have therefore been able to conduct research with other types of families as well (I use the plural since I continue to work in a team with my colleagues Boscolo, Cecchin, and Prata). An important area of our research involves families presenting psychotic children or adolescents (the first results of our work in this area are presented in our *Paradox and Counterparadox*, appearing in English translation this year for the first time— Jason Aronson, 1978).

We are convinced, after ten years of hard work, that we have only just begun what will be a very long but extremely promising task, one which will engage generations of researchers. As I emphasized in my preface to the British edition, changing our linear way of thinking in order to acquire a new epistemology, systemic and circular, is a tortuous process. Sometimes we fall prey to the illusion, rather widespread, of having achieved this, only to discover ourselves, with some dejection, confronted with failure. Detecting our error, we realize that the goal is still far away. It is our constant concern to maintain the most rigorous conceptual and methodological coherence. We dream of reaching the point where we can think and act in a systemic manner through the entire course of a therapy: in the first telephone contact with the family, in the exquisitely relational style of conducting the session, in organizing the discussion among ourselves in the team, and in the modalities and content of therapeutic interventions. And this, of necessity and paradoxically, through the use of language, which, linear in its essence, impels us to the very causal punctuations we are striving to transcend.

Some advances have been made. The number of families interrupting treatment has decreased: during the last two years, none have left treatment prematurely. When we are faced with failure, our increased capacity to detect therapeutic error is useful to us in saving the situation or, at the very least, in improving our knowledge. By the same token, we would not consider an inexplicable improvement a success. As to the anorexic patients who dropped their symptom in the family treatment of ten sessions, we now have years of follow-up. Not only have none of them relapsed: we have noted, as well, undoubtedly better results compared to those I had obtained with individual therapy. These patients had completely abandoned any sort of feeding worries, had realized a rich affective life, and were socially integrated, at times carrying on socially significant initiatives. This fact contradicts a widespread prejudice, namely, the unwarranted supposition that individual treatment effects more profound behavioral change. Additionally, the adoption of the systemic model represents real progress in that it provides persuasive answers to many puzzling questions, of which I mention here the two most common: (1) Why does the number of anorexic patients seem to be increasing in Western cultures? (2) Why don't all girls who go on slimming diets become anorexic?

A convincing answer is reached precisely through application of the systemic model to the entire cultural field in which the anorexic symptom develops: the culture of the "first world." The strange fashion whereby women are required to be slim just where there is plenty of food deserves deeper study. Here I shall only remark that quite often the slimming diet seems to begin, for the future anorexic patient, simply on account of the current fashion. She sometimes begins dieting with the approval of her parents. *But very soon her parents' reaction to her thinning informs her of the great power she has acquired through fasting.* And, of course, she secretly thinks: "I am the ruler now; nobody will succeed in making me change my behavior." In transactional contexts like those described in this book, escalation becomes unavoidable—just as unavoidable as the reinforcement of the reciprocal behavior: "The more you insist I should eat the less I will eat." Once imbued with the erroneous belief that she has gained power *over* the others (in actuality she is simply obeying *with* them the rules of the game), the identified patient is hardly ever willing to give up her symptom.

The widespread cultural cliche of the slender woman seems therefore to act as a trigger in the outbreak of crises in *certain* family systems. This explains why girls who put themselves on slimming diets, following the dictates of fashion, do not all become anorexic: for pathology to develop, there must be a peculiar dysfunctional organization of the family system. It follows that the therapeutic aim is change: change precisely of those organizational parameters which, governing in a repetitive way the relationships between members of the family, block their latent but everpresent potential for development

Milan, February 1978   MARA SELVINI PALAZZOLI

Preface

This monograph sums up experiences and reflections gathered during some twenty years' work on the fascinating problem of anorexia nervosa, a disease that should really be called 'mental anorexia' to avoid confusion with certain neuro-endocrinological syndromes. In fact, until only a few years ago this confusion was still so widespread that many patients whose emaciation was quite plainly based on psychological motives were still being treated for endocrinal insufficiency – an extremely rare condition associated with quite·a different type of alimentary and general behaviour. The result was a series of costly and futile laboratory tests and a waste of precious time that could have been spent much more fruitfully on psychotherapeutic treatment.

This book originally appeared in 1963, under the imprint of Feltrinelli of Milan. In this new edition some of the original chapters have been omitted, others have been changed, and new chapters have been added to bring the book up to date. The final section, devoted to family therapy, is the most recent of all, and describes some preliminary results of my work at the Milan Centre of Family Studies, where I have been working for the past three years with a team of family therapists – Luigi Boscolo MD, Gianfranco Cecchin MD and Giuliana Prata MD – to whom I am deeply indebted. That part of the book, as the reader will see, reflects a conceptual jump that is a radical departure from the approach used in the earlier parts – it expresses not so much a change in therapeutic method as a change in orientation. This transformation, though I welcomed it with enthusiasm, has meant a great deal of soul-searching; it is exceedingly difficult to abandon deep-rooted ideas. In particular the new orientation has forced me to discard the conceptual models of individual psychiatry and psychoanalysis on which I had previously relied, and to focus my attention on transpersonal interactions. To that end I have come to rely increasingly on the pragmatic theory of human communication, on cybernetic models and on general systems theory. The promising results have persuaded me to keep to this new road.

My sincere thanks are due to all those who have encouraged me, and quite particularly to Dr Paul Senft, whose friendly and warm interest in my work has made it possible to bring out this English edition.

Milan, August 1972   MARA SELVINI PALAZZOLI

PART ONE

1 *Historical Survey*

During the past decades few diseases have been studied and discussed at such length as anorexia nervosa, mostly by neuro-psychiatrists and endocrinologists. The results have been some-what obscure and confused; moreover, though many of the vast number of papers and books devoted to the subject are original, a much greater number is repetitive or full of 'rediscoveries' that betray a lack of familiarity with the earlier studies.

As a result there has been a revival of pathogenetic and nosographic controversies that has added nothing substantial to ninteenth-century observations. Moreover the term 'anorexia nervosa' has often been applied indiscriminately to other types of psychogenic inanition (chronic infantile anorexia and functional eating disorders of a neurotic or psychoneurotic type), with a consequent confusion and complication of the diagnostic and prognostic problems.

It might therefore prove helpful if I began with a brief historical review, in which we can distinguish four periods. The first saw the earliest attempts to identify the disease and produced a number of interesting case histories; the second was that of the identification of anorexia nervosa as a modern clinical entity with distinct morbid and pathogenic features; the third began after 1914 with the publication of Simmonds' work and ended in a spate of contributions confusing Simmonds' disease with anorexia nervosa; the fourth produced a host of psychoanalytic, phenomenological and existential attempts to reconstruct the psychogenesis of one or several cases of anorexia nervosa. These attempts were not so much concerned with nosographic and systematic problems as with the underlying psychological aspects of the disease.

First period
It is quite possible that cases of anorexia nervosa have been

known since time immemorial; in any case the history of medical psychology makes it clear that the disease was not uncommon in the Middle Ages (among witches, women possessed by devils, and pseudo-mystics). It also seems likely that inanition due to voluntary starvation was observed by ancient physicians, though Hippocrates, Galen and Celsius do not mention it explicitly in their writings. Two Italian authors, Accornero and Baraldi, have claimed that the earliest account of anorexia nervosa was given by Simone Porta, a sixteenth-century Genovese, but the more general view is that the first detailed description came from the pen of Richard Morton, a seventeenth-century English physician. In his *Phthisiologia, seu Exercitationes de Phthisis* (1689), Morton used the term 'nervous atrophy' to refer to a form of consumption that was not accompanied by fever or dyspnoea but went hand in hand with a loss of appetite and digestive difficulties. Morton not only gave two fairly detailed case histories but also described the chief characteristics of the disease – namely amenorrhoea, lack of appetite, constipation, extreme emaciation ('like a skeleton only clad with skin') and overactivity. Since Morton could not discover any pathological signs and symptoms other than hypothermia he concluded that the appetite of these patients must have been depressed 'in a singular manner'. He also mentioned their characteristic indifference to their condition or cure and assumed that 'nervous consumption' stemmed from 'sadness and anxious cares'. It is not clear, however, whether he attached any aetiological importance to the latter.

Morton was succeeded, after a very long interval, by Whitt, an eminent eighteenth-century English neurologist, who, in a treatise published in 1767, alluded to anorexia nervosa and attributed it to a disturbance of the gastric nerves, and by Naudeau, a modest French physician who published a lengthy description of a fatal case of anorexia nervosa in 1789.

Second period
During the second half of the nineteenth century anorexia nervosa emerged as a modern clinical entity, with a clearly defined symptomatology.

The first to describe it as such were Ernest Charles Lasègue, Professor of Clinical Medicine in the University of Paris, and William Withey Gull of London, one of the most famous clinical surgeons of his day. In April 1873 Lasègue published a definitive paper 'On hysterical anorexia', in which he argued that the term 'anorexia' ought to be replaced by 'inanition', which was the most characteristic feature of the disease though it was often absent during the earliest stages.

It is a fact [Lasègue observed] that while we use the term anorexia to describe a pathological state, our language lacks the word orexia (orexis = desire or yearning) to describe the normal state. As a result, we can only express the absence of, or changes in, a healthy appetite – a gap in our vocabulary that bears clear witness to our lack of knowledge.

According to Lasègue the cause of the disease was a peculiar mental state, an intellectual perversion, resulting from emotional disturbances which the patient either admitted or disguised. Lasègue claimed that the disease involved three phases. The first was said to be characterized by digestive difficulties, a reduction in food intake, and marked overactivity; the second phase was one of mental 'perversion' reinforced by family anxiety about the patient's condition and by the patient's own preoccupation with her environment, and emaciation. During the final or third phase, said to be characterized by extreme depression, loss of skin elasticity, abdominal retraction, pallor, amenorrhoea and constipation, overactivity made way for asthenia. This was the cachectic phase.

Lasègue's original description of that phase, though written a century ago, is still worth quoting in full:

After a few months, the patient finally arrives at a state that can rightly be called one of hysterical anorexia. The family is in a turmoil. Persuasion and threats only produce greater obstinacy. The patient's mental horizon and interests keep shrinking, and hypochondriacal ideas or delusions often intervene. The physician has lost his authority; medicaments have no effects, except for laxatives, which counteract the constipation. The patients claim that they have never felt better; they complain of nothing, do not realize that they are ill and have no wish to be cured. This description would, however, be incomplete without reference to their home life. Both the patient and her family form a tightly knit whole, and we obtain a false picture of the disease if we limit our observations to the patients alone.

Lasègue also showed the importance of the physician's attitude to his patients, thus heralding the advent of psycho-therapy. He has, however, been criticized for ignoring the role of isolation in therapy, and for paying insufficient attention to amenorrhoea, which he described as a late symptom when, in fact, it is usually present from the start of the illness. Moreover the term 'hysterical anorexia' has had to be dropped, because the same syndrome can also be observed in various mental conditions to which the term 'hysterical' does not apply.

Soon after a translation of Lasègue's paper was published in London, the same journal also carried the report of a communication submitted by William Gull to the London Clinical Society on 24 October 1874. In it Gull described 'a peculiar form of disease' which he proposed to call 'apepsia hysterica'; he considered it a malfunction of the gastric branches of the pneumo-gastric nerve, accompanied by a mental attitude reminiscent of hysteria. Subsequently, however, he decided to change the name to anorexia nervosa since there was no absence of pepsin and the disease was not confined to women, though women accounted for the vast majority of all known cases. In his original paper he had already stressed that the condition was due to psychopathological factors.

Gull also claimed that neuropathological processes could spread from the brain to the tissues and *vice versa*, and that morbid cerebral forms could give rise to a variety of disorders. He showed that emotional factors could well be responsible for a host of functional disorders, and the moral influence of the physician and the isolation of the patients from their families could play an important therapeutic role.

Gull's assertion that anorexia must be distinguished from hysteria was supported by several French authorities (Deniau, Sollier, Regis, Girou, Ballet and Charcot) all of whom centred their attention on the nosological problem. Writers in other countries followed suit soon afterwards.

In 1883 Huchard proposed to call the disease *anorexie mentale*, the name which has been retained in France. In particular Huchard and his pupil, Deniau, distinguished mental from gastric anorexia on the grounds that, while the latter, which is chiefly associated with digestive disorders and inade-quate intestinal absorption, may be attributed to hysteria, the former is a 'pure' psychiatric disease and poses mental rather than digestive problems. Sollier (1891) followed by Bouveret (1893) questioned the validity of this distinction. Sollier claimed that both types of anorexia were of mental origin, and that the only valid distinction was between a primary type of anorexia with no hysterical symptoms, and a secondary type associated with hysterical symptoms that often replace, or are replaced by, it.

Duvet and Janet then complicated the nosographic problem when they reported the presence of the same syndrome in 'psychoasthenic' subjects and stressed that this group must be differentiated from hysterical anorexics. Finally in 1909 André-Thomas argued convincingly that anorexia nervosa is not a simple disease, but a syndrome involving various abnormal states such as melancholia, paranoia, hypochondria, mania and neurosis. For all that the term 'anorexia nervosa' and its synonyms were generally reserved for neurotic as distinct from psychotic subjects.

Other attempts to classify anorexia nervosa were made by Gilles de la Tourette (1895) and by Déjérine and Gauckler (1911).

By the turn of the century it was thus widely agreed that anorexia nervosa was a mental illness. In particular most authorities believed that the patients' obstinate refusal to take food under all sorts of pretexts, and the resulting inanition, were the sole causes of the severe and often fatal organic sequelae of the disease. This was corroborated by the fact that cures could often be obtained by the mere isolation of the patients coupled to feeding by persuasive methods.

Third period

In 1914 Morris Simmonds, a Hamburg physician, described a fatal case of cachexia which, at autopsy, showed atrophy of the anterior lobe of the pituitary. Two years later Simmonds gave an anatomical as well as a clinical description of two further cases.

Simmonds' discovery misled physicians into attaching too much importance to the emaciation. As a result cases of anorexia nervosa were commonly mistaken for Simmonds' disease, and in about 1916 the term 'anorexia nervosa' was allowed to fall into disuse. Typical cases of adolescent anorexia nervosa were treated as cases of pituitary marasmus or of Simmonds' disease, and this confused state of affairs continued until the late 1930s.

It is an exceedingly odd fact that a condition so plainly due to deliberate fasting and 'bad faith' should ever have been mistaken for an endocrinological condition, on the false assumption that both ought to lead to a dramatic loss of weight. The confusion reached its climax in 1937 when E. Kylin described what he called 'emaciation of girls during late puberty' and attributed it to a dysfunction of the anterior pituitary lobe. Most of the fifty cases he observed were clearly cases of anorexia nervosa. The same is true of many other conditions mentioned at the time, for example of Bickel's simple pituitary emaciation, of von Bergmann's hypophysial emaciation, of Wahlburg's grave hypophysial asthenia, of Dogliotti's juvenile hypophysial asthenia and of May's and Lavani's cachexia of adolescence.

This muddle had crucial repercussions in the therapeutic field where pituitary grafts and injections of extracts (Kylin, Ehrhardt and Kittel, Curschmann, von Bergmann, and others) were widely prescribed as cures for what was, in fact, a purely psychological disorder. And though there was a mounting body of evidence to show that anorexia nervosa had no connection with Simmonds' disease, the success of a few pituitary grafts (or rather the suggestive powers of those prescribing this kind of treatment) persuaded doctors and patients alike that anorexia nervosa was, in fact, a glandular disease. Even those few who acknowledged the distinction between Simmonds' disease and anorexia nervosa, nevertheless saw fit to prescribe 'specifics' or pituitary transplants for patients whose emaciation was only too obviously due to mental causes.

I might add here that the reinstatement of the classical concept of anorexia nervosa during the past twenty years or so has largely been due to H. L. Sheehan who, following in the footsteps of E. Reye, dispelled the mistaken belief that the destruction of the pituitary must lead to cachexia. It was because of this mistaken view that many patients suffering from anorexia nervosa but having unimpaired glands had been diagnosed as cases of Simmonds' disease, while others without weight loss but whose pituitary glands had been destroyed by embolic or haemorrhagic processes had gone unrecognized.

Fourth period

We saw that early in its history anorexia nervosa was considered a mental disease. Gull and Lasègue clearly defined its psychic genesis and Morton, too, attributed it quite unequivocally to psychological factors. But though it was correctly identified, the patients' negative attitude prevented them from communicating their inner experiences to the physician, and obstructed all attempts to delve into their psychological motives, the more so as most of them showed a marked lack of introspective powers. Thus even cured patients, when pressed to state how they used to feel, could often do no better than repeat monotonously: 'I just couldn't eat, you know, but for the rest I felt perfectly well.'

This explains why psychogenetic research into anorexia nervosa, based on detailed case studies, began to take precedence over nosological investigations. And while some psychiatrists conducted these investigations for their inherent interest (phenomenological psychiatry, existential analysis), others, and especially those with a psychoanalytic approach, tackled them in the hope of combining the psychogenetic study of the disease with the discovery of an effective psychotherapeutic method.

The first attempt to think along these lines was made by the great Janet who, in his *Les obsessions et la psychasthénie* (1903), described a case of 'mental anorexia' – that of Nadia – with great acumen, and defined psychoasthenia as an obsessive form of disgust with one's body. He also suggested that mental anorexia reflected the patient's refusal to play a feminine sexual role. Freud, who did not make any special study of anorexia nervosa, took much the same view when he defined the disease as 'melancholia of the sexually immature'.

Important and fundamental studies of anorexia nervosa were also made by psychiatrists with a phenomenological orientation, including particularly Binswanger, Kuhn and Zutt. Binswanger's 'The case of Ellen West', though it has given rise to keen controversies (was Ellen a schizophrenic or was she a true anorexic?) remains a model of psychiatric research informed by phenomenological principles. R. Khun has examined the phenomenological categories of space and time in anorexics, thus throwing an interesting light on the lives of these patients. Zutt, in one of his extensive case studies, has argued that the primary or specific symptom of anorexia nervosa, namely the refusal to eat, constitutes not only a biological disturbance but also a serious lack of social adaptation.

In Italy, equivocal studies of Simmonds' disease have more recently made way for a much sounder, psychologically orientated, approach (Rossini, Basaglia, Canestrari, Cioffari and Ninni). In the United States the great majority of studies of anorexia nervosa has been conducted by psychoanalytically-minded workers, most of whom have relied on the observation of a single or a small number of cases (Gero, Leonard, Alexander, Deutsch, Cobb, Eissler, Benedek, and others). Particularly important is the contribution of Hilde Bruch, who has made a special study of psychological and psychopathological problems of alimentation. As far as anorexia nervosa is concerned, her attempt to come to grips with the primary disturbances has culminated in a psychotherapeutic attitude specially geared to the fundamental needs of these patients.

As evidence of the ever-increasing interest in anorexia nervosa two monographs deserve special mention. The first was written by E. L. Bliss and C. H. Branch (Utah College of Medicine) and may be criticized for its diagnostic approach, and its multiple psychogenetic perspectives. The second, which came from the pen of H. Thomä, an able German psychoanalyst, is remarkable for many of its insights though it, too, strikes me as being open to certain objections. In particular his presentation of the case histories suggests that he is not always an impartial observer of the facts, but allows himself to be swayed by the exegetic concerns and theoretical assumptions of his school. As a result, his therapeutic attitude, too, is not as open to the real needs of his patients as it might otherwise have been.

In 1965 a symposium on anorexia nervosa was organized in Göttingen by J. E. Meyer, Director of the University Psychiatric Clinic. It was attended by psychiatrists, psychologists, sociologists, psychoanalysts and endocrinologists from all over the world, and their various contributions and viewpoints have since been combined into an excellent monograph. A more recent monograph was published by Peter Dally of Westminster Hospital, London. Dally, who had the advantage of working with a very large number of anorexia nervosa patients, set out to study the diagnostic problem, the possible causes, the effects of various forms of treatment and the possible factors affecting the outcome. Dally's clinical approach was to divide all anorexia nervosa patients into three categories: an 'obsessional' group; a 'hysterical' group; a group of mixed aetiology. He suggested that the first two groups probably represent the primary form of anorexia nervosa, while the third group represents the secondary form. With the help of this system of classification Dally sought to dispel the confusion surrounding anorexia nervosa, and to establish more precise therapeutic and prognostic guidelines. Unfortunately his criteria for classification – hunger or lack of appetite, concern about one's physical condition, and the voluntary or involuntary nature of neuromuscular overactivity or vomiting – are highly subjective because they are chiefly based on the patients' own statements. Now it is a well-known fact that anorexics rarely if ever tell the whole truth, except after prolonged and positive psychotherapeutic contacts. More particularly many of these patients are completely unable to identify, and distinguish between, their various inner states, impulses and desires. For that very reason Hilde Bruch's separation of these patients into two groups – those suffering from *true* anorexia and those suffering from pseudo-anorexia – strikes me as being more valid than Dally's or, for that matter, any other system that has been suggested so far.

2 Clinical Aspects

Physical Examination

A decrease in weight constitutes the chief feature of anorexia nervosa. It varies in extent from one patient to the next, and becomes increasingly apparent as the illness develops. The degree of emaciation of the final stages is found only in very few organic diseases. In my own case studies, which were conducted at the Clinica Medica Universitaria, by kind permission of Professor I. Villa, and completed with clinical and laboratory tests, the minimum registered body weight was 68 lbs in a twenty-year-old girl, 5′ 3″ in height; the maximum was 95 lbs in a seventeen-year-old girl, 5′ 6″ in height. The weight losses recorded ranged from 15 lbs 6 ozs to 55 lbs, or from 20 per cent to 40 per cent of the patients' original weight. These figures are highly significant seeing that weight losses of 30 per cent occur in only the most severe physical illnesses. Some of the patients were so emaciated that they looked like walking skeletons. The fatty layers disappear and so do the characteristic curves of the female body. Only the breasts retain their shape to some extent, and this helps to distinguish anorexia nervosa from glandular insufficiency. The skeletal muscles atrophy to a greater or lesser but always noticeable extent. Yet, emaciated though these patients are, they are far more active than any other patients with a comparable degree of malnutrition. Another remarkable fact is that they retain their axillary and pubic hair and that they often show a faint down, especially on the face, the back and the limbs; however their lanugo never develops into hirsutism. No abnormal skin pigmentation has been observed, except in some cases in which it turns yellow because the patient's diet has consisted almost exclusively of carrots and marrows (*carotenes*).

No pathognomonic changes in the various organs have been detected. Arterial hypotension is fairly common; the heart is rather small and displaced to a vertical position because of the emaciation. Bradycardia is usual. The abdominal viscera show no particular changes except for a more or less marked tendency to ptosis. All patients are severely constipated, dental lesions (multiple caries, loss of teeth) are common; the hands and feet take on a bluish colour; the nails are abnormally brittle, but subcutaneous oedema is rare, which distinguishes anorexia nervosa from other forms of malnutrition, probably because the protein intake of anorexia patients is relatively greater. With the deterioration of the general state the feet and calves turn oedematous. Facial oedema appears only with a sudden return to normal eating habits or during compulsive bouts of overeating.

The body temperature of all my patients has been normal, though cases of hypothermia have been reported in the literature. Most of my patients were of the microsplanchnic type, had good posture, and their height seemed to exceed that of the average Italian woman. Dorsal scoliosis was observed in only three cases.

Laboratory tests

The results of laboratory tests in anorexia nervosa are not specific for any organic disease. Though a degree of anaemia was observed in all my patients, the blood count never fell below 3,500,000, the globular value fluctuating between 0·85 and 1·20. This contrasts sharply with the intense whiteness of the face found in more severe anaemics. The blood-sugar level is rather low – values ranging from 68 to 80 mg/100 cc have been observed in roughly half my patients; upon the administration of glucose, the blood-sugar curve generally rises and falls less sharply than the normal curve; sensitivity to insulin, on the other hand, is greater but never to the abnormal degree found in typical cases of pituitary deficiency. Tests of the hepatic and renal functions produced normal results; nearly all my patients were oliguric, but their response to water load was normal. The protein fractions were not significantly altered. Radiological examinations of the digestive tract revealed gastroptoses and a slowing down in the evacuation of the stomach in roughly half the cases. Cranial X-rays showed that the sella turcica remained within the normal limits. Electrocardiograms frequently revealed bradycardia, a low-voltage QRS and a reduction in the height of the T-wave.

The endocrinological study of anorexia nervosa patients has been intensified during the past few years in a vain effort to discover an abnormal hormonal factor; the persistent confusion of anorexia nervosa with Simmonds' disease has led many physicians to seize on anything that might confirm the presence of pituitary insufficiency. Amenorrhoea and the drop in the basal metabolic rate are – endocrinologically speaking – the two most obvious and essential symptoms of anorexia nervosa. It is generally agreed, however, that these are not necessarily the result of a primary pituitary insufficiency, but may very well be physical reactions to a low-calorie diet and its resultant: a lowered metabolism. A great deal has been written on the genesis of the amenorrhoea; everyone agrees that anorexia nervosa leads to a reduced elimination of gonadostimolin – in the ten cases I have examined the observed values were always below the normal. Lower than normal figures were also obtained by urinary estimations of the 17-ketosteroids and the 11-oxysteroids. Despite the low, and sometimes extremely low, value of the basal metabolic rate, radioactive iodine tests have shown that the thyroid function and the protein-bound iodine level are normal. That the function of the suprarenal cortex, too, is unimpaired may be deduced, *inter alia*, from the normal response to ACTH stimulation; anorexia nervosa patients show no eosinophilia, have a normal tolerance to desalination, and show no tendency to Addisonian crises. Post-mortem histological examinations have shown no change in the thyroid, the suprarenals and the anterior pituitary. The amenorrhoea of these patients is the result of an isolated gonadotropic insufficiency; whether the latter, in its turn, is due to a purely psychogenic mechanism involving the cortico-thalamo-hypophysial system, or rather to general physical depression, remains an open question. The first mechanism probably intervenes in anorexia nervosa with precocious amenorrhoea, the second in the more common form in which amenorrhoea is consequent upon severe organic depression. Cases of both types of amenorrhoea are well documented in the literature. Amenorrhoea is accompanied by a reduced elimination of oestrogen; the ovaries shrink, the endometrium becomes fibrotic and the vaginal mucosa atrophies.

Mention must also be made of changes in the electrolyte balance. As the adipose tissue shrinks, the percentage of water in the body as a whole tends to increase. At the same time the total amount of potassium (which is mainly intercellular) tends to decrease as a result of muscular atrophy, while the total amount of sodium tends to increase. What is of more immediate interest here is that the potassium and sodium levels of the extracellular fluids are not subject to constant variation. It has, however, been noted that, when patients have systematic recourse to purgatives or express their refusal to take food by vomiting, they develop hypokalaemia and natropenia, often followed by dehydration or metabolic alkalosis. Rational electrolyte replacement therapy based on infusions of, say, saline or Darrow's solution are likely to prove highly effective in these circumstances.

Another common feature in the most advanced stage of anorexia nervosa is the appearance of morbid complications consequent upon the general debility and the breakdown of the defence mechanisms. Our own cases include one patient who died of acute pulmonary tuberculosis and two who developed tuberculosis but were subsequently cured.

Clinical diagnosis

Since anorexia nervosa is primarily a mental illness, its identification calls for a study of the patient's memories and behaviour, and for the isolation of the specific psychodynamic factors.

From the purely clinical point of view the chief diagnostic criterion is the patient's general emaciation. It is quite simple to differentiate the emaciation consequent upon anorexia nervosa from that consequent upon juvenile diabetes mellitus, hyperthyroidism, adrenocortical insufficiency, chronic enteritis, pulmonary tuberculosis, tumours, etc. The main diagnostic problem is the differentiation of anorexia nervosa from Simmonds' disease.

To this day many physicians are reluctant to identify cases of anorexia nervosa; they consider this identification an admission of their lack of diagnostic skill – to their minds an organic debility of such exceptional gravity must needs have an 'organic' cause, which they usually try to attribute to glandular malfunction. As a result they commonly mistake anorexia nervosa for Simmonds' disease. In fact this diagnosis cannot be justified even on purely physical grounds, since the clinical, somatic and laboratory pictures of the two conditions are quite distinct – only in the rarest of cases is it possible to confuse anorexia nervosa with Simmonds' disease.

It should be remembered that the syndrome Simmonds described in 1914 was based on his treatment of an emaciated woman who died and was found to have post partum destruction of her pituitary gland. Now subsequent observations have shown that hypopituitarism (the post partum destruction of the pituitary is nowadays called 'Sheehan's disease') is rarely accompanied by emaciation – most patients suffering from pituitary insufficiency look well-nourished long after the onset of the disease.

Other types of hypopituitarism are generally caused by such tumours as eosinophilic adenomata, which produce changes in the sella turcica with signs of intracranial hypotension, bitemporal homonymous haemianopia, or are the result of cranial pharingioma in the young. Other conditions producing hypopituitarism such as gliomatous, sarcoid and granulomatous lesions (Hand-Schiller-Christian disease) are extremely rare, as is hypopituitarism resulting from cranial injuries.

The obvious pituitary insufficiency of these patients is due, above all, to understimulation of the thyroid and suprarenal cortex and to the secondary degeneration of these glands (myxoedema, hypocorticoidism). The patients seem torpid, asthenic, apathetic; they suffer from sexual frigidity and amenorrhoea, and are highly sensitive to cold. Outwardly, however, they show no signs of malnutrition; their faces often look swollen and pasty, and their skin is pale because of a lack of melanin. The axillary and pubic hair falls out altogether or becomes sparse; the eyebrows are thinned; the breasts often shrink. The atrophy of the suprarenal cortex manifests itself by arterial hypotension, marked hypoglycaemia, an abnormal sensitivity to insulin, and the possibility of an Addisonian crisis. The excretion rate of the 17-ketosteroids and 17-corticoids is very low. In contrast to anorexia nervosa there is a very poor response to ACTH – only repeated treatment over several consecutive days produces a gradual rise of the 17-ketosteroid level. In some cases pituitary insufficiency assumes less clear-cut forms, and is then exceedingly difficult to diagnose, the more so if there is no loss in weight.

3 *The General Picture of Anorexia Nervosa*

Patients suffering from anorexia nervosa are easily identified, even on first acquaintance: their attitude to the therapist, to whom they are often brought by members of their family against their will, is generally studied, cold and forbidding, though quite a few are fatuous, loquacious, hypocritical and inconsistent. But no matter what particular stance they adopt, all alike seem determined to discourage or exasperate the physician. They all insist that they are perfectly well and appear to be completely unconcerned about their grave physical condition or their amenorrhoea. (It is only when the disease has persisted for many years that some of them realize that all is not well and make up their own minds to visit a physician, but even then they never co-operate with him.)

The relatives usually tell the same monotonous story. They claim that the patient suddenly changed from a normal and peaceful girl into a hostile and solitary character. She refuses to make new friends and has dropped all her old ones. In particular she has no friends of the opposite sex let alone any sexual relationships (some of these patients express completely fanciful wishes for Platonic friendships). At work or school she is completely withdrawn, and tends to be shunned by others. She is reported to be overactive in whatever she does, but her expression is doleful, her lack-lustre eyes are usually glazed and her bearing is stiff. The physician, too, is immediately struck by the rigidity of these patients, and by the length of time that they maintain any one posture. They never lean back in their chairs, and rarely gesticulate or change their facial expression.

In conversations with their family, and quite especially with their mothers, they show intense irritability about all sorts of matters. They are often hypocritical of their brothers and sisters, whom they keep under constant observation, and whom, strangely enough, they often accuse of not eating enough; or of eating the wrong food. Many will try to force food down the unwilling throats of their mother, brother or sister – their chosen victim. They themselves are extremely intolerant of critical remarks about their own dietary habits and even resent any compliments about their looks. In spite of this professed attitude, they spend a good deal of time mirror-gazing, and are strangely preoccupied with their general appearance, their hairstyle and dresses, of which some can never have enough though they only wear one and leave the rest untouched in the wardrobe. Many of them are social snobs: they admire the upper classes but fear any contact with them.

Almost without exception and despite the obvious family tension, they resolutely refuse to leave home. The whole family is usually deeply disturbed by, and involved in, the pathological situation, in a kind of *folie à deux ou à plusieurs*. The entire household revolves round the patient. Nevertheless, the parents and even the family doctor generally resist all attempts to bring the underlying emotional conflict into the open. They insist that the home environment is 'perfectly normal' and that the patient is the sole disturbing factor.

Whatever spurious explanations the patient herself may give for her refusal to eat, the result is always the same: a drastic reduction in the food intake. This is usually a gradual process, and some time may elapse before it is noticed. The patients say that they have lost their appetite, that they feel bloated and replete, and complain of stomach aches, indigestion and nausea. They claim that they only like certain foods, particularly sweets, and this is especially so in the stable phase of the disease. Some crave exotic or monotonous dishes. Fatty foods are rejected with disgust, and farinaceous foods are spurned. There is no longer any question of regular meals; the patients take a mouthful of this or that at irregular intervals. In some, especially in chronic, cases there are occasional bouts of voracious eating interspersed with periods of fasting. During such bouts these patients will raid the refrigerator and gorge themselves with whatever cold titbits, sweets and unsavoury mixtures they can lay their hands on.

They never discuss what they eat, preferring to make a great mystery of the matter. No one can ever tell just how much or when they have last eaten. They never sit down voluntarily at table with others. They prefer to eat alone, standing up in the kitchen or their bedroom while nibbling casually at a snack. (One of my patients lived exclusively on food scraped out of saucepans.) They are often revolted by the sight of a fully-laden table. If they are made to eat, they will secrete their food, and later give it away to animals or throw it into the dustbin. At times, however, they will steal food and hoard it in their wardrobe. The thought of not having free access to food terrifies them, even though they have not the least intention of eating it.

All these patients are stubbornly self-willed and rarely worry about the effects of their behaviour on other members of the family. They are always ready with excuses, and will tell you the most far-fetched lies. They readily burst into tears at the least sign of opposition, often sobbing their hearts out in the privacy of their rooms, but occasionally causing dramatic scenes.

At the inception of the disease the patients simply refuse to eat enough, but during the subsequent, active phase they swallow enormous doses of laxatives and give themselves enemas. They will also make themselves vomit repeatedly, at first with great and painful effort and later almost at will.

The uncontrollable impulse to keep moving about, to do secret gymnastics is a common feature of anorexia nervosa especially during the initial stages. Some patients seem to have a fakir-like insensitivity to painful sensations: to cold (they are inadequately dressed in winter, have an obsession with keeping their overcoats unbuttoned and scorn underclothes); to fatigue (they always stand while studying, working, knitting or travelling by public transport, and even when they do sit down they are perched on the edge of their seats; they go to bed late and rise very early). Later, when the disease begins to take its toll, the fakir-like attitude disappears: they become highly sensitive to cold and complain constantly of this and that. Moreover, as Bliss and Branch have so rightly observed, their overactivity is more apparent than real: they seem overactive merely because the least activity in such skeletal people takes the uninformed observer completely by surprise.

4 *The Term 'Anorexia Nervosa'*

While the continued use of the term 'anorexia' to describe the condition that was first diagnosed by that name avoids the coining of a neologism, it has also led to a great deal of confusion. The German name *Pubertätsmagersucht* (literally 'compulsive pubertal emaciation') is much more expressive of the condition, and when we speak of 'anorexia' today we should be clear that we are not using that term in its etymological sense (ἀν-ὄρεξις = absence of desire) or doing justice to the psychological world in which anorexics live – their ἀν-ὄρεξις is no more than the façade they put up.

Because of the difficulty in probing into the private world of patients who become increasingly secretive and tend to dissimulate, those who have described anorexia nervosa have generally been forced to base their conclusions on the patients' own and false explanations: lack of appetite, a loathing of food, stomach aches and a bloated feeling. The fact that these very symptoms also occur in certain hypochondriacal conditions has misled many students into thinking that the same cause is at work. In fact anorexics, unlike hypochondriacs, take a keen, indeed an obsessive, interest in food, but manage to hide this preoccupation from all but the most scrupulous observers. Food is by no means a distasteful subject of conversation to these patients, provided only that the talk does not turn to 'their' food. They are usually fascinated by culinary matters, collect recipes, know all about the best delicatessen shops and make a point of reading cookery books and the menus displayed in restaurant windows. Cooking for 'others' is quite a hobby with them, and they will gladly prepare elaborate sweets and other tasty dishes.

These girls are extremely fussy about what little they themselves eat (in contrast to melancholics and schizophrenics) and have temper tantrums if the food they require is not readily available. When it comes to food they have a prodigious memory and will often recite whole menus they have enjoyed in the past. Thus one of my patients recalled the complete birthday dinner she ate prior to the onset of her disease eighteen months earlier. Another of my patients, who, during a relapse, lost some 13 lbs in weight during a twenty days' unhappy stay in a boarding school, repeated, when suitably prompted and without realizing how incongruous her behaviour was, every single menu she had been offered during that relatively long period. Finally another of my patients repeated a dream in which she saw a table laden with various foods, and which she recognized without hesitation as a meal she had eaten some fourteen years earlier!

These patients are not truly 'anorexic' during the initial stage of the illness. Many of those, who, after a time, have succeeded in establishing a good emotional relationship with the therapist, will confess that, especially before the onset of the chronic phase, they suffered terrible hunger pains. They rarely pass through periods of a genuine lack of appetite but fast quite deliberately, often in anticipation of a banquet or consequent upon one in order to offset the supposed consequences of overeating.

I myself have noticed that even my chronic patients have been unable to rid themselves of their obsessive interest in food, which reflects their desperate struggle to control their inner drives. Thus a thirty-two-year-old colleague, who had been a severely emaciated anorexic for some eighteen years, told me that she used to feel utterly frustrated and panic-stricken whenever she found herself in places where food was not constantly and abundantly available. During her recovery in a clinic, where she ate hardly anything at all, she encouraged the sisters and nurses to prepare the most fantastic dishes. 'Those women,' she told me, 'didn't have a clue. One day, when I'm rich enough, why don't we open a special clinic for anorexics? You can take charge of the psychotherapy, and I will look after the kitchen. I know most of the tricks to make them eat.'

The mere fact that food figures so prominently in the dreams of all these patients is enough to distinguish their condition from that of patients whose hunger sensations have been suppressed for purely organic reasons.

We have only to think of hepatics: to them food is so repulsive that they cannot bear to look at it or hear anyone speak about it.

Our patients, by contrast, show no disgust with food, let alone with discussions about it. In the most advanced and chronic stages of the disease, hunger frequently manifests itself through feelings of fatigue, vertigo, palpitation, irritation, repletion, nausea and even a loathing of food. Such sensations are often mistaken for indigestion. But even with such gravely ill patients ostensibly nauseated by, and indifferent to, food, once the conversation is skilfully brought round to topics indirectly connected with eating (good-food guides; special characteristics of regional or traditional dishes; memorable dinners, etc.) it will immediately lead to a revival of interest in food, accompanied by a lively expression and a tone of voice that betray a hidden desire. How many of my conversations with some of my patients did forcibly remind me of the favourite subject of general conversation during the bleakest days of the war!

In their monograph on anorexia nervosa, Bliss and Branch have put it all as follows:

What is common to all patients with anorexia nervosa is not the 'anorexia' but the 'nervosa' that causes a loss of weight. The appetite may be absent but also may be present, increased, or perverted. Some have a true anorexia and genuinely have no desire for food. Others crave food but refuse to eat. Some eat and then vomit; whereas others surreptitiously hide or dispose of their meals so as not to arouse the suspicion and disapproval of their families and physician. There are those who fear to eat because digestion may cause fearful somatic distress or lead to obesity; and there are a few who eat docilely and then purge themselves of the offensive nutriments by cathartics and enemas. But in every case, although the reasons and stratagems will vary, the final result is a reduction in the intake of calories, a loss of weight and semi-starvation.

But though Bliss and Branch have come close to the crux of the problem, they have apparently failed to grasp its full import. While it is perfectly true that the final result of the various stratagems employed by these patients is a loss in weight, the sole motive for their strange behaviour is a *desperate need to grow thinner*. This need (and the entire congeries of symptoms associated with it) is the sole motive force involved in the condition described as 'anorexia nervosa' which thus assumes a clearly defined and quite specific picture distinguishing it from all other morbid forms of inanition.

B

In other words anorexia nervosa is not primarily an absence or a perversion of the appetite, but a deliberate wish on the patient's part to lose weight.

As for the various ruses they use (or rather the various justifications they offer), my experience with my cases has made it clear to me that all of them are secondary adaptations to environmental conditions. The more unsympathetic the reactions of the patients' circle of acquaintances, friends and relatives the more impenetrable, astute and deceitful they become.

In a hypochondriacal environment they will make hypochondriacal excuses; in a suspicious environment they will lie astutely and persistently; in an authoritarian environment they will use all sorts of ruses to get rid of what food is forced upon them; in an overtly hostile environment they will simply reject all food without bothering about justifications, and so on.

It may be useful to note in this connection that the initial form of anorexia nervosa is usually a passive one: the patient simply refuses to eat enough. The so-called active forms which involve self-induced vomiting, enormous doses of laxatives and enemas are generally secondary and often partly iatrogenic, that is result from forced-feeding. They often set in after unsuccessful treatment, especially after forced-feeding without adequate psychotherapeutic support, and tend to distort the psychological picture beyond recognition. As for the biological picture, it is aggravated in the active form not only by the effects of inanition but also by the protein and electrolyte imbalance.

It cannot be stressed enough that, since lack of appetite is a subjective factor, no one has been able to demonstrate that patients suffering from anorexia nervosa are, in fact, not affected by hunger. Thus all the cases I have investigated not only showed a keen though disguised interest in food as an indirect sign of their real needs, but generally ended up by confessing that their continuous struggle against that very interest had become their chief concern.

It is therefore not the lack of appetite (or the bizarre explanations the patients volunteer for it) that holds the key to anorexia nervosa – the true cause is a deliberate wish to slim. This very fact, as I have said before, stamps anorexia nervosa a specific clinical entity.

5 *The Differential Diagnosis of Anorexia Nervosa*

As I have pointed out the publication of Simmonds' results in 1914 confused the clinical picture of anorexia nervosa. The reason for this confusion is easily explained: at the beginning of the twentieth century the general enthusiasm for, and pride in, the stream of discoveries in histopathology, biochemistry, endocrinology and empirically verifiable laboratory tests, often held up as examples of objective research, threatened to denigrate the most sensitive of all medical instruments – man – and to reduce clinical medicine to a mere branch of biochemistry. Small wonder then that the ancient clinical method of observing the patient carefully, not only in his impaired physical state but also in his personal and interpersonal behaviour, began to fall into disuse. Thus many articles devoted to anorexia nervosa stated quite simply that the disease takes the form of extreme emaciation accompanied by amenorrhoea and constipation; various authors enlarged on the anatomy and physiology of the hunger centres, on their pathology and on the experimental results of endocrinological research based on the administration of a host of biochemical substances in varying doses, but did not find it necessary to devote a single word to the associated behaviour patterns. Had they done so, they would quickly have realized that these patients do not really suffer from a lack of appetite or an inability to assimilate food, but are engaged in an active struggle against their normal biological needs.

In my view – and I stress this again – the term 'anorexia nervosa' should be reserved for a special clinical syndrome occurring in pre-pubertal and pubertal girls. It is associated with a series of clinical symptoms and signs: a deliberate and increasing refusal to eat enough which eventually causes severe emaciation (though there is never a total rejection of food); amenorrhoea (usually precocious); constipation, and neuro-muscular overactivity. It is characteristic of the disease that it usually strikes well-to-do young girls in perfect physical health, and often gourmets. Their mental health too is good in the premorbid phase; they are highly disciplined and 'good-natured', and only a tiny minority have neurotic symptoms that point to their subsequent illness.

According to Bliss and Branch the chief characteristic of anorexia nervosa is a loss in weight (at least 25 lbs) due to psychological causes which, however, they have failed to define in any great detail. As a result they have robbed the clinical picture of anorexia nervosa of those specific characteristics that the earliest authors clearly recognized.

In fact so broad a definition as theirs necessarily includes all such forms of emaciation due to neurotic or psychoneurotic abstention from food as dysphagia, phobia of swallowing, oesophageal or pyloric spasms, chronic anorexia due to hypo-chondriacal dyspepsia and hysterical vomiting – which have nothing to do with anorexia nervosa. The result is diagnostic and prognostic confusion. Thus Massermann has wrongly described as anorexia nervosa the condition of a patient who, though emaciated by vomiting due to unresolved sexual con-flicts, disliked her own emaciation and tried to have it cured.

I greatly prefer the approach of J. A. Meyer, who has distin-guished anorexia nervosa not only from emaciation due to functional eating problems but also from other types of emacia-tion readily confused with it, that is from chronic anorexia and secondary neurotic anorexia. In contrast to primary anorexia nervosa, chronic anorexia starts in early infancy and is always associated with serious and recurring intestinal disorders. This type of anorexia shows a clear if transitory improvement during adolescence, only to make way for chronic inanition coupled to a host of hypochondriacal disorders, especially of the digestive tract. It invariably goes hand in hand with severe psychoasthenia.

Secondary neurotic anorexia can appear at any stage of life. It is generally a response to an intolerable existential situation following upon a traumatic humiliation (failing an examination, losing a job, the breaking of an engagement, etc.), and takes the form of a transitory physiological change in the appetite. It does not lead to extreme emaciation, nor is it complicated by other mental disorders.

Some of these cases do, however, become chronic as a result of family and personal problems, and most of them are poorly endowed intellectually and emotionally immature. Their reduced food intake (and consequent physical debility) reflects an attempt to manipulate the home environment to their own advantage, to shirk the demands of school, work or marriage, and to avoid running the risks of existential failure in general. The reaction is directed much more strongly at the outside than at the patient's inner world. It is motivated on the one hand by fear of failure, and on the other hand by personal resentment. Unlike true anorexia nervosa this reaction does not involve any attempt to resolve psychological conflicts, to gain control over one's body or a desperate search for self-esteem.

Neurotic reactions in these potentially chronic cases generally appear much later in life than they do in true anorexia nervosa. I have been able to study (but not to cure) several cases that were triggered off by a 'difficult' engagement, or by the problems of early married life. When these patients do not come to see the psychotherapist before the chronic phase, he often has great difficulty in distinguishing their condition from true anorexia nervosa – the presentation, and the overall preoccupations are so similar as to demand a detailed and complete reconstruction of the patients' problems. Moreover, thanks largely to the dominant asthenic component of their personalities (fear and withdrawal from daily life) and the advantages they expect to gain from their condition, many of these patients are reluctant to gain clearer psychological insights into their problems and hence even less open to therapeutic persuasion than are true anorexics. They prefer tonics and rest cures, which may bring them slight, if temporary, relief. The prognosis *quoad valitudinem* is poor: these patients will drag out their dreary and incredibly restricted existences as invalids in the bosom of their families.

Hilde Bruch has based her definition of anorexia nervosa on the presence of the following three fundamental criteria:
1) A disturbance of the body image so delusional as to lead to total disregard of the severe emaciation, in the belief that it is a perfectly proper state. The true anorexia nervosa patient identifies herself with her skeletal appearance and vigorously

denies that there is anything wrong with her figure. This sets her aside from patients who cannot eat properly but deplore their loss of weight.

2) A loss in the ability to perceive and identify body stimuli and a consequent failure to interpret hunger signals. The outward symptom is a drastic reduction in the food intake. Eating habits become disorganized, and strange predilections appear. This disorganization has two distinct aspects: fasting interspersed with uncontrollable impulses to gorge oneself, often followed by induced vomiting. The loss of control during this bulimic phase is astounding; it sometimes leads to obesity, followed by renewed abstinence. Another characteristic feature of the failure to appreciate and interpret body signals is over-activity and a non-response to fatigue. There is also an absence of sexual feelings and patients show a marked inability to identify their own emotions.

3) A paralysing sense of ineffectiveness pervades every thought and activity of the true anorexia nervosa patient. They feel that all their actions are responses to the demands of others.

While the first two criteria are easily recognized, the third is not because it is masked by a negativistic attitude which means that the patients will not co-operate with the therapist. In fact their negativistic façade and obstinacy merely serve to hide their lack of initiative and autonomy.

I fully agree that Hilde Bruch's third criterion is characteristic of true anorexia nervosa, and pay tribute to her for having been the first to stress this fundamental psychopathological factor. As for her first criterion I should like to add the following observation: in my own experience I have found that, no matter what they say, many patients are not *truly* convinced that their skeletal figure is perfectly normal. Thus they will often refuse to wear low-necked dresses, bathing suits or other articles of clothing that might reveal their emaciated bodies (though a few will do the precise opposite, in order to put their mothers to shame). They merely *pretend* that they are normal as a buffer against their imaginary fears of obesity, which also allows them the occasional indulgence.

As for the second criterion, that is the loss in the power to perceive and interpret body signals, or what Hiltmann has called the loss of *Leibgefühl*, I myself have found that it occurs regularly in the most advanced forms of anorexia nervosa, in which bouts of bulimia are quite common. I have not observed it in static cases of anorexia nervosa, who generally manage to control their food intake, a point with which I shall be dealing at some length in a later section.

The differential diagnosis of anorexia nervosa also involves other types of psychogenic emaciation: psychoneurotic forms with mechanico-functional feeding difficulties, hysterical vomiting, dysphagia, fear of swallowing, cardiac spasms, etc. These forms differ from anorexia nervosa, not only in that they do not produce the same grave physical sequelae, but also in that the resulting emaciation is a secondary phenomenon and above all in that those suffering from them are acutely aware of, and concerned about, their condition, for which they generally seek therapeutic help. True anorexia nervosa patients, by contrast, are not only indifferent to their own emaciation, but are terrified by even the slightest increase in weight.

The schizophrenic forms involve clear delusions about food (poisoning, messianic fasts, etc.), the presence of which distinguishes these cases from anorexia nervosa. They are moreover part of the characteristic complex of symptoms which includes alienation and inactivity and thus contrasts with the overactivity and emotional involvement of anorexia nervosa patients.

The melancholic forms, too, present a clinical picture quite unlike that of anorexia nervosa. In particular the associated lack of initiative and inactivity are clearly distinguished from the 'perpetual motion' of anorexia nervosa patients (and, incidentally, produce quite different Rorschach protocols).

In distinguishing anorexia nervosa from glandular insufficiency (Simmonds' disease, Sheehan's disease) the observation of the patients' behaviour as the authentic expression of their mental state matters much more than the results of laboratory tests – it is only by very careful observations of the patient's mental state that the physician can hope to separate anorexia nervosa from all other types of inanition. Thus Kind has shown that the psychopathological picture of pituitary insufficiency differs markedly from anorexia nervosa. In dealing with the behaviour of various patients suffering from Sheehan's disease, he mentions not only the absence of any active desire to lose weight and lack of opposition to treatment (two typical findings in anorexia nervosa), but also general apathy and indifference to the vicissitudes of daily life and family reactions, which, again, is in sharp contrast to the ambivalent, but always active, reactions of anorexia nervosa patients.

To sum up: the diagnosis of anorexia nervosa calls for attentive observation of the patients' behaviour in order to determine whether or not they are deliberately trying to lose weight under one pretext or another, and whether or not they seem genuinely unconcerned about the grave physical consequences. Patients suffering from anorexia nervosa do not even seem to be worried about their amenorrhoea, as witness their refusal to eat when it is pointed out to them that the amenorrhoea is a consequence of their emaciation. Their behaviour as a whole can be summed up under a single heading: anorexic behaviour. The illness tends to appear characteristically in thirteen to sixteen-year-old girls who were previously considered physically fit and in perfect health. It is of the utmost diagnostic importance to establish whether or not the patients were overactive, at least in the initial phase of the illness.

True anorexia nervosa must be distinguished:

1) From secondary neurotic or reactive anorexias which may appear not only at puberty but at any, even a late, phase of life, following an emotional trauma (humiliation or frustration);

2) From chronic anorexia which starts during early or late infancy, remits temporarily during adolescence, only to reappear again and to persist for the rest of the patient's life, coupled to disturbances especially of the digestive tract with clear psychoasthenic overtones;

3) From emaciation due to mechanico-functional difficulties of a neurotic or psychoneurotic type (dysphagia, fear of swallowing, oesophageal and pyloric spasms, uncontrollable vomiting), in which the refusal to eat is not deliberate but consequent upon the functional disturbances, and in which the patients are worried about their condition and seek help (however unsuccessfully);

4) From food refusal of melancholic or schizophrenic origin which is never associated with overactivity;

5) From anorexias of endocrine origin (Simmonds' disease, Sheehan's disease) which present a quite different psychopathological picture. In particular anorexia nervosa patients do not

exhibit the characteristic apathy, dullness and psychotic episodes associated with primary destruction of the anterior pituitary; they remain mentally alert, energetic and receptive, except in the terminal phase. Anorexia nervosa invariably involves an active and deep wish to lose weight and a reluctance to seek help, a state of affairs that does not obtain in endocrine disorders.

PART TWO

6 *Anorexia Nervosa and the Contradictory Roles of Modern Woman*

There is little doubt that the modern girl is weighed down by a host of cultural and social pressures that tend to aggravate the inner conflicts and all those generic predispositions to neurotic and psychotic reactions in Karen Horney's sense (for a discussion of these problems in the context of the family see Chapter 27, p. 244).

The most important of these conflicts are due to such factors as the admission of women into traditional male preserves (universities, the liberal professions, commerce and so on) when previously they were confined to the home to play the role of good housewife and mother. At the same time female narcissism has, if anything, been increased rather than diminished by constant pressure to keep up with the latest fashions. Today, in fact, women are expected to be beautiful, smart and well-groomed, and to devote a great deal of time to their personal appearance even while competing in business and the professions. They must have a career and yet be romantic, tender and sweet, and in marriage play the part of the ideal wife *cum* mistress and *cum* mother who puts away her hard-earned diplomas to wash nappies and perform other menial chores. It is quite obvious that the conflict between so many irreconcilable demands on her time, in a world where the male spirit of competition and productivity reigns supreme, exposes the modern woman to a terrible social ordeal.

In addition to these quite general pathogenic factors, young girls are subjected to more specific pressures: the fashionable need to appear slim and sophisticated, the widespread publicity of dietetic aids, the constant discussion, at home or among girlfriends, of calories and weight, and above all the social ridicule in which women of Rubensian proportions are held. Modern fashion rejects the fat girl, who is destined to remain a lonely spinster.

In this context it would be highly instructive to study the reactions of those societies in which female obesity is considered a positive advantage. We know, in any case, that in periods when food was short, corpulence was considered a mark of distinction. This may explain why in the modern West, where food is plentiful, the obese female has become a figure of fun.

That social and psychological pressures can block the perception of hunger stimuli was shown by Stunkard in 'Obesity and the denial of hunger'. Adopting the classical principles of Cannon, according to whom hunger sensations are due to the contractions of the empty stomach, Stunkard went on to investigate the relationship between contractions of the stomach (recorded by means of a balloon probe) and hunger pangs in two groups of female subjects: one obese and the other non-obese. The second group regularly reported hunger sensations during gastric contractions and no hunger sensations in their absence. A third, control, group was made up of obese males, who responded in the same manner. Obese women, on the other hand, often failed to report hunger pangs or any desire for food during stomach contractions.

That the denial of hunger pangs must be due to a specific difficulty in recognizing gastric contractions was suggested by the observation that obese and non-obese women alike denied hunger sensations in the absence of gastric contractions.

Obese patients with a 'night-eating syndrome' (lack of appetite in the morning, insomnia, and hyperphagia at night), described for the first time by Stunkard in 1955, had a much more pronounced tendency to deny hunger during movements of the stomach than did patients without this syndrome.

To explain these facts Stunkard suggested that the denial of hunger sensations is confined to subjects who have sharp conflicts in respect of food in the wake of intense psychological and social pressures. The fact that obese males recognize gastric contractions confirms Stunkard's hypothesis: obese males are not exposed to social ridicule or rejection.

Stunkard's view received support from an unexpected quarter. Two women suffering from severe mental conflicts as a result of prolonged social pressure to cut down on their food, claimed that they had no hunger sensations during gastric contractions. Now these women were not obese; they were, in fact, suffering from anorexia nervosa.

These and similar investigations have thrown some light on the connection between anorexia nervosa and psychogenic obesity, and show the importance of considering the psycho-social aspects during physiological studies in general and quite particularly during studies in alimentary pathology.

7 *The Parents of Anorexic Patients*

Thomä, quoting the detailed family studies of schizophrenics by Lidz and others, believes it is impossible to draw equally reliable conclusions from the thirty cases of anorexia nervosa he himself has investigated, without a deep analysis of their nearest relatives.

I, too, can only draw on the data of my own psychotherapeutic experience (as reliable as a series of data filtered through one's own personality can be), but with this advantage: my patients, unlike Thomä's, were not confined to hospitals. They lived with their families or as paying guests in hostels or communities, and I was able to engage in frequent discussions with their parents and relatives, often continuing these discussions, for the purpose of dealing with family neuroses or connected problems, even after the patient was clinically cured. In that case the information I obtained (for example about the mother's difficulties in adapting herself to her daughter's greater independence and maturity) was often much more telling than the data I collected while the patient was still critically ill.

After the cure, the greater confidence of the parents in the therapist and the diminution of their sense of guilt and defensive inhibitions generally make them much more forthcoming and, in particular, allow them to express themselves with much greater ease. This is in sharp contrast to what so often happens during the phase of clinical improvement when the attitude of the mother or of both parents to the daughter tends to become blatantly pathological. My observations of the patient's home environment are the more convincing in that they tally with those of Hilde Bruch.

All the parents of the anorexics I have treated seemed to have intense neurotic conflicts, to have fallen prey to many of the conflicting forces that are typical of our society. At no time did

I come across parents with a mature emotional relationship to each other, superficial appearances to the contrary. Many of the parents seemed utterly devoted to their work and their home, observed all the conventional social norms, were acutely concerned with external appearances, and often puritanical and bigoted. But even though they did not engage in vulgar squabbles they all lived in a constant state of tension, had a tendency to be bad-tempered and – most characteristically – a propensity for interminable arguments about the most trivial subjects – so many symptoms of their latent aggression. With very few, if any, exceptions, the conspicuous figure in the home of anorexic girls is the mother; the father is usually an emotional absentee, generally overshadowed, and secretly or openly belittled, by his wife. And whenever he tries to lay down the law, the mother enlists the support of the children by playing the part of the innocent victim.

I have spoken of the monotonous clinical picture presented by anorexia nervosa patients; similarly one might speak of the monotonous behaviour of the mothers of anorexics. Like their daughters, they are a characteristic though less desperate product of the ambiguous state of modern woman. They feign acceptance of traditional behaviour patterns, and merely pretend to submit to the head of the family (often for purely economic reasons), and to be devoted to the home, the children and the accepted mores.

They never court social disapproval by open acts of rebellion or resistance, but act the part of long-suffering guardians of the hearth. But 'inside' they never acquiesce in the role of the good wife, let alone in that of the responsive lover. Instead they evince open or secret disgust with the flesh, with sex, with excrement and with physical lust. They foster ambition and assertiveness in their children but, in so doing, distinguish sharply between their sons and daughters. The boys are more immune to the mother's wiles and demands, largely because their experience and prospects make it more difficult for them to identify themselves with her. The girls, by contrast, are more easily subdued: they become the model children of a domineering, intolerant and hypercritical woman, who prevents them from standing their own ground and stunts their emotional development. The daughters grow up in the shadow of the maternal super-ego, so much so that the observer often gains the impression that, at puberty, these girls change abruptly from totally inexperienced children into young women, without any transitional phase of gradual emancipation from an all-powerful presence. As a result they lack any true knowledge of themselves, and are quite incapable of coping with the shattering and quite unexpected advent of puberty.

As a rule the mothers of anorexic girls look after their daughters extremely, even excessively, well, but they rarely derive any real pleasure from these attentions. They are scrupulous and attentive cooks but generally do not enjoy good food themselves and despise gluttons.

Often such families have a complicated dietary pattern that tires the mother and makes a martyr of her: certain courses must never be omitted, and the rest must be varied almost ritually. In any case the importance of regular meals is constantly stressed, but the meals themselves are consumed in an atmosphere of mutual recrimination and ill humour.

The reader may be interested in the transcript of a few snatches of conversations taken down verbatim during various sessions and interviews. (These quotations are not meant to prove any particular point, but to serve as illustrations of the mothers' general attitude to food and bodily functions and of the daughters' reactions.)

Ira's mother (who asked for an interview ostensibly to seek advice about Ira's elder sister who was out and about every night, working herself into a rage and with an expression of unspeakable disgust):

This craze for getting together after the cinema and stuffing themselves with bread and salami or spaghetti late at night – it makes me quite *sick*. Can't they find anything better to do?

Signora Mirin (a patient who alternates between anorexia and bulimia, speaking of her mother):

My mother had eleven children. . . . We were a very distinguished family. . . . My mother told me that whenever she had to breast-feed me she shut herself up in her bedroom because she *was embarrassed to let the servants* hear the noise I made while suckling . . . and the way I smacked my lips. . . .

Azzurra's mother:

At table I get edgy. Sometimes I just have to get down because of the *disgust* I feel at the *greed* with which Maria Grazia polishes off *even* a bowl of salad.

Since my girl took ill I have stopped wanting intimate relations with my husband. I am too worried about my little girl. . . . I told him we must make this sacrifice for her sake.(!)

Ira:

Yesterday I helped myself to the biggest piece of steak. Mother was watching me. She didn't realize it herself . . . but I'm sure she hated me that moment. I wasn't her daughter. I'm only her daughter when I come first at school and she can tell everybody that I am the best in my class. . . .

Ira's mother:

Ira was her father's favourite because she looked like him. . . . A glutton we called her, a real dustbin. . . . She would eat just any-thing. . . . I myself need very little. As for *him*, I must always prepare a whole lot of little titbits, otherwise he pulls a long face. For 365 days a year, it has to be minestrone and woe betide me if it isn't there. . . . If I had known what it would be like I would never have had any children. Perhaps just one (the eldest sister) and then – *basta*!

When she was one year old, I took her to the pediatrician because she was still wetting herself and I wanted her cured.(!)

Rita's sister:

When I was swotting up for my matriculation, Mother drove me mad with her constant talk about food. According to her anyone who didn't eat twice the normal amount was bound to plough – they would be too weak from all that studying. When I passed my exams I was gross, as big as a house. Two years later it was Rita's turn but she did the precise opposite. She dropped to 77 lbs! And yet mother told her the same story.

Lena (who asked for an interview two years after her recovery; her mother was trying to arrange a marriage of convenience for her):

I've only just come to see my real relationship with my mother. . . . She can't even imagine that I might be different from her. . . . If she thinks that something is good for me and I refuse it, she turns icy. She can say the most cruel things, things that not even my worst enemy would say. . . .

Liliana's mother (who came from her home town to visit her daughter. The daughter was flourishing, and quite unlike what she used to be: apparently much too self-possessed, free and easy, and quite happy about all the young men who kept running after her):

We certainly expected much better of her. . . . We hoped she would go to university . . . Still, I suppose we should be thankful that she is living it up and is no longer the walking skeleton she used to be. . . .

One patient, Azzurra, pasted Modigliani reproductions into the notebook in which she kept a record of her dreams. She identified the *Portrait of Leopold Zborowski* with her father, the *Portrait of Lunja Czechowska* with her mother, the *Child in Blue* with herself as a young child and the *Portrait of a Young Girl* with herself as an anorexic. What struck me as being highly significant was not only her own associations with the portraits, but also the similarity between Modigliani's gothic verticalism and the vertical and ethereal world of anorexics.

8 Learning Patterns and Body Awareness

When studying the psychological problems of child feeding we must bear in mind that, from the very first day of life, feeding is a co-operative venture.

The new-born child, who is completely dependent on the nursing mother, is part of a dyad the two terms of which constitute the basis of his first interpersonal relationship (transaction). Feeding is thus rooted in an experience full of perceptual and emotional overtones, as a result of which the simple nexus between hunger pangs and their pleasurable satisfaction becomes highly complicated.

The primitive relationship between mother and child might be represented by the following schema:

hunger

↓

signal by the child

↓

reception (decoding) of that signal and satisfaction of the signalled need by the mother.

It should be added that, when the child emits his hunger signal, he is probably conveying a state of anxiety to the mother, and that once his needs have been satisfied he communicates to her his sense of relaxation and pleasure, which the normal mother then shares with him.

Now it is my firm conviction that it is by the precise degree of satisfaction he obtains in response to his hunger signals that the infant learns to recognize, and to differentiate accurately between, his various physiological needs and the behaviour patterns most likely to satisfy them. In short he becomes *conscious of his corporeal identity.*

More precisely it is by the response to the various signals expressing his physiological needs which he himself finds utterly confusing (anxiety) that he gradually learns to differentiate between them. At the same time, the mother becomes aware (if only within certain limits) of his personal needs and body signals.

By awareness of body sensations I thus refer to the result of a particular learning process, namely that in which the child is taught, through his transactions with the mother, to identify and conceptualize his precise bodily needs and how to satisfy them, regardless of the mother and his own unconscious fantasies, through direct and stable contact with his basic source of experience: his own body.

In this connection I would refer the reader to the writings of R. Spitz whose work with very young children was based on direct observation and experimental psychology, which sets him off sharply from all those who have preferred to reconstruct the process of child development from studies of adult behaviour.

In his *The First Year of Life*, Spitz (paraphrasing Head, Wallon and others) contends that the child's bodily and emotional responses are gradually organized into two systems, namely the coenaesthetic and the diacritic. The sensations of the coenaesthetic system are extensive, diffuse and visceral; its effectors are the system of smooth muscles, while its nervous organization is vested mainly in the sympathetic and parasympathetic systems. The sensations of the diacritic system, by contrast, are intensive and involve the sense organs; its effectors are the striated muscles and its nervous organization is vested in the central nervous system. In the newly-born the diacritic system does not yet function properly, so that he operates chiefly on the coenaesthetic level.

The physiological organization of the diacritic system is attained along two paths:
1) through the gradual development of the child's innate biological structure, and
2) through psychological empathy with the mother which, according to Spitz, ensures not only that the child's earliest contacts with the mother's breast are felt to be gratifying but also activate the diacritic system, which eventually takes over from the more primitive coenaesthetic organization. Now it is precisely at this stage, that is during the maturation of the child's

perceptive and cognitive system, that his transactional relationship with the mother may become severely disturbed.

In her *Normality and Pathology in Childhood* Anna Freud argues that, before the child can obtain body independence, he has first to pass over a long road, involving the following stages:

1) being nursed at the breast or bottle, by the clock or on demand, with the common difficulties about intake caused partly by the infant's normal fluctuations of appetite and intestinal upsets, partly by the mother's attitudes and anxieties regarding feeding; interference with need satisfaction caused by hunger periods, undue waiting for meals, rationing or forced feeding set up the first – and often lasting – disturbances in the positive relationship to food. Pleasure sucking appears as a forerunner, by-product of, substitute for, or interference with feedign;

2) weaning from breast or bottle, initiated either by the infant himself or according to the mother's wishes. In the latter instance, and especially if carried out abruptly, the infant's protest against oral deprivation has adverse results for the normal pleasure in food. Difficulties may occur over the introduction of solids, new tastes and consistencies being either welcomed or rejected;

3) the transition from being fed to self-feeding, with or without implements, 'food' and 'mother' still being identified with each other;

4) self-feeding with the use of spoon, fork, etc., the disagreements with the mother about the quantity of intake being shifted often to to the form of intake, i.e. table manners, meals as a general battleground on which the difficulties of the mother-child relationship can be fought out; craving for sweets as a phase-adequate substitute for oral sucking pleasures, food fads as a result of anal training, i.e. of the newly acquired reaction formation of disgust;

5) gradual fading out of the equation food-mother in the oedipal period. Irrational attitudes toward eating are now determined by infantile sexual theories, i.e. fantasies of impregnation through the mouth (fear of poison), pregnancy (fear of getting fat), anal birth (fear of intake and output), as well as by reaction formations against cannibalism and sadism;

6) gradual fading out of the sexualization of eating in the latency period, with pleasure in eating retained or even increased. Increase in rational attitudes to food and self-determination in eating, the earlier experiences on this line being decisive in shaping the individual's food habits in adult life, his tastes, preferences, as well as eventual addictions or aversions with regard to food and drink.

The infant's reactions to the changes in phase 2 (i.e. to weaning and to the introduction of new tastes and consistencies) reflect for the first time his leaning toward either progression and adventurousness (when new experiences are welcomed) or a tenacious clinging to existing pleasures (when every change is experienced as threat and deprivation). It is to be expected that, whichever attitude dominates, the feeding process will also become important in other development areas.

The equation food-mother, which persists through phases 1–4, provides the rational background for the mother's subjective conviction that every food refusal of the child is aimed at her personally, i.e. expresses the child's rejection of her maternal care and attention, a conviction which causes much oversensitiveness in handling the feeding process and underlies the battle about food on the mother's side. It explains also why in these phases food refusal and extreme food fads can be circumvented by temporarily substituting a stranger, i.e. a noncathected or differently cathected person, for the maternal figure in the feeding situation. Children will then eat, in hospital, in nursery school, or as visitors, but this will not cure their eating difficulties at home, in the presence of the mother. It explains also why traumatic separations from the mother are often followed by refusal of food (rejection of the mother substitute), or by greed and overeating (treating food as a substitute for mother love).

The eating disturbances of phase 5, which are not related to an external object but are caused by internal, structural conflicts, are not affected by either the material presence or the material absence of the mother, a fact which can be utilized for differential diagnosis.

After phase 6, when the arrangements for food intake have become the mature individual's personal concern, the former food battle with the mother may be replaced by internal disagreements between the manifest wish to eat and an unconsciously determined inability to tolerate certain foods, i.e. the various neurotic food fads and digestive upsets. . . .

Battles about eating the mother's food express the toddler's ambivalent relationship to her. An excellent clinical illustration of this was a toddler who, when angry with his mother, not only spat out what she fed him, but also scraped his tongue clear of any morsel of food adhering to it. Literally he 'would have none of her'. Battles about the amount of food intake alternate with battles about the type of food which is preferred or rejected, i.e. food fads, and those about the mechanics of eating, i.e. table manners. More in the nature of symptoms is the disgusted avoidance of particular shapes, smells, colours, and consistencies of food, an avoidance which is derived from defence against anal trends; or vegetarianism which (if not produced and maintained by environmental influences) results from defence against regressive cannibalistic and sadistic fantasies; or refusal of fattening foods, sometimes of food altogether, in the service of warding off fantasies of oral impregnation or of pregnancy.

Since these various forms of symptomatic behaviour are developmental manifestations, each in its own right, there is no need to fear, as parents often do, that the milder forms, such as the food fads, are presages of the more severe ones, such as far-reaching food refusal, and that the one will change into the other if they are not treated. They are by definition transitory and open to spontaneous cure. Nevertheless, any excessive upset in the eating process on an earlier stage will leave residues which increase and complicate disturbances on the later ones. In general, the eating disturbances of childhood leave the area of food intake vulnerable and this prepares the ground for the neurotic afflictions of stomach and appetite in adult life.

When Anna Freud argues that the psychological eating disturbances of childhood prepare the way for 'the neurotic afflictions of stomach and appetite in adult life', I find myself in whole-hearted agreement with her. The case histories of those of my own patients who suffer from neurotic alimentary or digestive disturbances (relatively late anorexia as a neurotic reaction to humiliations or delusional traumata, hypochondriacal preoccupations with the digestive tract, alimentary idiosyncrasies, etc.) fully justify her claim.

However my own study of the structuring of body awareness through alimentary experience shows that other psychological syndromes must be taken into account as well. Thus, basing himself on the observation of certain pathological phenomena in his patients' body awareness and then carefully analysing their development from both the genetic and the psychotherapeutic points of view, the therapist can, as we shall see, show that many adult aberrations of the 'stomach and appetite' are, in fact, so many alimentary syndromes *in which the infantile disturbances described by Anna Freud play no part.*

Serious nutritional syndromes such as passive anorexia nervosa with near-total refusal of food; active anorexia nervosa with repeated vomiting and purging to the point of endangering life by dehydration, disturbance of the electrolyte balance and chloropenic hyperazotemia; severe bouts of bulimia (whether or not they follow more or less periods of fasting); acute intoxication, hypercatabolism and acute renal and cardio-circulatory insufficiency; certain forms of obesity (Rossini) – none of these is preceded by infantile feeding disturbances of the type described by Anna Freud.

Thus in early or late infancy and even during the latency period, these patients appear singularly free from reaction formations and neurotic defence mechanisms, both in the nutritional and also in many other spheres.

If we approach the mother, or better still both parents, for the purpose of filling in some detail in the patient's case history, they will usually produce nothing of interest. It almost seems that they had lived with their child as one might live with an object that had no particular attributes other than being 'good' (especially in his eating habits). There is a marked lack of significant episodes, of emotional changes or upsets in the filial relationship. According to the parents the illness 'came out of the blue' – until that moment the child was a normal happy being 'who never gave them the least trouble', 'was a joy to have around', 'a sensible girl who never worried us', 'one who always ate up her food', 'a girl we called a mop because she always cleaned up her plate', 'an affectionate little girl easy to bring up', 'a happy child full of fun'.

When, after such discussion, we take on these model children, they usually tell us much the same uninformative stories. They seem quite incapable of verbalizing any internal experiences or emotions. The therapist has an uphill struggle trying to get them to talk of their feelings, moods and humours, and often gets nowhere at all. In particular when we ask them to speak of their inner reactions to such bodily stimuli as hunger and feelings of anxiety (and also to fatigue, cold and even to bladder and intestinal pressure) they seem seriously perplexed. If we go on, as we invariably do, to the appetite and sense of satiety their confusion becomes total. They can never rely on their own sensations to tell them whether it is time to eat or to stop eating. They are always afraid of being out of control – of having eaten too much or too little. Quite often their case histories show that these anxieties first appeared when they left home with its regular meal routine for a college or school camp, or else at the time of some change in the household regime. It might be useful at this point to describe two typical cases.

Paola, who lost her mother at the age of three, was sent to a smart college in the North when she was thirteen. She and her sister had been brought up by their paternal grandmother, a highly neurotic woman with an obsessive and ambivalent attitude to her grandchildren. Paola was never allowed to help herself at the table, but was handed a full plate, which she was never permitted to put aside. She had sporadic bouts of 'indigestion', probably because her physiological needs were not always attuned to the large amounts of food her grandmother put before her. In the moralistic, old-fashioned and hyper-critical atmosphere in which she lived, any initiative she took was frowned upon. Then, when she went on to college and all the students had to help themselves, Paola did what her grandmother had always done for her: she crammed her plate with food and then finished it off together with anything left over by those of her friends who disliked certain dishes on the menu.

In a short time she became obese, and when her friends called her a 'dustbin' she was left with the humiliating feeling that she could never do right. Her only solution was to cut down stringently on her food, regardless of her increasing hunger pangs. This was the beginning of her incurable anorexia nervosa.

Berto, the fifteen-year-old first-born son of two teachers (his mother taught mathematics and his father philosophy) received an education in table manners that can only be described as contempt for, and the systematic deconditioning of, his own biological needs. These were regularly sacrificed to the opinions and rituals of his obsessive and perfectionist mother. Since Berto was an unusually intelligent boy, she was determined to turn him into a perfect little gentleman and scholar. Every day, just before lunch, when she hurried home from school to do the shopping, Berto would tag along behind her. At the baker's he would invariably be presented with a slice of *pizza*, an old custom in Liguria, but his mother would never allow him to eat it on the spot. He was expected to carry it home, enjoy its fragrant smell and disguise the fact that it made his mouth water. If he ate it, he was called a 'naughty boy'.

But once back home and at the ritually sanctified hour he became a 'good little boy' if he not only ate the slice of *pizza* but all the other food his mother put in front of him, which regularly included a fried egg.

At the age of thirteen Berto had to change schools. He now attended a foreign language institute some distance away from his home and did not return until 3 pm each day, by which time his parents had long finished their lunch and had gone back to work. He had to look after himself, and this made him strangely anxious. He had felt hungry at school at the usual hour, but all he felt now was very tired. Very often he would throw himself on his bed without eating, completely oblivious of his biological needs. His mother's constant reproach that he was wasting away gradually made him aware of his inner conflict and set off a perverse struggle between fleeting hunger sensations and an intense need to master them.

To give the reader another glimpse of his family background, I might add that, during a conversation, the father volunteered the following information:

You know, doctor, if you can cure this lunatic son of mine, I shall bring you my eight-year-old son as well. He is even worse. Imagine, at his age he thinks he can tell whether or not he has eaten enough! As if he knew better than his own mother!

The root causes of the confused body awareness of anorexia nervosa patients have been examined by Hilde Bruch, according to whom their hunger signals become blurred by anxiety and emotional stultification, the more so as their body awareness has been incorrectly programmed in the first instance (Bruch [1961]; Bruch and Palumbo [1961]). Thus she quotes the case of a fat little boy who had few opportunities of learning to correlate his hunger sensations with the need for food, since right from infancy his mother had responded to every least sign of anxiety on his part by thrusting food into his mouth. Bruch stresses that it is wrong to presuppose the human organism 'knows' its own body feelings and the nature of its instincts. The recognition of bodily needs and of the appropriate behaviour to satisfy them depends on a *learning process* that begins in infancy.

Similar programming errors affect the physiological needs, the creation of the body image, the consolidation of behaviour patterns and the interpretation of experiences: all these errors seriously distort and confuse individual attempts to solve problems, to achieve a sense of autonomy, and to act on *one's own initiative*. (As quoted by Lidz.)

Hilde Bruch's view is, as we have seen, fully corroborated by the now famous experimental researches of Stunkard, who has shown that obese patients (especially those suffering from the night-eating syndrome) and female anorexics are quite unable, even after prolonged fasting, to identify stomach contractions with hunger sensations, whereas the control group had no such difficulties.

Spitz was referring to the same phenomenon when he claimed that there has been a breakdown during the transition from the vague and diffuse coenaesthetic phase to the diacritic phase.

This takes us beyond psychodynamics into neurology or rather into neurodynamics, that is the relationship between wrong conditioning and the structure of the nervous system.

The child can only acquire an adequately structured diacritic perception of his own body stimuli, that is identify them correctly, if his mother responds to them in appropriate ways.

An overprotective and impervious mother, for instance, can never conceive of her child as a person in his own right, with original needs of his own. The result is neuropsychological confusion and malconditioning, which make the child doubt the legitimacy of his own sensations. My use of the term 'legitimacy' requires some qualification.

Before the child can assent to his own basic perceptions, they must first be 'legitimized' in his interpersonal relationship, particularly with the person in authority (given his state of dependence).

In early infancy this legitimization is provided by the optimal satisfaction of the child's particular need:

$$hunger = food$$
$$cold = clothing$$
$$tiredness = bed$$

need
↓
signal emitted by the infant
↓
satisfaction and legitimization of the need.

This can only be achieved if the parents consider the child as 'another', as an individual with a right to have needs, perceptions and conceptions of its own. For this to happen the parents must, in turn, have maintained a distance from their own parental figures, must be mature people, and as such capable of flexibility in handling the dialectic of their active and passive attitudes to the child, as Sylvia Brody has shown so lucidly in the tables accompanying her study entitled *Passivity* (pp. 149–53). In the final chapter of that study, she makes the following comment:

Without specific positive findings of organic defect, deficit or arrest, and without extensive knowledge about the course of the patients' maturational progress, we have no way to approach an answer to the problem of constitutional determinants. From a psychoanalytic point of view, the problem is made more complex by inexact definitions of constitutionality. . . .

For psychoanalysis, it might be economical to think of constitutionality as referring primarily to bodily events that have their basis in inheritance. . . . The organic condition might be one of low resources of energy, or of too low threshold for tension tolerance. . . . [Unfortunately] we lack the means to evaluate drive endowment. Drive endowment at this time cannot be considered a datum, but only something inferred. . . .

In view of the limits of the clinical data, it is more fitting here to pursue the psychological relationships that could be found between the patients' observed and reported experiences and the formation of their psychic structures. . . . In all phases of development, the possibility of establishing environmental conditions that are important for the balance of active and passive aims will vary with the character and personality of the child's parents. Ideally, they would be adults whose own instinctual aims would permit them to be passively receptive enough to recognize the infant's signs of instinctual need with a mixture of composure, concern, and pleasure, and to be active enough in their aims to try to satisfy the instinctual needs (not the demands) agreeably, and to offer additional satisfactions according to the infant's developmental capacity to be pleasurably stimulated and psychologically enriched by them. As the infant becomes a young child, the parents, while continuing to provide support and pleasure, would also be able to enjoy increasing inner freedom to let the child experience delay in need satisfaction. They would feel no less free actively to protect him from too easy discharge of impulses, lest he arouse excessive anxiety in them or in himself. Later, but still in his early childhood (prelatency), they would enjoy a 'passive' tolerance of his efforts toward independent functioning, or toward a preference for dependence upon contemporaries of his own age, yet they would provide him with ample opportunities to return for parental protection, education, and love.

But let me return to my own patients. If the rigid attitude of the parents persists after early infancy, the confusion eventually spreads to the child's verbalization of his inner stimuli, that is to language itself. Percepts can no longer be distinguished from concepts. Now it is generally admitted that as far as the higher mental functions are concerned the ability to verbalize and consciousness are one and the same thing:

$$
\begin{array}{c}
\text{need} \\
\downarrow \\
\text{signal emitted by the child} \\
\downarrow \\
\text{non-satisfaction of that need} \\
\downarrow \\
\text{naming of another need by the parent} \\
\downarrow \\
\text{imposition} \\
\downarrow \\
\text{confused conceptualization by the child of his own body stimuli} \\
\text{(and therefore of his body awareness).}
\end{array}
$$

At this point it is necessary to stress another aggravating factor: that of role attribution. These patients are cast in a fixed role, that is in the *only role* their parents can accept without anxiety.

Among such roles the most common, as we saw, is that of 'the good little boy or girl' (that is of the meekly dependent child who does nothing untoward, who always obeys the parental commands he has introjected, 'who empties his plate', etc.). Quite often such children play their role so well that the contented parents begin to laugh indulgently at their antics. Pietro, one of my youngest patients, had identified himself with his role of 'good and contented feeder' to such an extent that, as he himself put it during psychotherapy, he constantly acted the clown. Thus, when he was three years old and attended a Christmas dinner at his grandparents', he started licking the hors d'œuvre plates to the accompaniment of general laughter. Again, at the age of four, he celebrated St Barbara's Day in his father's mess by consuming the rations of two soldiers, to the applause of all those present and severe indigestion.

In such extreme cases the child rarely dares to shed his role, but if he does he is met with shocked surprise. To the child that response not only means putting the precarious relationship of his parents to his role (not to 'him') at risk, but also endangering his own precarious identity (which he himself confuses with his role). If he stops playing his part, those near him will be unable to 'recognize' him. . . .

As for the parents, such role-shedding poses a threat to their emotive and cognitive schemata by introducing an unexpected element into their narcissistic security system, and hence fills them, too, with anxiety. 'Aren't you eating up? Is there anything wrong with you?'

To escape from the vice of his own anxiety and that of his parents, the child quickly returns to his role and becomes even more reluctant to throw it off. Let us try to analyse this process.

The child can only accept the propriety and legitimacy of his own body sensations when those in authority over him encourage him to do so. Most often his parents will insinuate their own views into his body feelings, perceptions and attitudes. They will say quite peremptorily, in phrases brooking no contradiction: 'You are hungry, you are tired, you are cold.' Just as he is not allowed any physiological changes in appetite, so he is also denied changes in mood: 'He must be happy – he has no reason not to be!' A bad mood on his part inflicts an unbearable narcissistic wound on parents so devoted to him.

Now the very fact that the child cannot turn to anyone else who might confirm the legitimacy of his perceptions makes him suspect the very element that ought to shape his experiences. He ends up by doubting his own sensations; surely if his feelings were not *wrong* his parents would not continually deny their validity. As a result he becomes more and more dependent and submissive. And by accepting unreservedly what *others* think of *his* experiences, he loses touch with his *own body*. During infancy and the latency period he will do just as he is expected to do: he will eat, dress and sleep in the 'right' way. In some cases, however, he retains enough energy to put up some kind of defence. At puberty, when he has to abandon his primary objects, make closer contacts with the outside world and begin his desperate search for a socially acceptable identity, he will often feel totally inadequate, and try to play a new role. The anxious and aggressive reactions of the parents merely serve to dramatize and aggravate his predicament.

What happens if such a patient comes for psychotherapeutic treatment? In the therapeutic relationship he will gradually develop the attitudes to food that Anna Freud has described so well for the primary phases of infant life: he will build up ego defences and engage in an ambivalent struggle against those interfering objects that were unknown to him or could not be structured in the proper time, that is during the first years of life. But in that case his neurotic defences will rest rather precariously on his prior perceptive-cognitive distortions.

Let me again take the case of Pietro, the adolescent pre-psychotic who came to me for treatment at the age of fifteen.

He was, as I said earlier, a model child and pupil, a veritable paragon of good manners and submissiveness. At the age of ten, though remaining the 'perfect' little boy, he began to adopt a host of obsessive ceremonials of a rhypo-phobic type. He was not sent for treatment because his parents were told by a neurologist that his obsessive fear of dirt was a superstition characteristic of his age group, and that it would eventually disappear.

But at the age of fourteen he began to deteriorate rapidly: his school record became deplorable; he obstinately refused to speak and turned completely rigid. Next came induced bouts of vomiting which Pietro blamed on a gastric obstruction due to excessive salivation.

During psychotherapy Pietro proved quite incapable of verbalizing his inner experiences and conflicts; he merely acted out his hatred of the little saint he had always been expected to be by a series of pseudo-delinquent actions that I lack the space to describe and analyse in detail. I shall simply confine my comments to his attitude towards food: Pietro seemed quite incapable of perceiving, and responding adequately to, hunger stimuli.

After every meal, which he swallowed voraciously in the company of his anxious parents, he would have prolonged fits of vomiting that led to severe hyperazotaemia, hypochloraemia

C

and the appearance of albumen and blood in his urine. This happened during the fifth month of his treatment, which Pietro attended three times a week after a very long journey from his home town: he refused steadfastly to be separated from his familiar surroundings for more than a day. At this point his physical condition had deteriorated to such an extent that I had to insist on his hospitalization. He would only go to a hospital in his home town, from which he kept sending me ambivalent letters. As soon as his condition had slightly improved he insisted on returning to our sessions. He no longer had vomiting fits but adopted increasingly bizarre eating habits. When his frantic mother kept serving him the most delicious dishes she could think of, he refused to eat them in the proper order – he would mix all the dishes up in the most repulsive manner, pouring beer over his spaghetti and sweet cream over his salad, and consuming it all with obvious satisfaction.

When I asked him to explain his odd behaviour, he at first shrugged his shoulders and pretended not to understand. Then, after a long silence, he added: 'It's on account of my taste buds . . .' and refused to volunteer any further information. For a moment I was at a loss, but then the meaning of his strange reply dawned on me: he was determined that his 'taste buds' should no longer have his mother's food preferences imposed upon them. He had taken refuge in these small sensory organs, from whose safety he was trying to build up the first conscious defence of his own autonomy! (The reader will have noted the similarity between his case and that quoted by Anna Freud: the toddler who scraped his tongue clean whenever his mother fed him. But Pietro was an adolescent and the toddler was only two years old!)

In discussing the importance of interpersonal influences in the discernment of sense stimuli, Spitz (*The First Year of Life*) quotes at length from von Senden's account of his work with a group of blind adults who had been cured of congenital cataract by surgery. Now, far from evincing delight in the recovery of their sight, they were regularly observed to show signs of severe anxiety and a refusal to reorganize their perceptive system. Many would not make use of the restored organ *until they had entered into an intense re-educative, emotionally motivated, relationship*. As a result von Senden felt entitled to reject all studies of human perception that neglect the emotions. The emotions, according to him, are the most powerful incentive to learning.

This becomes even more obvious from a case described by Balikov. It is unique in psychological literature and deserves far greater notice than it has received, the more so as similar circumstances are very unlikely to recur.

Three perfectly normal children had been brought up by blind parents, who though very affectionate and attentive to their children's needs, generally left the the shades drawn so that the children grew up in semi-darkness. As a result, though their eyesight was quite normal, these children behaved like blind people – even when entering well-lit rooms they would feel their way with their hands. They identified all objects by touch, and only put food into their mouths after careful tactile inspection.

Balikov's study deals with the re-education of Carl, the youngest of the three children who, at the age of two years and eight months, was sent to a nursery school for normal children.

It took eight months of rehabilitative training and psychotherapy before little Carl ceased to identify himself with his parents, came to *trust* his own eyes and lost his fear of forfeiting the approval and protection of those he loved. Let me quote Balikov's own comments (the reader would do well to read the whole article):

My attempts to understand this unusual material led me to the following speculations. I believe Carl and his siblings perceived their environment correctly and adapted to it appropriately with those sensory functions which were stimulated by their environment and the people in it. Furthermore, a sensory organ must be stimulated by appropriate stimuli of adequate intensity in order to be brought into useful function. This dark home did not provide adequate visual stimuli although the stimuli in other areas such as touch and hearing were sufficiently adequate. Thus the working model of the physical character of the home, which the children internalized, and which became a source of security, was a model built on impressions received from the functioning of only those sensory modalities which were adequately stimulated. This did not include adequate visual impressions. Secondly, through the experience of being reared by blind parents, a model of the parental techniques for adaptation was internalized. These parents suffered from a sensory loss and were unable to provide for their children an experiential model in that modality which could be perceived, appreciated, and internalized. Thirdly, the function of seeing was not cathected, or given value, by these parents. Other modalities such as hearing and touch, which were used by the parents, were valued.

By the use of the normal adaptive processes of imitation and identification, these children acquired a model from the parents which was incomplete so far as their own physiological endowment was concerned. As a result the three children were left with an impairment of a particular sensory function by virtue of their adaptations to an environment which offered insufficient stimulation to this sensory function and to parents who offered no stimulation because it had no value representation of function for themselves. This adaptive pattern was later utilized as a defense. Correction of the functional lack or impairment occurred when the child was offered an experience with an environment which provided visual stimulation and in which the important persons placed a high value upon the function of the specific sensory system involved.

I have quoted a clinical example that has no obvious connection with the perceptive and cognitive development of hunger sensations in the shaping of body awareness, because this unusual case provides an *outstanding illustration* of the *fundamental importance of the primary interpersonal relationship in the process of learning to perceive and satisfy one's own body stimuli.* In fact instincts never reveal themselves as pure biogenetic tensions, but are moulded from the outset by learning within an interpersonal relationship.

This is borne out by neurophysiological research. According to Hebb, the sub-cortical centres regulating visceral and emotional responses during relatively advanced phases of life have all received 'information' on need satisfaction during the earliest phases of existence.

Hence the great importance of Balikov's case study. If a faulty learning process can, indeed, impair the use of such specific and localized sense organs as the eyes, will its effects not be much more insidious on the far less specific and emotionally influenced psycho-sensory functions, such as the sense of hunger and satiety, the thermic sense and the sense of fatigue and exhaustion?

Before he can regulate his own diet rationally on the basis of his *own* needs and appetite, the child must first undergo a long process of learning in the confines of a highly flexible interpersonal relationship. Thus, while Balikov's children were prevented from learning how to use their eyes by their relationship with parents who were *actually blind*, the cases I have been describing had their body perceptions deformed by a relationship with parents who were *emotionally blind* to their children's individual needs.

This makes such cases of anorexia nervosa patients particularly complicated and points to a poor psychotherapeutic prognosis. In Balikov's case we merely had a failure of learning and a gap in experience, complicated by a unilateral, and I would say physiological, anxiety on the part of the children that they might forfeit the love of their blind parents if they used their eyes. The parents themselves, however, in no way tried to impose their own blindness on the children.

In our own cases, by contrast, the flaw in the learning process is reinforced by *mutual* anxiety. While his own anxiety prevents the patient from learning to come to terms with his own bodily needs (thus risking the loss of the reassuring object) the parents are anxious that their son (or daughter) might escape from total dependence by re-organizing his body sensations.

The analysis and treatment of such cases involves us directly in the recent polemics between psychotherapists with a purely neurodynamic and reflexological orientation (Eysenck, Platonov, Salter and others) and orthodox psychoanalysts. I hope that my own case presentations have shown that both orientations can and must complement and enrich each other in an effective therapeutic methodology. With these patients, confused and alienated as they are from their own bodies as the primary source of experience, it is, in fact, essential to begin with the kind of re-education that enables them to recognize and trust their own body signals, but it is equally important to realize and drive it home to them to what extent their interpersonal relationships stand in the way of their re-education and real autonomy.

It is only thanks to this dual psychotherapeutic approach that it has been possible to cure many anorexics including very severe cases.

The cases I have mentioned are not, in my view, neurotics,

but suffer from psychotic distortions of their body awareness in general and of their awareness of hunger and satiety in particular. Needless to say, between these extreme cases and those with purely neurotic disturbances, there exists a whole spectrum of intermediate conditions.

9 *The Development of Anorexia Nervosa*

Having dealt briefly with the social and family background of anorexic patients, we must now turn our attention to the strictly psychiatric problem of the psychodynamic basis of anorexia nervosa.

Despite the great nosographic range I myself have encountered, I refuse to follow other authors in describing anorexia nervosa as a simple symptom associated with a variety of mental illnesses. The fact that all true anorexics are absolutely determined to remain emaciated, refuse to admit they are ill and keep justifying their condition with all sorts of pretexts has convinced me that anorexia nervosa is a distinct and well-defined clinical entity.

I have accordingly made a point of searching for the *common elements* in the clinical and family histories of all my patients, paying particular attention to their premorbid personality, to their attitude towards the therapist and also to the phenomenal aspects of their illness as a possible key to their existential choice of starving themselves to death.

One obvious common element is their attitude to food which, as we saw, none of them ever reject as such. Unlike other patients suffering from sitophobia, anorexics consider food a matter of the utmost importance and are constantly preoccupied with it. They never think of it as being poisonous in the way schizophrenics do, or pointless in the way melancholics do (except for a superficial pose that does not stand up to careful clinical observation). Rather is it the *act* of eating that fills them with fear and anxiety, and that they consider degrading and self-defeating.

There is thus a clear split in their approach, which can be schematized as follows:

food = positive
eating = negative.

In other words what they reject consciously is the need to still their hunger. At first sight this attitude might appear as an extreme attempt to reconcile premorbid strains with an ideal body image. Other personality manifestations of many of these patients – their Spartan habits, perfectionism, intellectual ambition, overactivity and refined aesthetic and cultural tastes – seem to point in the same direction.

However some of my patients did not behave in this way at all: they seemed timid, without ambition, apparently without ideals or aims. And yet they, too, showed the same clinical symptoms, the same determination to starve themselves, and the same indifference to their dangerous physical condition. They, too, were thus reaching out for the same pathological objective as the rest. In my attempts to get to the bottom of this matter I was greatly helped by the work of Sullivan and especially by his writings on interpersonal relationships and personality development.

According to Sullivan three major and closely connected factors preside over the primary interpersonal and social development of the infant, namely:
1) the search for satisfaction;
2) the search for security;
3) the implementation of the power motive.

The power motive, which is the highest factor in the scale of human biopsychological development, represents an evolutionary impetus to test one's own capacity and ability. It is consolidated on the one hand by the attainment of satisfaction and security (basic trust) and on the other hand by successful attempts to establish the validity of one's own actions. As Hilde Bruch has pointed out, the normal implementation of the power motive involves the balancing of external stimuli with the validation of personal initiatives.

According to Sullivan secure personal development depends on the infant's discovery of his own power to attain desirable ends with the means at his disposal. In the absence of this fundamental discovery, the infant will feel inadequate, impotent and incapable – feelings against which he deploys all his mental resources.

In other words the need for satisfaction and security, and the implementation of the power motive, are jointly responsible for the survival of man as a distinct social being. The three integrating factors are inseparably interlinked: in the mature personality they blend into a harmonic whole.

Now in the case of anorexia nervosa patients it is my firm belief that this dynamic interrelationship has suffered a split or dissociation. More precisely their rejection of oral satisfaction (and hence the denial of the need for food) is the direct result of a feeling that such satisfaction runs counter to the need for security, autonomy and effectivity.

We have seen that most anorexics come from well-to-do homes where food is never in short supply, indeed that the importance of food is *pedantically* stressed by their mothers, so much so that it often assumes an almost magical, and in any case heteronymous, significance. We also saw that these mothers are scrupulous nurses, but that they offer their breasts joylessly, thus envincing their inability to accept and relish the most elementary aspects of life. As a result, though their daughters grow up surrounded by an abundance of the best food, their early experiences, together with frustrations in their subsequent contacts with their mothers, cause them to feel that what satisfaction is to be obtained from food is purely physical or even bestial and hence threatens their security. Eating to them is never a positively reinforced experience, and it is on the basis of this primary oral distortion that they develop premorbid personality traits. All their interpersonal experiences served only to undermine their sense of achievement and power.

Hilde Bruch, too, has noted that all the severe anorexics she has treated show a paralysing sense of helplessness. They all feel that they are merely acting in response to external demands and behave as if they did everything not because they wish to do so but because they must. Whereas the other two characteristics mentioned by Hilde Bruch – the disturbance of the body image and the misinterpretation of the body stimuli – are quite obvious, this particular disturbance is masked by the enormous negativism and diffidence with which these patients protect themselves against personal contacts. The indiscriminate nature of this defence mechanism shows that it is a desperate attempt to disguise an equally undifferentiated feeling of impotence, coupled to the fear that if they take even one mouthful of food, they will lose what little control they still have. According to Hilde Bruch this sense of impotence is in sharp contrast with the patient's earlier history, and also with the fact that the parents usually claim that their daughter used to give them no trouble at all. She was an exceptionally good, quiet and obedient little girl, ready to please in every way, trustworthy and extremely successful at school. Her downfall thus came with adolescence, when she was suddenly thrown on her own resources and found that she was utterly lacking in them.

In this connection I can do no better than quote in full the dream of one of my patients (Azzurra), as she herself related it to me. It has the power of a parable.

The dream of the ugly yellow dog

It was very dark, and I was in a nasty old house near the cemetery. It was spooky and I hid away behind the unheated boiler because I was afraid that a whole lot of gipsies might break in. But Mother could see my every move, because she was behind me, facing a small window. Then Mother gave me a yellow dog, and I was suddenly out in the street holding it on a leash. Then I saw another huge dog coming towards me. I looked at my own dog and noticed that he was hideous: his head was growing all the time on its tiny body. He filled me with utter disgust and I dropped the leash. The dog stopped dead because without the leash he couldn't walk. Then the other dog ordered me to give him something to eat, and then he bit him.

Translation of the dream into non-symbolic terms

The little girl was trembling in the dark because of a lack of affection (the dead boiler) and filled with terror (the gipsies – Klein's schizo-paranoid phase). At one point she realized that her mother, though emotionally detached (she was facing a small window), was omnipresent (Klein's depressive phase) and also that she could gain Mother's approval by playing the obedient, faithful and passive role of a dog on a leash (latency period). On reaching adolescence, she became partly conscious of herself: social contacts had revealed the weakness of her own ego, a weakness resulting from the divorce between her conformist behaviour and her personal experiences (the dog with the large head and the tiny body). She was filled with panic and could not stand on her own legs ('without the leash he couldn't walk'). Next came regression and recourse to anorexia as the concrete expression of her psychic situation (the dog with the large head and tiny body 'stopped dead'). The horrified reaction of those around her was such as to transform the invitation to take food into naked aggression ('he ordered me to give him something to eat and then he bit him'). In other words she had come to experience even the positive interhuman relationship expressed in the offer of food as an act of aggression.

I must stress that this dream was no arbitrary fantasy. If, in fact, she experienced her mother's feeding as an imposition then the subsequent offers of food by members of her family must needs have struck her as so many acts of aggression, the more so as constant battles were waged during every meal.

And so the young anorexic was caught in a cruel trap. She refused to eat in order to preserve her personal identity, but in order to preserve her life she simply had to eat and this she experienced as an act of self-betrayal. What she could not do, in any case, was to adapt her own food intake to her real needs.

This was borne out eloquently by another of her dreams, at a time when she was gradually improving under treatment and had begun to eat when nobody was looking.

The dream of the ferocious penguins

I entered a large poulterer's shop. This shop was very cold – the whole place was one huge refrigerator. People kept stealing chickens, and to stop them the shopkeeper had put all the chickens into display cases. Next to each case two penguins stood watch. They were hideous, frightening and enormous and had sharp beaks.

When asked for free associations, Azzurra came out with a story she had been told at school. A polar expedition whose starving members were desperately trying to get hold of anything they could to eat, found itself among an unknown species of penguins, three times larger than the normal kind, and aggressive to boot – one blow of their wings was enough to knock a man down.

The poulterer's shop was obviously the refrigerator in Azzurra's own home – from which she used to help herself from time to time. Whenever she did so, she felt that she was being watched by the chilling images into which her super-ego had transformed the parental figures (ferocious penguins). It was they alone who were entitled to dispense food; helping herself was a serious crime, a case of blatant theft.

We saw earlier that the typical home environment of anorexics is completely closed on itself and centripetal (the 'inward family' of American analysts). A detailed reconstruction of the childhood of these overprotected and often spoiled patients invariably reveals a conspicuous lack of support on the part of their parents for any spontaneous activity. The result, in the premorbid phase, is a compliant life-style that cuts off at its roots any sense of self-awareness or self-identification, and produces a severe atrophy of the feeling that it is possible to influence people or things in any significant way. The deep needs, the emotional drives and the very individuality of these patients have been damaged by the lack of understanding and oppressive attitude evinced by their all-powerful parents.

In the case of one of my patients (Ira) the subtle intolerance of the mother was such that the daughter became ashamed not only of having needs of her own but even of having a separate physiological constitution. The mother, who suffered from dramatic attacks of dysmenorrhoea and from a host of hypochondriacal symptoms which she used as an excuse to tyrannize her husband and family, let it appear that her daughter's painless menstruations made her something of an animal, as did her vigorous appetite and excellent digestion. Moreover the girl's build and character reminded her of her husband's family, whom she went out of her way to run down on every conceivable occasion. Ira's illness was one way of evening the score by the unconscious caricaturing of her mother's unjust accusations.

To understand this reaction we can do no better than follow, in our mind's eye, the gradual development that causes a fictitious anorexic to make an existential choice of her particular illness.

No special traits in her hereditary or constitutional predisposition distinguish her from others; a primary endocrine insufficiency (of the kind that organically oriented authorities used to cite) must also be ruled out; indeed her endocrinal glands are, if anything, extraordinarily resistant (cf. M. Bleuler, *Endokrinologische Psychiatrie*).

In the psychological domain, by contrast, she has a number of specific negative features, the most important of which are: 1) an unusual sensitivity to the modern cultural demand that young women play a highly ambiguous (passive-active) role, a demand that exposes them to sharp conflicts between the traditional residuals and the contemporary call for more active forms of behaviour;

2) a special relationship with what is (or are) the most important person (or persons) in her life. This interpersonal relationship is characterized by excessive domination on the part of this person (or these persons), to which she responds with passive compliance, the more so as she has been prevented from experiencing a *real sense of autonomy*, that is, her power to influence people and things *regardless of what others expect of her* (and this is equally true of those anorexics who were vivacious or even tomboyish pre-adolescents).

But, as we shall see, this psychobiological sensitivity invariably goes hand in hand with a remarkable *élan vital*, a passionate though suppressed love of life, a 'sthenic spur' which alone explains her heroic defence reactions. Let me add that it is this very spur (*der stenische Stachel*) which has made her choose anorexia in preference to, say, toxicomania or obesity, two conditions that spell surrender to one's own greed. (It should be noted that though frequent recourse to massive doses of amphetamines serves to maintain overactivity by overcoming the sense of inertia and inner emptiness, only one of my patients, Alda, ended up as a morphine addict, twenty years after the onset of her illness.)

H. Hieltmann, a German psychologist, who has made a psychodiagnostic study of anorexics, also speaks of their *explosive vitality*. Such 'sthenia within asthenia' and the various attitudes to which it gives rise pose many difficult problems even to the expert.

The pubertal crisis

It is with this heavy burden that our subject enters the critical phase of puberty. Here we cannot enter in detail into its full repercussions, particularly on girls. Suffice it to recall that adolescence usually goes hand in hand with a more or less intense rebellion against parental authority. This reaction is the unavoidable concomitant of detachment from the omnipotent parental image and of the affirmation of that autonomy which is the mainspring of originality and personal initiative.

Adolescence normally leads to the rejection of adult conventions, impositions and petty restrictions and to a search for higher ideals. It is, moreover, characteristic of the normal adolescent that such goals are always sought with the help of a close friend and comrade, who can be expected to share one's thoughts, feelings and resentments.

By contrast, our future anorexic has to face adolescence unsupported, not only because of her restricted home life but quite especially because of her attachment to her mother. She has no friends at all or else superficial acquaintances with whom she competes or about whom her mother's thinly disguised jealousy makes her feel guilty. These solitary little girls are full of fears: fear of life in general; fear of scholastic failure; fear of falling short of all sorts of expectations, and fear of doing the wrong thing. In short they have an apparently inexplicable and obscure feeling of fatal impotence, of a total lack of control over their lives.

It is in this precarious pyschological situation that the physical developments associated with puberty suddenly overtake them.

This calls for a brief digression about the differences between puberty in boys and girls. To begin with girls reach puberty at an earlier age than boys, so much so that the more psychologically immature amongst them are often taken completely by surprise. In purely physical respects, too, puberty leads to much more drastic, and potentially much more traumatic, changes in girls than it does in boys. Thus while boys develop larger genitals, begin to sprout facial, axillary and pubic hair, and change their voices, the general aspect of their bodies remains largely unchanged. In girls, on the other hand, the development of the primary sexual characteristics goes hand in hand with a radical change of the secondary sexual characteristics. The whole body becomes rounded and loses its angular lines; within a matter of months there are breasts, full hips and a curved belly. Often these changes attract strange looks and comments or even catcalls from passers-by that often wound the fragile and immature young girl to whom they are addressed.

Simone de Beauvoir in her autobiographical *Memoirs of a Dutiful Daughter* has dealt with the subject most movingly:

During the day, I had dizzy spells; I became anaemic. Mama and the doctor would say: 'It's her development'. I grew to detest that word and the silent upheaval that was going on in my body. I envied 'big girls' their freedom; but I was disgusted at the thought of my chest swelling out; I had sometimes heard grown-up women urinating with the noise of a cataract; when I thought of the bladders swollen with water in their bellies, I felt the same terror as Gulliver did when the young giantesses displayed their breasts to him. . . .

I was going through a difficult patch: I looked awful; my nose was turning red; on my face and the back of my neck there were pimples which I kept picking at nervously. My mother, overworked, took little trouble with my clothes: my ill-fitting dresses accentuated my awkwardness. Embarrassed by my body, I developed phobias: for example, I couldn't bear to drink from a glass I had already drunk from. I had nervous ticks: I couldn't stop shrugging my shoulders and twitching my nose. 'Don't scratch your spots; don't twitch your nose,' my father kept telling me. Not ill-naturedly, but with complete absence of tact, he would pass remarks about my complexion, my acne, my clumsiness, which only made my misery worse and aggravated my bad habits.

Nor must we underestimate the traumatic shock of menstruation: the sudden flow of blood seems far more dramatic than the first ejaculation of seminal fluid. The menarche is a sudden, mysterious and humiliating bodily happening over which the poor girl has no control.

In fact the female with her curved body, *exposed* as she is to sexual cupidity, to coitus, to pregnancy, to breast-feeding, to the physical demands of her husband and children, is much more inextricably involved in the biological sphere than is the male. But what is far more traumatic to the adolescent girl is that she experiences her feminine sexuality in a passive and receptive way: she is exposed to lewd looks, subjected to menstruation, about to be penetrated in sexual embraces, to be invaded by the foetus, to be suckled by a child, etc.

As a complement to Simone de Beauvoir's remarks, I must also quote the following extract from *La Femme*, by Buytendijk:

Man, we have said, is aware of his body because he is conscious of his grip on the world. He treats his body as an instrument that helps him to act, to exert his power, to fight. This includes the function of his sexual organs: they are part of the actions man can perform. It is one of the great merits of Simone de Beauvoir that, in dealing with resentment, she underlines how uncertain is the feminine hold on the world. Women, she suggests, do not experience encounters as occasions for taking but as occasions for being taken – in the most abstract sense of these terms. This means that a woman has a body that allows her to be taken.

This passive-receptive aspect of feminine life, which is 'experienced' so suddenly during puberty, is an unbearable climax to the potential anorexic: it is the concrete manifestation of that passivity and impotence that had vaguely plagued her for so long. She now looks upon her body (or for that matter upon her physical development) in two conflicting but equally intolerable ways: on the one hand, her oral needs and sexual characteristics make her body an essentially receptive-passive object and hence the 'guilty' representative of that excessive passivity ('the self') that she abhors; on the other hand, its 'indiscreet' and uncontrollable development makes her look upon her body as an irresistible intruder, that is, as part of the external environment ('the others').

Hence she fights her body on two planes:

1) because she considers it the concrete expression of the unacceptable part of her self (passive receptiveness) she attacks it as the source of her impotence and anxiety;

2) because she considers it an all-powerful invader, she attacks it as an alien force.

In my view the behaviour of these patients fully bears out Sullivan's contention that the power motive is much more pronounced during a particular stage in the development of certain people than are hunger and thirst (though, I hasten to add, anorexics deliberately *choose* their particular form of privation).

An understanding of the power motive is fundamental, both psychologically and logically. For Sullivan, the power motive means much more than the usually restricted meaning of power in 'power drive'. A person is born with this power motive, or, in his cautious words, with 'something' of the power motive. This does *not* mean, however, that one is born with a 'power drive'. For Sullivan, power refers to the expansive biological striving of the infant and states characterized by the feeling of ability, applying, in a very wide sense, to all kinds of human activity. A 'power drive', in the narrow sense, results from the thwarting of the expansive biological striving, and the feeling of the lack of ability. In other words, a 'power drive' is learned, resulting from the early frustration of the need to be, and to feel, capable, to have ability, to have power. A 'power drive' develops as a compensation when there is a deep, gnawing, inner sense of powerlessness, because of early frustration of the expanding, developing latent potentialities of the organism. Later acculturation and experience may, and frequently does, add to the early frustration and sense of powerlessness. A person who has a feeling of ability or power does not need to gain, and will not seek, dominance or power *over* some one (Mullahy).

Anorexia nervosa patients who have lost the ability to experience their 'power motive' in affective *interpersonal* relationships seek to express it in an *intrapersonal* relationship with, and fight against, their own body. They look upon their illness as a struggle against their incapacity, and attempt to regain lost power.

The ego of the anorexic, deformed as it is, cannot experience its autonomy in external reality, that is, outside the inner conflict with the body – the sense of autonomy is so lacking that the anorexic can only reconstruct it in her mind's eye in the guise of autarchic corporeal *non-receptiveness*.

This is the basis of the great anorexic lie: to live 'as if' the entire blame for one's misfortunes lay with one's body.

This is so, first of all because the body's very appearance suggests that it is open to invasion, that it is a palpable manifestation of that receptivity which has led the patient to feel so impotent and inadequate; and secondly because its irresistible development and growth forces the anorexic constantly to re-experience the tyrannic constrictions of interpersonal relationships past, present and (presumably) future. The body becomes the scapegoat: to let it grow fat means giving passivity free rein, submitting to the demands of an arrogant usurper. Hence the anorexic keeps spying on the body, is totally preoccupied with it even while disowning it, keeps fighting its demands and lulls himself or rather herself into a false sense of security with its emaciation.

For far too long various writers have been repeating the old fable that anorexics are people who refuse to grow up and who reject their femininity, and this on the slender grounds that anorexia is largely confined to women. But, as J. E. Meyer has observed most shrewdly, *the true counterpart of anorexia nervosa in the male is the pubertal depersonalization syndrome which often lasts for years.* However he saw fit to add that, 'unlike female anorexics, these boys long to be adults and to be fully accepted; but their apparent impatience to grow up hides a fear of responsibility and independence.' Now this is precisely what happens with anorexic girls; they, too, want to be adults and wholly accepted.

It is therefore an oversimplification (and therapeutically harmful) to insist that the anorexic wants to revert to infancy and rejects her femininity because she is afraid of the consequences. What she shows instead is a keen desire, however distorted, to become an autonomous adult. This she does by rejecting those aspects of feminine corporeality that conjure up the terrifying vista of turning into a succubus and passive vessel. For all that, the pubertal development is only an incidental trauma which, while revealing the actual state of the ego, wrongly identifies the enemy with the body. Hence emaciation becomes the symptomatic expression of the search for security and power (and therefore a defence against insecurity, inadequacy and impotence). Emaciation means the suppression of oral satisfaction (and thus of all basic needs) for the sake of security and power. The result is an ambivalent attitude that can be schematized as follows:

$$\text{fasting} \rightleftarrows \text{voracity}$$

Within this schema the achievement of the two main objectives, security and power, assumes different forms depending on the subjects' inner state. Thus while less sthenic patients look to emaciation for security, for *escape from* the negative aspects of social existence, the more sthenic and more intellectual subjects see emaciation as the magic key to greater *power*, to a more positive social existence. We can schematize the whole process in the following way:

Security from	Emaciation as escape from
the negative aspects of social existence	non-acceptance
	ridicule
	exposure to lustful glances
	to critical remarks
	to aggression
	to sexual advances
Pull towards	Emaciation for the sake of
the positive aspects of social existence	freedom
	beauty
	intelligence
	morality

The most pronounced sthenic types tend to adopt a precise and active social attitude and employ the same motivations that impel most of us to realize the most essential part of ourselves. Needless to say with anorexics this realization is illusory: they are in the grip of a conflict, and pathologically impaired by their voluntary emaciation, which they see as the bodily expression of their aspirations.

As a *search for freedom*, the rejection of food strikes these patients as affording the only possible proof of their autonomy. 'They can force me to do anything they want,' said Azzurra of her parents, 'but they can't make me swallow even a single

mouthful more!' In fact parents who keep stuffing their children but do not respect them as persons, who try to force food
down reluctant throats with threats or supplications, often strike
anorexics as blatant hypocrites who are determined to have
their own way at any price. Thus one of my patients, commenting
on her mother's tears which flowed freely at every meal, said
bitterly: 'She isn't crying because she is unhappy; she just cries
because she can't get the better of me!' Moreover in its extreme
form – the hunger strike – the refusal to eat becomes an idealistic
blow for freedom: the total rejection by the weakest of the
impositions of the strongest.

In the sphere of *aesthetics*, the withdrawal of primary cathexis
from one's own body calls for a regressive reinvestment of
libidinal energies that produces a perverted image of physical
beauty. One of my patients, who felt this problem with particular
force, dreamt of being admired in public as she stood on tiptoe
looking very tall and slender. In other dreams she saw herself
as a delicate silver amphora surrounded by coarse earthenware
vessels. Another of my patients, who was highly intelligent, told
me that before her recovery she used to identify extreme slenderness with simplicity and straightness. Slenderness to her was thus
the physical demonstration of that very authenticity from which
she was psychologically debarred.

The problem of *intelligence* or of intellectual *power* is reflected
in the anorexic's firm conviction that eating blunts one's mental
acumen. We all know how hard it is to solve a difficult mathe-
matical problem, to improvise an intelligent speech or to produce
a telling argument on a full stomach, and these patients merely
carry this knowledge to outrageous extremes.

Similarly their ascetic approach reflects a rigid belief in the
split between body and mind: one has only to crush the one
(the strong body) to enhance the other (the weak spirit), thus
magically reversing their respective roles. Every victory over the
flesh is a sign of greater control over one's biological impulses,
a sort of athletic training against the expected bouts of voracious-
ness. This type of asceticism should not be confused with the
religious: the saint becomes an ascetic not as an end in itself but
as a means to attain mystical communion with God and all His
creatures. The religious sentiments of anorexics, in so far as we
have looked into them at all, do not, by contrast, involve this

mystical element: what religious beliefs they profess are schematic, rigid and quite without love. If they pretend to be giving and outgoing (as many of my patients do indeed) they are aggressively so and their attitude oppresses rather than relieves those at whom it is directed. Anorexics do not become ascetics after a slow and arduous process of inner development – they are in a hurry to reach a pathological goal, they 'jump to conclusions'. Hence they achieve no more than an ascetic 'appearance', a hastily constructed somatic shadow of the true ascetic.

Great religious teachers have always been alert to the psychological, no less than to the physical, dangers of penitential fasts, and they have warned particularly against the mistaken sense of power and euphoria that often affects those who engage in such practices. Duncan *et al* have mentioned the sense of blissful well-being associated with hyperketonaemia due to fasting. But perhaps the most telling account comes from the pen of a famous theologian, Romano Guardini. In those who deliberately refrain from food, he writes, the body and spirit are set free; the whole person becomes more agile and nimble.

Material worries and irritations drop away. The confines of reality are yes and no, the horizon of the possible grows ever wider. . . . The spirit becomes more sensitive; more far-seeing and more acute, and the conscience more quick and lively. The sensitivity to spiritual choices increases. The natural defence system, meant to protect the individual against occult or harmful influences and against other forces that threaten his existence from all sides, is badly shaken. The inner life is, as it were, laid bare. . . . The awareness of spiritual power is increased and with it *the danger of losing sight of what is assigned to each one of us, of the limits of our finite existence, of our dignity and our abilities.* Hence the dangers of pride, magic and spiritual intoxication. . . .

It is worth stressing that Christ, too, after fasting for forty days in the desert was tempted to sin against His own humanity.

10 *Anorexia Nervosa and Sex*

The fact that anorexia nervosa does not generally appear as a clear clinical entity until puberty, and that it is chiefly confined to girls and is associated with amenorrhoea, has misled many writers into thinking that it is causally related to sexual development and the ensuing sexual problems (fear of pregnancy, fantasies of oral impregnation, sexual traumata, lack of sex education, etc.).

In fact sexual problems have much the same bearing on anorexia nervosa as they have on schizophrenia, which, too, is generally a post-pubertal illness. This explains why organically-oriented psychiatrists have tried to trace the genesis of schizophrenia back to a disorder of the gonads, though so far without any success. From the psychodynamic point of view sexual problems, while playing an important part in schizophrenia, do so to a limited extent and in no way overshadow the many personal and interpersonal problems that stand in the way of emotional and sexual maturity.

My own experience has convinced me that in anorexia nervosa, too, the sexual problem is not the basic one. All my women patients were fixated at the pre-genital levels. Puberty and the sudden, overwhelming physical developments it entails then trigger off traumatic, but in any case quite unexpected, situations that shake the apparent emotional equilibrium of these subjects. In our discussion of their family background we saw earlier that the emotional 'absenteeism' of the father vitiates the transition from the dyadic relationship (mother–child) to the triadic relationship and hence impedes normal psychological growth.

B. Sommer has argued that:

In these patients the primary oedipal conflict proved to be highly traumatic and could not be surmounted because their fixations to objects appropriate to earlier stages prevents the resolution of the oedipal conflict on a plane appropriate to their age. The patients are not only fixated in respect of their oedipal conflict, dynamically weakened though it may have become, but have moreover been impaired in their elementary and vital pre-oedipal development, i.e. during the oral phase, and hence frustrated in the widest sense of that word.

This is also the view of Meng who has observed that the physical developments associated with puberty tend to frighten the young girl: she sees her body growing 'bigger' while her ego, fenced in as it is by the fixation, keeps regressing.

As Binswanger has so rightly noted in his analysis of Ellen West, the dread of becoming fat must be considered anthropologically not as the beginning but as the end of an insidious pathological process. 'It is the "end" of the encirclement of the entire existence, so that it is no longer open for its existential possibilities.' As Ellen West herself explained, her existence had become 'confined to a steadily diminishing circle of narrowly defined possibilities, for which the wish to be thin and the dread of getting fat represent merely the definitive [psychophysical] garb'.

In short puberty drives home to the young girl her incapacity to tackle a new problem over and above the many others she has been unable to solve in the past. The illness generally bursts upon the adolescent at a time when she ought to be affirming her own presence and ability to face life with a greater measure of independence. At puberty, the normal young girl must realize her potential not only as an individual, but also as a distinct and unique person who assents to her existence, that is to her own body and sex. And this is precisely what the potential anorexic is quite unable to do.

Obviously such subjects cannot even imagine that sexual relations are a form of self-fulfilment based on a personal choice. Some patients simply ignore the whole problem and shut their minds off whenever the subject is broached by others. A few will permit themselves to engage in academic and completely detached discussions of something that may well concern others but certainly not themselves. A fair number indulge in romantic fantasies of ideal Platonic friendships with unknown or distant lovers, thus evincing an intuitive or purely imitative interest in a problem the happy solution of which would so greatly enrich their lives. Such fantasies are confined to relatively 'old' subjects – girls in their late teens – and are very rare indeed among the pubertal. One twenty-five-year-old chronic patient (who later died following an uncontrollable bout of bulimia) confined her 'love life' to a sentimental correspondence with various young Italian emigrants in Australia and South Africa, whose addresses she had procured from matrimonial advertisements. She hurriedly broke off the correspondence as soon as one of the 'pen-lovers' announced his impending arrival in Italy.

Of all my patients, only one (Rita, aged twenty-one) pretended to be open-minded about sexual matters. She told me that on festive occasions or at student reunions she would seek out a boy (or even several boys) and engage in heavy petting, but never 'go the whole way'. During psychotherapy it became obvious that she was merely trying to assuage her paralysing sense of impotence and inadequacy; she was simply making sure that she could still evoke some response in herself and in others. These sexual 'experiences', unlike eating, posed no real threat to her. 'I couldn't be caught out because I always knew just when to stop.'

What she was obviously afraid of was oral, not sexual, satisfaction. She thus provided me with an excellent illustration of what Zutt has called the 'clear antinomy between appetite and eroticism on the one hand, and hunger and sexuality on the other'. In fact appetite and Eros have a close social affinity: they are both delightfully human. They both call for a refined sense of *discrimination*. Appetite does not mean swallowing anything that comes your way, but *savouring* food and drink suitably prepared and presented, if possible in the company of relatives, friends and favoured guests. In the same way the true lover does not seek his pleasures indiscriminately but has personal standards of what he thinks desirable in his or her partner; he refuses to be fobbed off with substitutes.

Appetite and true eroticism are therefore quite different from hunger and lust, which reflect a blind quest for satisfaction by any available means, in the second case with a faceless partner, whose name is legion.

However anorexics in whom food binges go hand in hand with

indiscriminate lechery are very uncommon. Generally these patients are frigid and obsessed with maintaining their precarious equilibrium by following the most respectable and conventional patterns of life. It is very rare indeed that such patients confess to manual masturbation or to conscious sexual needs – at most they will admit that they occasionally create vaguely pleasant sensations by squeezing their legs together or by contracting their pelvic muscles. They often misinterpret the nature of their own sexual stirrings and become filled with all sorts of obscure fears. Their problem is the control not of their sexual drives but of the tyrranical physical demands that are reflected in their hunger pangs.

11 *The Problem of Death and Suicide in Anorexia Nervosa*

Many authors have stressed that anorexics have a strong self-destructive urge; thus Boss speaks of suicide in 'refractive doses' when referring to those patients who, in their innermost selves, refuse absolutely to live as beings of flesh and blood. 'They are totally lost to the therapist: using their own method right to the end, they allow themselves to evaporate and dissolve.'

This highly suggestive interpretation of gradual suicide raises a number of questions. In the first place we must ask ourselves whether the desire for self-annihilation, the suicidal drive of these patients, is conscious, even though dissimulated, or unconscious. In the second place we must determine why, having discovered the apparently intolerable burdens of the flesh (the pressure of physical demands and the body's inevitable decay) they do not put an end to themselves there and then, instead of soldiering on at the price of atrocious sacrifices over many years.

Let me try to answer these difficult questions by drawing on my own therapeutic experience.

From my direct contact with anorexic patients, and from reading their diaries and hearing the confessions of those I was able to cure, I am convinced that not one of them has ever had a conscious wish for annihilation by suicide. (As pointed out on p. 120, the suicide of Anna Maria was in fact unconnected with her anorexia as such.) Nosographically, too, I have never observed anorexics in the kind of depressive state that often leads to suicide, and, in fact, anorexia nervosa patients never deliberately end their lives by direct measures. This, we found, is also reflected in their Rorschach protocols. Moreover, their pathological picture does not even involve an unconscious suicidal wish: psychodynamic studies have shown that their 'choice' of emaciation does not serve to remove or displace the real object of their conflict in the manner that common neurotic mechanisms do. It was precisely this bias on the part of many psychoanalysts that was responsible for the failure to cure such patients. Their wish to be thin is perfectly conscious, as is their struggle to keep control of their oral needs and the resulting sense of security, however precarious and unrealistic it may be. No authentic anorexic ever considers her symptom absurd or makes a real effort to eat copious meals; all of them consider their behaviour perfectly justified (I am speaking of the pre-chronic phase, that is of the phase before various clinical and therapeutic interventions persuade them to *feign* illness).

The true anorexic has a deep and lasting horror of obesity, completely untempered by introspection – it reflects a deliberate decision that must never be renounced. The resulting struggle takes the form of alternate bouts of bulimia and the most stringent fasts, or of unbridled greed and total self-abnegation; but however often the patient succumbs to the demands of the body, her mind is made up that the body can and must be subdued in the long run. But this *type of acarnality is not a death wish* – quite the contrary. It is, essentially, an unrealistic tension and a rejection of existence *qua* living and dying in one's body. More precisely it is a rejection of death as a biological fact, and with it a rejection of ageing, corpulence and existential decay. In short, the anorexic turns her back on the existentially inevitable, on everything that is imposed by, and inherent in, her corporeality.

In two of my cases, the illness appeared quite suddenly after the death of someone they loved, and was preceded by a state of shock and of intense revulsion at the idea of such irreparable loss. In a third case (a probationary nurse) the illness started immediately after her first attendance at an autopsy, for which her rudimentary training had ill prepared her.

This patient, to whom I was the first to give a psychological examination through she had been chronically ill for ten years and had been hospitalized, had never once mentioned this unfortunate episode. It was only when she was given a Rorschach test that she suddenly 'saw' an open abdomen and the exposed intestines in many Rorschach cards, thus reliving, and offering associations with, the traumatic experience of the autopsy. 'I saw that open abdomen . . . full of stinking bowels . . . and I thought to myself . . . there used to be a soul here . . . and I rebelled!' This patient, who had reached the most extreme state of cachexia (height: 5' 2''; weight: 50 lbs) but was still remarkably lively, looked highly sceptical when her doctor told her that she was close to death. She was firmly convinced that she had finally broken through the barrier of physical corruption.

In fact anorexics look upon their possible deaths as so many accidents, but never as something they themselves may be courting. We saw that anorexics, unlike certain psychotics, do not refuse food altogether but merely reduce their food intake to absurdly low levels. Their emaciated bodies are their guarantee that they are winning the fight against passive surrender to greed, so much so that whenever they lose weight for inter-current reasons (fevers, dental complications, etc.) they pride themselves on this extra loss as yet another victory over their demanding bodies.

These patients play with death like children who think they can disappear by shamming dead. Incapable as they are of facing reality or even, as we shall see, of comprehending their own physical needs, they delude themselves into thinking that they can tamper with their bodies as they please. This I have observed with utter astonishment even in one of my patients who was a doctor, who, in theory at least, was fully familiar with her biological processes and nevertheless treated her own body in the most absurd and anti-scientific, and sometimes even magical, way, thus ignoring the most elementary tenets of medical science.

All those who have observed patients in the terminal phase of the disease have been struck by their severe state of psychological regression and their divorce from biological reality. They are in no way depressed or sorry for themselves and do nothing to avert their impending death; but they also take no deliberate steps to hasten their end, and show no signs of waiting or hoping for death. This attitude is maintained obstinately and persistently, until extreme organic exhaustion sets in. The accompanying mental state is one of emotional dullness and indifference reminiscent of that of patients debilitated by a long history of chronic organic disease. The suicide of Ellen West described by Binswanger was an exceptional case: to this unusually gifted woman, death was the mystical personification of salvation from an imprisoned existence, and hence an authentic choice, a *dies festus*. Ellen did not, as Boss would have put it, trade total suicide for a suicide in *refracta dosi*: to the last she tried bravely to preserve her existence through anorexia, but when, after fifteen years of torment, she came to appreciate the futility of her struggle, she tragically put an end to it.

12 *Interpretation of Anorexia Nervosa by the Object-Relation Theory*

My psychotherapeutic observations of patients whose capacity to recognize, and distinguish between, body stimuli had been impaired in various ways have convinced me that only a psychodynamic theory based on object relations (particularly on relations with the negative aspects of the introjected object) can make a substantial contribution to the psychopathology of body experience. I was led to this conviction in a very simple way: because all authorities are agreed that the child's original experience with the primary object is a corporeal-incorporative experience, I was persuaded that the incorporation of the negative aspects of the primary object, with the ensuing repression and defence against the return of that object to consciousness, must provide the dynamic foundations of psychopathological body experiences.

In the early phase, the incorporation of the object is inevitable. There is no other way of relating to it. The child's fundamental experiences with his object are body experiences. The experience of goodness and well-being is a body experience, and so is that of evil and discomfort. Moreover the child can only distinguish himself bodily from his object at a comparatively advanced stage.

We must now discuss what we mean by a child's 'good' and 'bad' body experiences. This is a point on which the literature is extremely vague. Terms such as oral frustration or poor feeding conditions often recur, but the types of mothers and the different children discussed vary very considerably.

I would like to suggest the following general definition of a *good* body experience: to feel one's body, in the relationship with the mother, as a source of predominantly pleasurable sensations, but without premature genital excitation which, because of its aggressive component, would lead to anxiety. This means treating the child's primary relation with the good object as a pleasant erotization of the cutaneous, mucous, oral, gastric and passive-motor elements of the body. Only later does the genital aspect come into play, associated with a small amount of aggressiveness (the genital play studied by Spitz). The child, who cannot yet perceive distinct objects, experiences his own body as a good object.

When this process is thwarted by defective emotional relations with that object, a pathological situation arises. In that case the child, because he cannot perceive himself as distinct from the object, may feel his own body as a source of unpleasant or bad sensations. As a result he comes to consider it as bad in itself or else as being inhabited by a bad object.

Psychoanalysis has taught us that personality development is based on the individual's relation with his own body, *from the moment he perceives it as a whole, as existing outside the maternal object. In cases of psychopathological body experience*, the condition of being 'outside' is realized in part only. Most of the 'bad' experiences of his own body, which the child has met during the incorporative, primary narcissistic, phase of his object relationships, remain immured inside his body. *In these circumstances, all the 'bad' experiences he encounters during the subsequent phase of secondary narcissism and later* (dis-identification) will be repetitions of the patterns laid down during the primary-incorporative, archaic phase.

In my attempt to account for the patient's 'choice' of psycho-pathological bodily experience, I have emphasized the primary incorporative phase. However I do not wish to give the impression that I underestimate the importance of all the later inter-personal experiences of childhood, the latency period and adolescence. In different cases they may compensate for, or aggravate, the consequences of the defective primary object relation. The negative consequences of defective interpersonal relations in early childhood on the later phases of development will become apparent in what follows.

On the basis of the above assumptions I suggest the following working hypothesis.

Psychopathological body experiences are a direct expression of a libidinal and aggressive emotional relationship with negative (exciting-rejecting) aspects of the incorporated object.

Let us now consider the bearing of these remarks on anorexia nervosa.

What is the body experience of the anorexic? Should anorexia nervosa be considered a defence against an oral-sadistic impulse? Some writers, under the influence of Melanie Klein, have suggested that the anorexic girl tries, by not eating, to deny her impulse to destroy the primary object; in brief, she tries to repress her cannibalistic impulses. I am rather sceptical of this interpretation. I consider it arbitrary, because it fails to consider the clinical and phenomenologic data which alone can provide a basis for a valid psychodynamic theory.

Patients in a predominantly schizo-paranoid situation with oral-sadistic impulses organize their defences against a reactivation of their condition by developing either delusional ideas about being poisoned, or fears of not being able to eat or an actual block against food. This block is completely involuntary and is accompanied by severe irritation, a preoccupation with starvation, and intense feelings of physical damage and decay. Thus one of my non-anorexic patients always carried a bottle of milk with him. He would take advantage of any loosening of his block by taking a few sips from the bottle.

The clinical picture presented by the anorexia nervosa patient is altogether different. She is not the passive victim of a total or sporadic block in her food intake, but reduces it to absurd levels with consistent determination. The most important point is that, once she has consumed food, especially in what, by her standards, are large quantities, she does not feel that her body is being *threatened* or destroyed, but thinks that it has become bloated, ominous and in the way.

The basic symptoms of anorexia nervosa are therefore: persistent hunger (which is generally disguised and only admitted after long familiarity with the therapist), and a deliberate struggle against it. Hunger pangs may completely disappear in the terminal phases or when excessive starvation and the continuous use of laxatives cause disturbances in the electrolyte balance and lead to ketonaemia.

In short *the body has become a threatening force that must be held in check rather than destroyed.* This is the crucial phenomenon by which anorexia nervosa can be distinguished from similar syndromes. In my view the classic oral-sadistic approach cannot explain why the anorexic should feel after every meal that her body, far from being damaged or threatened, has become intolerably bloated.

This raises the problem of whether the anorexia nervosa patient is afraid of food or of her body. My answer is that she is afraid of her body, and that *she experiences food intake as an increase of the latter at the expense of her ego.*

To the anorexic, *being a body* is tantamount to being *a thing.* If the body grows, the thing grows as well and the 'person' starts to shrink. The fight against the body is thus a desperate fight against reification – paradoxically so, because while refusing to be a thing the anorexic fights her battle, not on a spiritual plane, but rather on a purely material one: that of her own body.

Now let us ask how the anorexic acquires this particular experience of her body. In my view she does so by equating it with the incorporated object, namely the mother, in its negative, overpowering aspects, the better to oppose it and to separate it from the ego.

I should like to emphasize that the body of the anorexic does not merely *contain* the bad object but that it *is* the bad object. From the phenomenological point of view, the body is experienced as having all the features of the primary object as it was perceived in a situation of oral helplessness: all-powerful, indestructible, self-sufficient, growing and threatening. No active aggression enters into the clinical picture or into the patient's dreams: there is an unconscious feeling that the object is far too strong to be destroyed. The result is a dejected feeling of complete helplessness. Liliana, for instance, had the following dream: 'I am standing in front of my mother. I would like to do something, but my feet are two bleeding stumps.' (Very occasionally a feeble compensatory aggressive fantasy makes its appearance.) She was still a poor and totally helpless child, both biologically and psychologically, when confronting the impervious object. That object did not so much frustrate her *oral* drives and needs as it frustrated the needs of her ego. As another patient, Rita, put it:

I have never been left to experience things in my own way. This is the worst loss anyone can suffer. It leads to emptiness, to a lack of

D

emotional contact with life, to a lack of real vitality, of whatever makes you feel yourself instead of a heavy, shapeless thing.

The typical mother of the anorexia nervosa patient is an aggressively overprotective and unresponsive woman, and as such incapable of considering her daughter as a person in her own right. It is often the parental couple, with its own pathology, or the whole family group, who sabotage the basic needs of the patient's ego, and quite especially the feeling that she is unique, capable and worthy of respect. My own observations show that the most common basic interpersonal experiences of anorexics are the following:

During infancy the ritual aspect of feeding takes precedence over the emotional relationship with the mother, who derives no pleasure from nursing the child; control prevails over tenderness and joy. Parental stimulation serves to stifle any of the child's own initiatives (Bruch).

During childhood and the latency period, an insensitive parent constantly interferes, criticizes, suggests, takes over vital experiences and prevents the child from developing feelings of his own.

These pathogenic interpersonal experiences give rise to a paralysing sense of ineffectiveness pervading every thought and activity (Bruch). Hence, though few anorexics have had to go short of material goods in their childhood, they were nevertheless severely deprived: their spontaneous expressions were ignored or frowned upon, unless they accorded with the mother's possessive ambitions. In the latency period these patients accordingly developed a life style of passive surrender. Their self-awareness, and quite particularly their body-awareness, and the feeling of being separate from others and from their expectations were severely impaired.

It is thus – bound to a possessive mother who treats her as a mere appendage and never as an individual deserving uncritical support – that the patient enters adolescence, and is faced with what to her is an unbearable traumatic situation. She has to withdraw her libidinal cathexis from the parental figures and to face the difficult problem of establishing new interpersonal relationships. Her body undergoes rapid changes: it is transformed almost beyond recognition and yet it remains her own. She has to discover a new self, which means that she can no longer identify herself with her mother but must play an independent social role. All these problems push her fragile and premorbid personality into a state of depression: she fears that her ego cannot measure up to so many new tasks. If we examine the stage prior to the onset of anorexia – as we should always make a point of doing – we shall invariably discover such signs of ego depression as a transient sense of unreality; boredom; the feeling of being different from others, and especially from one's schoolmates who seem either much more childish or much older; a sense of isolation, and an obscure feeling of helplessness and uselessness. During this prodromic phase, anxiety and depression often go hand in hand with an actual decrease in appetite, which may draw the patient's attention to the problem of food. At this point the depressed ego, faced as it is by impossible tasks, *reactivates* the overwhelming *sense of helplessness* experienced during the infantile period, when the patient was quite incapable of satisfying her own vital needs.

At this point I should like to express my agreement with E. Bibring that the emphasis should not be laid on oral frustration and the ensuing oral fixation, but on the infant's and child's experience that her ego is totally helpless. This approach

does not invalidate the accepted theories of the role which orality and aggression play in various types of depression. It implies, however, that the oral and aggressive strivings are not as universal in depression as is generally assumed, and that, consequently, the theories built on them do not offer sufficient explanation but require a certain modification.

We can now try to answer the puzzling question of why it is that anorexia nervosa should occur almost exclusively in the female sex and at about puberty. (The three cases of male anorexia I have studied were not cases of true anorexia nervosa. One quickly developed paranoid delusions. The second entertained hypochondriacal ideas of a psychoasthenic type, centred on the digestive system. The third was the closest to true anorexia nervosa, not least because of his neuromuscular overactivity. This patient, however, had two atypical symptoms: an explicit longing for food, and obvious pride in his condition. Unlike female anorexics, who will invariably tell you that they eat more than enough, this patient would boast about his fasting feats.)

In my view this is due to a process of 'concretization'. Puberty, as we saw, is a sudden and traumatic experience for the girl. Narcissistic libido cathexis has to be withdrawn from the infantile body and directed towards the new, strange, adult, and rounded body, which, moreover, must be accepted as being part of oneself. This process, that is the separation of one's own body from the maternal object, is, however, impeded by the permanent incorporation of that object. In fact, because of the development of the breasts and other feminine curves, the body is experienced *concretely* as the maternal object, from which the ego wishes to separate itself at all costs. During this transitory phase of pubertal depression, the ego organizes a desperate defence system by splitting itself into two parts, in the hope of averting two major psychic catastrophes: a permanent state of depression and regression to schizophrenia.

The patient considers and experiences her body as one great incorporated object which overpowers her and forces a passive role upon her. Because she builds her defences at a comparatively advanced stage of psychological development, she is able to make a distinction between identification (an ego function) and oral incorporation (an instinctual process). Psychoanalytical writers usually treat the two processes as closely related if not identical. In the anorexic's defences, however, they are clearly distinct. The incorporation of the bad object (which becomes one's own body) not only persists, but is reinforced for defensive purposes, for gaining better control of the object. The libidinal parts of the ego remain attached to the object and its needs; as a result of the split, they become detached from the central ego (Fairbairn, see diagram, p. 91). Nevertheless, because the frustrating object is both bad and fascinating, an ambivalent attitude prevails. The central ego, associated with super-ego components, then identifies itself with an ideal that is a desexualized, acarnal and essentially powerful image. In fact, like hunger, nascent sexuality is re-experienced by the patient as an 'inner force' threatening the ego's idealized image.

Whereas, during the premorbid phase, the anorexic sensed unconsciously that the bad object was too strong to be attacked, now that it has been equated with her body, active aggression can be consciously directed towards the latter by starving it of food.

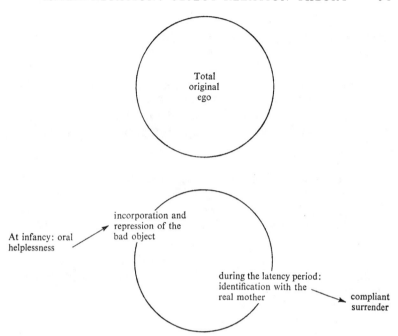

At infancy: oral helplessness

incorporation and repression of the bad object

Total original ego

during the latency period: identification with the real mother

compliant surrender

At puberty: Split between the incorporating ego (the body) and the identifying ego (the central ego)

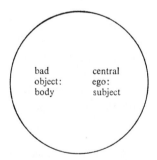

bad object: body

central ego: subject

The libidinal part of the ego attached to the bad incorporated object is split off.

The central ego disidentifies itself from the real mother and identifies itself with an idealized object (plus super-ego components).

The incorporation of the bad object (after Fairbairn)

The ego defence which is thus built up is characterized by the rejection of the body as such and of food as a bodily substance. The pathological control of the body is effected by an attitude that I would describe as *enteroceptual* mistrust. Once the body has been equated with the bad, overpowering object, namely with the threatening entity, the logical consequence is distrust of the body, and of its stimuli and needs. But, like the bad object, the body is also fascinating and therefore cannot be abandoned or decathected (in which case somatic depersonalization would set in). The body-object must simply be kept under control, not be allowed to swell and grow, must be subjected to hard work and strain. The ego becomes an avenger which transforms its master into a slave. However the slave, too, wields a knout. It is as if the patient says to herself:

The bad and overpowering object made me a slave by nourishing me: now this incorporated object has become my body and is still trying to enslave me by its demands, by luring me with its hunger which, once satisfied, makes it even more exacting and irresistible. I must not pay any attention to its signals: hunger, fatigue or sexual excitement. They are so many tricks the body employs to master me. Whose is the hunger I feel? It is most of all the body's. I must differentiate myself from it, pretend that hunger speaks only for itself and hence is not worthy of my attention. I am here and the hunger is there. So let me ignore it.

In this way, though the patient feels and recognizes the body as her own, she treats it *as if* it were not.

The failure to detect, and the mistrust of, body signals may therefore spring from two sources: psychologically, it may be due to the identification of the body with the bad object and its consequent rejection; *neuropsychologically*, it may be due to the maladministrations of an insensitive mother unable to recognize or satisfy her child's original needs.

Certain clinical aspects, however, vary according to whether or not the patient has reached the anal or phallic phase. After the shocking discovery that she is orally dependent on the object, she will resort to starvation as the simplest means of organizing an independent and self-sufficient image of herself. The anal defence is primarily organized around the fear of losing control over passive impulses and objects ('I have to keep dangerous impulses and interfering objects in check'), and reflects more highly organized aspects of the search for power. The reader will recall that, when dealing with that search in anorexia nervosa, I have referred to the *flight from* the passive side of existence (see p. 70). Girls of an intelligent ascetic type prevail in this group. The phallic defences, by contrast, are built up round the competitive efforts associated with the oedipal situation: the wish to beat the rival, to be admired, to be strong and unvanquished.

The ambivalent attitude towards the bad and fascinating object might also account for fantasies of oral impregnation. Many authors who have studied only a few cases of anorexia nervosa and have found that their patients were afraid of oral impregnation have concluded that this fear is the basis of their illness. In my own work, however, I have rarely come across this particular fantasy. When it did occur, I was always convinced that the fear of pregnancy must not be interpreted as a sexual fear but rather as a sexual symbol of a more frightening experience, namely that of being invaded and distended by the primary object, that is the mother.

My own conclusion, therefore, is that anorexia nervosa is a special defence structure midway between schizo-paranoia and depression. The incorporated bad object neither can be nor ever is split up, but remains whole, just as the body with which it is identified constitues a whole. Because the patient hovers between schizophrenia and depression, her body experience, too, is ambiguous: it lies half-way between the non-I and the bad I, is both alien and her own, persecutor and persecuted, a destructive non-self invading the self. The patient undoubtedly projects, but defends herself against the schizophrenic catastrophe by projecting the 'unacceptable' within the structures of her own personality into her own body. The body thus becomes the persecutor, but a persecutor on whom it is relatively easy to spy and impose controls. This type of projection thus protects the patient from interpersonal delusions and, in a way, preserves her ability to socialize and to relate to the world. Anorexia nervosa is also a safeguard against depression and deliberate suicide. The bad body kept at bay from the self protects the existence of a good, idealized, enhanced, acceptable and respected ego. No wonder therefore that, just as soon as the anorexic system is organized, these patients shed the depression of the premorbid phase, and begin to relate and act against the 'object': they become subjects.

The threefold meaning of the anorexic symptom may be schematized as follows:

$$\left.\begin{array}{ll}\text{to retain} & \text{the good}\\ \text{to ward off} & \\ \text{to control} & \text{the bad}\end{array}\right\} \text{object (body).}$$

In order to *retain* the body as the good object, the patient treats it as her own and invests it with libidinal cathexis; there is no somato-psychic depersonalization.

In order to *ward off* the body as the bad object, she keeps it out of the self. The central ego remains worthy of respect, so that there is no depression.

To *control* the body as the bad object, she must keep it at bay. She herself remains in the saddle, the object-world remains good, and there is no schizophrenia.

This schema may well explain the exceptional stability of the anorexic syndrome in the many mild forms that escape the clinician but have an identical structure. In these forms the ego defence is centred on keeping the weight to a fixed minimum that is neither too dramatic nor too dangerous.

I often refer to this minimum jocularly as *the magic weight*. As soon as it is violated, a red warning light seems to flash in the patients' minds. Many so-called recoveries in the wake of various medical treatments are based on this very factor. The *magic weight* adjustment often coincides with the resumption of the menstrual cycle: it provides a minimum level of psychological security for the acceptance of this typical feminine function.

In my view anorexia nervosa is an intra-personal paranoia (intrapsychic paranoid split). The power motive frustrated in interpersonal relationships is shifted to the intrapersonal structure, that is to a rigid control of the patient's body. The unacceptable is projected into the body, not into the environment. Can we then speak of an oral syndrome in anorexia nervosa? In a dynamic sense, no. We can merely speak of an oralized aspect of a problem involving the power and worth of the ego. In its primary relationship, the ego has found only three means of psychological survival:

1) preservation of the embodied object (this means that the object is not incorporated in a dependent or anaclitic sense, but embodied and imprisoned for the sake of independence);

2) preservation of the relationship with the other;

3) preservation of its own power.

The result is a cold, mutilated and far too often a tragic existence.

PART THREE

13 *The Organic Treatment of Anorexia Nervosa*

Since the organic treatment of anorexia nervosa is exclusively concerned with the symptoms, that is with malnutrition and its secondary effects, and ignores the basic psychological problems, we must now examine what value, if any, should be attached to it.

In practice, early cases are generally treated by the family doctor with tonics, stimulants or digestants. Sometimes, when secondary amenorrhoea appears prematurely, hormone therapy is added to stimulate the ovaries.

All such treatment is not only a waste of time but invariably does harm to the patient. Thus tonics and other appetizers which are designed to help the patient put on more weight merely encourage the anorexic to eat even less. Hormone therapy, for its part, when administered in small doses, has no effects at all and, when administered in large doses, not only produces psychological traumata in patients consciously or unconsciously averse to menstruation but may also cause uterine haemorrhages. Ideally, the general practitioner who sees such cases should immediately refer them to a psychotherapist, having first persuaded them and their families with all the tact he can muster that otherwise the continuous mealtime battles and the patients' gradual but inevitable physical deterioration are bound to complicate the clinical picture even further.

Attempts to force-feed such patients at home or in a clinic only serve to aggravate their mental state, to render them more obstinate and rebellious, and to persuade them to get rid of the 'offensive' food by induced vomiting and large doses of laxatives, with dire physical and psychological consequences.

It is, moreover, very difficult for the family doctor to treat the patient at home without becoming involved in the complex emotional situation. Quite frequently his behaviour is such as to make the patient feel he is siding with the parents and hence completely out of sympathy with her.

Cases that are treated by a psychotherapist from the very outset are always very much less complicated and have much better prospects.

Somatic therapy is, of course, essential when malnutrition is already so severe as to undermine the patient's powers of resistance and hence to threaten her life. Moreover patients who are severely debilitated are also psychologically impoverished, often to the point where they are inaccessible to psychotherapeutic contacts. Cases with a sudden and rapid loss in weight (20 per cent of the ideal weight and more) are particularly threatened because their bodies have no time to adjust. Cases in which the drop in weight is more gradual may only reach the point when the loss is of the order of 50 per cent.

However it is not weight losses alone but also the general clinical picture and attitude of the patient that may make immediate physical intervention imperative and that also determine what particular remedies are to be used.

An almost infinite range of such remedies has been put forward over the past thirty years. This very fact, and also the contradictory principles on which they are based, show that they are of no real or lasting value. Leading medical experts agree on only one point, namely on the uselessness and dangers of hormone therapy (oestrogens and anterior pituitary extracts) and above all of the pituitary transplants advocated by Bergmann, Kylin and Sauerbruch and many of their continental successors. Löffler, too, agrees that such treatment, when at all effective, is so only because it appears as a disguised form of psychotherapy. Cortisone preparations act as stimulants and, though they may prove useful in emergencies, they too have no lasting effects. The only hormone that can safely be administered is insulin, but only in hospitals and to patients who have come through the gravest phase of malnutrition because there is the risk of contracting severe hypoglycaemia. Löffler prefers isolation with controlled feeding and general treatment coupled with psychotherapy, and Cioffari and Ninni take the same view. In emergency situations, analeptic and cardiokinetic plasma transfusions (but not too many lest the blood mass become diluted) are preferable to blood transfusions which often revolt the patients: I know of one patient who deliberately injured her brachial veins so as to escape from further blood transfusions. Vitamins only prove beneficial in cases of anorexia with beriberi, when B vitamins should be administered.

In his recent monograph Peter Dally, basing himself on ninety-eight cases of anorexia nervosa treated mostly as in-patients at St Thomas's and Westminster Hospitals, London, concludes that the best and speediest methods of weight restoration involve the administration of chloropromazine and insulin. At the beginning of the treatment the patients are put to bed and told that they must stay there without visitors. Chloropromazine is administered orally, starting with as much as 300 mgm a day. If necessary this dose can be increased by 150 mgm a day to the limits of tolerance. It is essential to increase the intake until the patient's resistance to eating is overcome; at the same time the sense of panic at the sight of food will decrease and so will the post-prandial sense of discomfort. Modified insulin therapy is started at the same time, beginning with 10 units one hour after breakfast. This dose is progressively increased until the patient sweats and becomes drowsy. Interruption then takes place with a large meal. The average dose is between 40 and 60 units.

More recently Marino and Gambardella of the Institute of Pharmacology in the University of Naples have suggested that a combination of amitryptylene and chlordiazepoxide (Ro/4–6270/2, or Limbitryl Roche capsules each containing 12.5 mgm of amitryptylene plus 5 mgm of chlordiazepoxide) is more effective than chloropromazine, and this is because of:
1) the anti-depressant and tranquillizing effects of the amitryptylene;
2) the anxiolytic and tranquillizing effects of the chlorodiazeproxide;
3) the anti-colinergic effect of the amitryptylene and the appetite-stimulating effect of the chlorodiazeproxide.

The eleven cases they treated (all of whom had vainly been subjected to other forms of therapy) showed a surprisingly speedy return to a normal food intake.

Durand, for his part, has suggested that patients in a depressed state should also be given electroshock therapy, while agitated or hyperactive patients should be put on chloropromazine.

Various Italian authors, including Cerletti, Balduzzi and Martinotti, also set great store by electroshock therapy. According to Cerletti such therapy exerts 'a beneficial influence on the vegetative centres and a balancing and anabolic effect on the diencephalic centres'.

Of my own cases only three had been subjected to electroshock therapy before opting for psychotherapy. One of them had improved temporarily, but the other two had failed to respond in any way. There is thus a sharp division of views about the best method of restoring the patient's normal weight. At present, the prevailing opinion (Dally) is that the patient must be given a light diet which is steadily increased from 1500 to 4000–5000 calories per day over a fortnight. Unfortunately many hospitalized patients, though protected from family pressures, tend to see the home atmosphere reflected in the attitude of the nursing staff, who may misinterpret or even respond aggressively to what they consider the patient's intolerable obstinacy and to the attempts by many anorexics to apply the Roman maxim of *divide et impera*.

The painful method of tube-feeding, which is unavoidable in extreme cases, must be applied very sparingly because of the physical and psychological dangers it entails. Sometimes the mere threat of this technique is enough to persuade patients to take food in the normal way, but one of my cases, who died of extreme cachexia, actually tube-fed herself over a considerable period of time.

All forms of organic treatment must be adjusted to the needs of each individual patient, after careful examination and under the close supervision of a competent physician – there is no single therapy that can be applied indiscriminately to all anorexia nervosa patients.

The follow-up of patients treated exclusively by organic methods

Bliss and Branch, in their *Anorexia Nervosa* (p. 114), have drawn up a table of the therapeutic results obtained by some twenty-five authors. The one to score the greatest success was Hurst, who had fifty complete cures in the fifty patients he had treated.

Bliss and Branch have noted that malnutrition, unless extreme, is relatively unimportant as such – it is a symptom rather than an illness. Not that it can be ignored by the physician, but a mere restoration of body weight leaves the patient with the same personality defects that first made him ill. However, purely for the sake of convenience and accuracy, the success or failure rate is generally expressed in terms of weight changes. On that basis most of the authors examined by Bliss and Branch succeeded in curing one-third of their patients completely and in improving the condition of another third, but failed with the remaining third. The reliability of these figures, however, can only be established through a follow-up, five, ten and fifteen years after the alleged cures (as conducted by Kay, and Beck and Brochner-Mortensen).

Zutt, for his part, believes that anorexia nervosa is an incurable disease: not a single one of his patients turned out to have been completely cured when re-examined after a significant lapse of time. He suspects that many so-called cures have merely changed anorexia for other psychological aberrations. My own work shows that his pessimism is fully justified in the absence of psychotherapeutic support.

Meyer and Weinroth take much the same view. They note that the illness often oscillates between acute starvation and bulimia, inactivity or depression and overactivity and agitation. The mere admission of the patient to a clinic or hospital can lead to grave emotional crises, mainly because of the 'anaclitic' and regressive atmosphere of the new environment, in which nurses and doctors apparently assume the role of the severe parents. In my experience quite a few patients, especially on their first admission to hospital, quickly realize that the only way to be discharged is to put on weight. They accordingly eat up everything they are given, only to relapse again the moment they are back home.

To my mind the most important follow-up study of all is that published by J. Cremerius in 1965. He re-examined thirteen cases originally diagnosed as anorexics at the Psychosomatic Clinic of Giessen University, none of whom had received psychotherapeutic help. The onset of the disease went back to fifteen to eighteen years before the follow-up.

Of the thirteen patients, one had died. The remaining twelve fell into the following categories:

Five cases had turned chronic; the clinical picture was more or less identical with the original one except for a few slight improvements.

Five patients had put on weight and some of these were no longer amenorrhoeic. In two of these five patients anorexia had made way for a different psychosomatic disturbance (obesity, hemicrania); in the first this change went hand in hand with the construction of a different psychoneurotic symptomatology, in the second with the disappearance of the original psychopathological features. In the three other cases, only the physical symptoms of malnutrition had disappeared, while the psychoneurotic symptoms had either grown more pronounced or had been restructured.

One patient had become a chronic schizophrenic, another had died after an intercurrent illness (pneumonia): her condition prior to the pneumonia was such that her case should really have been included among the chronic group.

In short not a single one of these patients had been truly cured. The five who might have been pronounced cured on the basis of their improved feeding habits and increase in weight showed by their persistent neurotic behaviour that they had merely exchanged symptoms. We can therefore say of anorexics what Bleuler has said of schizophrenics, namely that 'the more accurate the follow-up, the fewer the cures'.

Dally, in the monograph from which we have been quoting, suggests the following criteria for assessing improvement:
1) the patient's weight;
2) menstruation;
3) psychosexual development;
4) degree of independence;
5) mental state.

Using these criteria his follow-up studies of the 140 patients he treated with large doses of chloropromazine, a method he considers superior to all others, shows that he had succeeded exceptionally well in restoring the patients' weight (69 per cent), but not nearly so well in respect of his other criteria, and quite particularly in respect of his fifth criterion – in 25 per cent of the patients whose body weight had been restored, persistent psychiatric symptoms had come to replace the original symptoms of anorexia nervosa.

14 *Introduction to the Psychotherapeutic Treatment of Anorexia Nervosa*

From what has already been said and from my own experience I have reached the conclusion that the most satisfactory treatment of anorexia nervosa must be based on psychotherapy. Obviously this must remain a theoretical desideratum so long as various economic, logistic and family problems and the lack of trained psychotherapists with experience in this field continue to stand in the way. In fact these external factors are the gravest obstacles to psychotherapy in all its practical forms. The enormous expenditure of time and energy demanded from therapists, the vast expense of the treatment, and general public disinterest jointly ensure that psychotherapy is confined to a chosen few.

I do not, moreover, agree with Bliss and Branch who, ignoring the external obstacles, maintain that only a minority of patients are suited to psychotherapy and that the psychiatrist must use his experience and acumen to sort them out from the rest, that is from those who will respond to physical treatment including lobotomies.

In my view, in the absence of material and other practical impediments, all anorexia nervosa patients, including the chronically ill and those whose physical condition is such that organic treatment has become imperative, must be given psychotherapeutic help. Such help has to be extremely *flexible* and adapt itself, in due course, to the intellectual capacity, special needs and above all to the past experiences of each individual patient. By 'flexibility' I do not mean some sort of wild improvisation, let alone ignorance of the fundamental principles of psychiatry or psychoanalysis. Psychotherapeutic flexibility must go hand in hand with sound training and the refusal to immure oneself in rigid and immutable rules; the therapist must be able to respond fully and spontaneously to the needs of these extremely vulnerable and withdrawn patients. For that very reason, and also because, as I said earlier, anorexics suffer from a severe ego impairment, I feel strongly that what is needed is an intense form of psychotherapy similar to, but not identical with, that used in the treatment of psychotics (though anorexics are much less seriously unbalanced) in which tact, delicacy, sensitivity, intuition and emotional warmth on the part of the therapist (coupled to keen self-awareness especially in respect of unconscious responses) play a paramount role.

During therapy it will become obvious to the experienced analyst – for reasons we shall be examining at greater length – that therapeutic and diagnostic considerations have become inseparable. Psychotherapy, not only as a method of treatment but also as a method of research, does much more than provide simple diagnostic data, or detached and static phenomenological descriptions. The rational and emotional dialogue which is so essential a feature of psychotherapy sets up a special dynamism of understanding that sometimes culminates in a genuine 'discovery' not only on the part of the psychotherapist, but on the part of the patient as well. It is to this singular dialogic dynamism that the psychotherapeutic method owes its un-doubted superiority, not only over standard diagnostic methods but also over Kierkegaard's ingenious method of introspective self-analysis.

As a result, psychotherapy, however restricted its present scope may be, can make a particularly fruitful contribution not only to clinical medicine but also, and above all, to greater human understanding especially in psychiatry, psychology and general anthropology. This is particularly obvious in anorexia nervosa which, because it involves the most various and complex psychopathological mechanisms and distorts the patient's most fundamental drive – the oral – with all the extreme consequences this entails, demands the utmost commitment from the psychotherapist. From this commitment he derives not only greater therapeutic powers and increasingly effective methods but also a quite unexpected insight into many problems of dynamic psychology that are apparently quite unrelated to anorexia nervosa.

15 *The Therapist and the Parents*

In connection with the psychotherapeutic treatment of anorexics, I must point out that it is essential not to exclude the patient's parents and especially her mother. In general we may say that the weaker the patient's ego the more essential it is to probe into, and if possible to change, the complex interactions between her and those among whom she lives. Moreover most of these patients are minors and economically dependent on their parents who, particularly during the most stormy but productive phases, often break off slow and expensive treatment to resort to quicker and cheaper organic methods. This they do the more readily because psychotherapy enables the patients to express hostility towards their parents more openly – they feel protected by the therapist's 'comforting shoulder'. However, quite often, and particularly during the the first month of treatment, such patients will deliberately distort or exaggerate the therapist's remarks for the express purpose of getting the family to terminate the sessions.

This may even happen, and has in fact happened to me, during the more advanced phase of the treatment, when a positive relationship has already been established. In that case, however, the patients have ceased to feel resentful of the therapist, and merely express an infantile need to show off how much progress they have made and to assert their newly-found autonomy.

Only during the final phase of their treatment do such patients become more tolerant of the obvious faults of others in general, and their family in particular. They do not only grow happier themselves but show a deeper understanding of the needs, and even of the neurotic needs, of their relatives. At the same time they are no longer prepared to have their own rights trampled underfoot – in short they are ready to play a fuller part in the social group to which they belong. I shall never forget the remarks of one of my patients who, with her father, came to take her leave of me at the end of a particularly difficult cure. When the father reproached her for letting his wife 'get away with murder', the girl replied:

I shall have to bide my time. I can't just suddenly face Mother with a completely new person. It would simply kill her. And I myself still have a long way to go before I can steer an even course with Mother instead of always squabbling with her.

This girl, who used to be the family's 'invalid' was now able to cope successfully with a traumatic series of personal and family crises, playing her full part in her home and business life.

In my dealings with the relatives of anorexics I used to make it a point not to probe too deeply into their own psychological problems, let alone attempt to change their personality structures. I felt that in so doing I should have elicited a totally negative reaction from people no longer young, precariously balanced and harbouring deep guilt feelings. Particularly at the time of maximum emotional commitment to the patient, the therapist must do his utmost not to criticize or offend perfectionist mothers whose self-esteem is bolstered up by the conviction that they have done wonders for their family.

The therapist who disregards this warning is bound to obtain neurotic responses from the mother that range from distrust, depression and fear of being mistaken and of having failed in everything, to frigid non-co-operation usually reflected in a rigid posture, crossed arms, calculated hostility and vitriolic attacks on psychotherapy.

Contacts with the family are also rendered delicate by the patient's own suspicions of the therapist to whom, after all, she has been taken by her parents, and who is therefore bound to be in league with them, no matter what he says. It is essential that these suspicions be allayed. Worse still, after such interviews the parents often make inopportune remarks about the therapist or about what he has told them of the patient's condition. Thus when the mother of one of my patients informed her that I felt more optimistic about her than about another, less intelligent patient, and added that, in my view, an intelligent girl ought to be able to solve her problems in a more rational way than by refusing to take food, the fifteen-year-old girl, who felt a strong need for intellectual appreciation, immediately abandoned her anorexic symptoms to convince me of her mental acumen but left all her basic problems unsolved. As a result her physical condition improved dramatically, but she became increasingly alienated and developed a syndrome with dangerous suicidal fantasies. It took a great deal of time and patience to reconstruct the origins of her sudden and psychologically harmful rejection of the 'rewards' she had previously obtained from fasting.

The therapist must therefore be extremely cautious in his discussions with the parents and make a point of refraining from communicating his opinion of the patient's condition (swearing the parents to silence does not help, as such promises are rarely kept). Instead he must simply try to listen, to gather what information he can, and probe as far as possible into the dynamics of the family relationship, into which he himself will be drawn unavoidably. Some writers have called the psychodynamic method of reconstructing the patient's family relationships a historical method (Arieti [1947]). In fact it ceases to be purely historical and becomes dynamic the moment the therapist transforms it into a dialogue about the present, for the present is open to change.

Before starting treatment the therapist must make a point of telling the parents, without dramatizing the difficulties, that it will take quite some time before the patient's physical condition improves and that they must expect stormy scenes. I always tell the mothers that they will grow jealous of their daughters' positive therapeutic relationships, which are difficult to establish but indispensable to the cure and hence must be treated with understanding. Such relationships, I always add, will only be temporary and will eventually help to restore a healthier and more affectionate relationship at home. Many psychotherapeutically counterproductive and hence harmful reactions on the part of the parents are highly predictable and can therefore be mitigated by friendly preparatory talks. Thereafter the therapist's dealings with the parents will be confined to occasional suggestions on how they should behave towards the patient, and to fostering optimism and faith in the outcome even during the worst crises.

Generally, save for those rare cases in which removal from

the family environment is openly welcomed by the patient, it is best to opt for a policy of wait and see. If there is positive therapeutic progress, the patient herself will come to realize that it is best to leave home for a while and there is therefore no need to exert any pressure on her. One of my patients, Liliana, who came from outside the city, insisted that her mother spend months and months with her in a hotel, before deciding quite spontaneously to let her go back home. The patient who freely demands separation from her family without too many guilt feelings is already on the road to recovery. In that case, moreover, the family, too, is generally much less anxious about the separation, which previously they either refused on the grounds that they alone could make certain that their daughter had eaten enough, or else demanded aggressively in order to escape from the everlasting ordeal at the dinner table. The therapist must, however, feel free to make his own decisions regardless of any family pressures and, indeed, do his utmost to keep such pressures from interfering with his relationship with the patient. It is better to procrastinate during critical moments, and not to engage in dramatic telephone conversations with the desperate parents, lest the therapist himself become over-anxious and too involved in the family dispute.

16 *Difficulties during the First Meeting with Patients*

By 'emaciation' Zutt has referred not only to the physical state of anorexics but also to the narrowness of their entire existence. Anorexics are, in fact, anything but warm, cordial, optimistic or sympathetic – so many attributes that the man in the street associates with fat people. Shakespeare, too, took the same view when he warned against Cassius's lean and hungry look.

Anorexia nervosa patients have no love for the therapist, who, in turn, finds it hard to respond with sympathy. At first their attitude is rarely aggressive or openly scornful; it is merely cold and passive. However, their frigidity is simply a screen for their acute fears and suspicions and for their determination to ward off all approaches. Some patients, especially the youngest, look like terrified children, or as if they had been tortured. In fact such patients never come for treatment of their own free will. Some have to be dragged along reluctantly; others resign themselves to what they consider a lesser evil than hospitalization and tube-feeding.

In these circumstances it is clear that the therapist cannot use the orthodox approach or even put such patients on a couch; the couch seems to terrify or horrify them, especially during the first few months of treatment. If pressed to use it, they will stretch out as if lying on a Procrustean bed, their legs tightly crossed, their hands squeezed together so hard that they change colour, and their faces full of anguish.

Far better, therefore, to put them in an armchair and to look them full in the face, while sitting out their inevitable silences or, more rarely, listening to their idle chatter designed to avoid awkward questions.

Anorexics not only refuse to be drawn into what they fear is yet another stifling interpersonal relationship, but are more determined than all other mental patients to cling on to a symptom they have been protecting tooth and nail against attacks from all sides and particularly from their parents, who think that once they start to eat properly all the remaining problems will vanish by themselves. More difficult still are those cases who have been treated unsuccessfully in psychiatric or general hospitals, and who feel particularly sceptical about all forms of therapy. They are invariably surprised to find that the psychotherapist, who has read their full case histories, does not reɪer to their dietary problems, but they look upon this strange omission as a suspicious mouse might look at the cheese in the trap. They are afraid of being cured, and hence feel defensive towards the therapist, much more stubbornly so in fact than do schizophrenics. But they lack the schizophrenic's sharp irony and great powers of symbolic expression. As an example of the latter I should like to mention the case of Francesco, a chronic schizophrenic who had stopped speaking years ago and was being treated by a colleague. One day she found him seated at his table, with the Bible opened at the story of Judith and Holofernes. He had wound a belt round his neck and was pulling one end through the buckle while fixing the therapist with a stare and signalling a desperate no, no. . . . The obvious meaning of this symbolic gesture was that though the blade might already be at his throat, he was nevertheless determined not to end like Holofernes at Judith's hands. He would never surrender his head, that is his madness (and the pseudo-security it afforded him). Anorexics, by contrast, feel no need to express themselves in such ways; they believe that all the therapist really wants is to fatten them up. Hence they look upon psychotherapy as a 'whole lot of talk to persuade them to blow themselves up like wine-skins' (Rita).

The therapist must therefore be perfectly frank and open with them from the start, for only in this way can they gradually be persuaded to collaborate with him. They are extremely sensitive to the least sign of insincerity and circumlocutions; they are always afraid of hidden motives and, though they themselves resort to hypocrisy for defensive purposes, they detest and loathe it in others. It is essential to tell them, if necessary in the most elementary manner, that their real problem is not food, as everyone else seems to think it is. Their fasting, they must be told, is merely a symptom of their problem, much as a high temperature is a symptom of typhoid. It is only the visible manifestation of something hidden deep in their history, their family problems, their outlook on life, their loneliness, sadness and secret fears.

With these patients the therapist's injunctions, however gentle, fall on deaf ears for a long time. They do not observe the basic psychoanalytic rule: they offer no free associations; if they associate at all they do so in brief spurts; they do not dream or fail to report their dreams. Faced with their long suspicious silences and their rigid stares, the therapist often feels embarrassed or impatient, and as soon as this happens he had best cut the silences short. How he does this is a matter of intuition and experience, but in any case it must never take the form of critical or bad-humoured remarks. Sometimes it is possible to break the defensive wall by sympathetic allusions to the patient's difficulty in expressing herself and to the disappointing experiences that might have been responsible for this. The therapist must, however, take care not to be too insistent with direct offers of help or display too much warmth, lest the patient think him an emotional blackmailer. Thus Azzurra, one of my young patients, warned me off (though I had tried to be as gentle and tactful as I knew how) by telling me that she had more than once dreamt of me as a thief.

(I might add that her identification of me with a thief, and hence with her overbearing and inquisitive mother, though undoubtedly a transference phenomenon, was also a direct critique of myself as a real person. By treating such reports as pure transference phenomena, the therapist simply ignores his own mistakes and effectively prevents himself from making the necessary adjustments. By admitting my mistakes quite frankly and with good humour, I was able to help Azzurra to take yet another step towards a completely new human relationship – one that merited her openness and full collaboration.)

Experience has taught me that direct interpretation of a patient's actions or dreams often has a beneficial shock effect: it suddenly illuminates the hidden source of her suffering. I say 'hidden' because very often the patients are so regressive that they are not even aware of their suffering. Frequently such incidents help to turn the scales in the therapist's favour.

Thus one of my patients produced the following dream fragment after a long period of latent hostility:

My mother was sitting with Signora F, her best friend, on the drawing-room sofa. I came in to say hello. As I passed Signora F, I spilled blood over her lovely white dress. I was horrified and apologized profusely, then I noticed that blood was pouring from the two truncated stumps that were my arms. But while I felt guilty about the dress, I was not at all surprised by my own condition.

In my interpretation of the dream, which was based not so much on the patient's sparse associations as on my intuitive feelings of what sort of person her mother was, I took care to avoid any references to jealousy, revenge or sado-masochistic impulses. Instead, I said in a rather subdued tone of voice: 'Mother, if only you knew how I longed for hands and arms to fend for myself. . . . But then I had them cut off. . . . I didn't even realize that they kept bleeding. . . .' Soon afterwards I noticed a clear change in the patient's attitude towards me.

Other serious cases present problems of a different kind. An eighteen-year-old working-class girl (Marisa), who was totally uneducated (she had not even passed her Grade III examinations) and who had, moreover, been deeply shocked when she was sent to a neurological ward where she was vainly subjected to repeated electroshocks, attended her psychotherapeutic sessions for weeks, turning up with great punctuality but conveying nothing beyond an occasional monosyllable or a slight nod of her head. In the case of this little, and apparently most backward, girl the Staab Sceno-test proved to be most rewarding: after suitable and patient encouragement she was able to construct several highly complex scenes divided into several blocs. Though she herself was as rigid as a robot, she bent the flexible models with so much dramatic realism that she left me in no doubt that only in this way could she vent her repressed feelings.

Another patient, Rita, had quite a different problem during the first six months of treatment. At the age of twenty-one she had suffered a third general relapse and was now in a state of serious but not extreme emaciation (height 5' 7", weight 100 lbs). During her first two relapses her mother had boarded her out for months with a second cousin, a psychiatrist, who lived in a small provincial town near a psychiatric hospital. Warned that she would be sent to that hospital for the least misbehaviour, Rita had submitted to a strict feeding routine administered with bureaucratic precision. She was served with enormous helpings of *pasta* which she swallowed mechanically. The bathroom was kept locked for several hours after every meal so that she had to keep back her vomit. For the rest she was kept in strict isolation – she was not allowed to go for walks lest she dissipate her energies, and she had no recreations or friends: the provincial family lived a monotonous and totally withdrawn existence. After four months of this kind of 'therapy' Rita returned home in what her mother considered an excellent state of health (she now weighed 157 lbs), but what she herself considered a state of revolting obesity. She felt desperate, humiliated and rebellious. Soon afterwards she started to lose weight again, and was again packed off to her cousin, but this time there were continuous tears and a less dramatic increase in weight. On her third relapse, after unsuccessful treatment by a clinical psychologist, she finally came to me for intensive psychotherapy. She started her treatment with obvious reluctance and for the sole purpose of avoiding the hated and fearful administrations of her dictatorial cousin. Her attitude to me was hostile and mistrustful, though masked by good manners and a show of gaiety. Occasionally she would enlarge about the treatment in terms that were far too exalted to have the least ring of sincerity. For the rest she stayed away from sessions and offered excuses that were as far-fetched as they were irritating. What rare dreams she produced were deliberately intended to mock me (though with some ambivalent overtones) and to express her firm intention to keep losing weight. In fact during the first two or three months her general state deteriorated markedly: she was down to 73 lbs, there were signs of oedema, and the family started to bombard me with dramatic telephone calls and demands for hospitalization. At that point the patient had, in fact, succeeded in gaining the upper hand in the psychotherapeutic situation: she was forcing me to shelve the analysis proper while concentrating on her refusal to take food, a subject she constantly brought up in floods of tears accompanied by dramatic scenes. However, soon afterwards I was able to let her catch some glimpses of her real motives. Her mother was pressing for her immediate hospitalization, and I promised Rita to stand by her and to ensure she was spared the pain of yet another detentive experience. In return I did not ask her to put on weight, but merely to maintain what minimum weight was compatible with her survival. I added that I fully understood her hostility towards me: she was merely trying to pay me back for all she had had to suffer in the past. I was just another psychiatrist, part of a detestable breed. My patience with her had obviously taken her aback and she was constantly putting me to the test. I was bound to have something up my sleeve . . . and any moment now I would pounce on her like the rest. . . . And not only was she trying to see how I really ticked by goading me with her obduracy, she was also avoiding the hateful process of being analysed. Hence her reluctance to come to the consulting room or to talk of anything other than food. But if I had perhaps passed the test, might we not start all over again at the beginning, quite calmly and in an atmosphere of mutual trust? And in fact we did just that: Rita grudgingly maintained a tolerable weight level, and we could get down to the psychotherapy proper, though with occasional stormy outbursts that had to be expected in view of her chronic condition and her disastrous psychiatric experiences.

Whenever the general deterioration of a patient's health makes her hospitalization unavoidable, the therapist must make certain that she does not feel betrayed or abandoned, by taking her fully into his confidence. She must be persuaded, not bullied, into realizing that such treatment is in her own best interests.

The therapist should moreover arrange with the hospital staff that no forcible measures will be applied, and should continue to visit the patient regularly lest their new relationship (already strained by the hospitalization) be completely jeopardized.

In any case, for the sake of the patient's psychological health, it is advisable to avoid hospitalization if there is any alternative. The very suggestion invariably strikes terror in the patient's heart and provokes uncontrollable crying fits and a flood of idle promises. These patients see all hospitals as places of torture, humiliation and oppression, and it is far better to have them treated organically *before* taking them on as patients. But when, as happens quite often, the patient's condition deteriorates during psychotherapy, experience has shown me time and again that if only one does not panic in the face of dramatic weight losses and runs the unquestionable risk of keeping the patient out of hospital even while the relatives clamour for it, one can often draw the patient into a positive psychotherapeutic relationship. Quite often the therapist will be tempted to agree to the patient's hospitalization – which is always justifiable on purely organic grounds – simply for his own peace of mind. But while hospitalization may benefit the patient physically it can ruin an inter-human relationship that is likely to have a much more decisive and profound curative effect.

The situation is quite different when psychotherapeutic treatment is started inside the hospital or clinic, but, since I have no personal experience of this matter, I must refer the reader to other writers (for example Bruch and Thomä). I nevertheless feel strongly that, particularly in Italy, the hospital atmosphere is, with few exceptions, not conducive to psychotherapeutic treatment, not least because the nursing staff lacks the necessary training.

From all the above it will have become clear that there is no single concrete method that can be applied indiscriminately to every type of anorexic patient. All the therapist can and must do is to aim, not at extracting a spate of psychologically interesting material, not at tangible results or at an outright 'cure', but at an honest and respectful understanding of his patients, for only in this way can he hope to offset the negative experiences that lie at the very heart of their so-called remoteness.

17 *Some Hints on Psychotherapeutic Conduct*

Preliminary structural diagnosis

Before beginning the psychotherapeutic treatment of anorexic patients it is essential to make a careful assessment of their general state. This puts the therapist on his guard against possible difficulties, and helps to determine the best therapeutic approach to any particular case. In other words the therapist must first decide whether his patient is a stable anorexic without marked mental aberrations, or a bulimic with a severe personality disorder, terrified by the thought of his inevitable food binges and seriously disturbed in his enteroceptive responses, his thoughts and his powers of communication (see p. 92).

Patients of the first type, provided that their symptoms have appeared fairly recently and that they have not had traumatic experiences, are capable of entering into a valid – albeit ambivalent – relationship with the psychotherapist fairly quickly. They can also accept the fact that they are expected to attend regular sessions, generally up to three a week.

The patients in the second group are much more seriously ill and also much more difficult to approach: they must be treated with extreme patience and sympathy. Because of their fragile personalities, they are terrified of any kind of intimate interpersonal relationship for which they nevertheless long with passion. With them the therapist must expect constant demands for a reduction in the number of weekly sessions, repeated absences justified in the most childish manner or requests for a temporary interruption of the treatment. Thus a perceptive colleague, starting the treatment of a gravely ill patient in this second group, realized that the long silence at the end of one of the first sessions was a terrified reaction of the patient to the deep tenderness my colleague felt towards her. This helped my colleague to respond sympathetically when the patient rang up to say that she found the treatment far too upsetting to continue with it. My colleague told her that she quite understood the position but hoped the patient would feel free to call on her services whenever she needed or desired them.

Only in this way can the therapist sometimes initiate a relationship with the patient. In fact some of the gravest cases will often show a marked deterioration to avoid falling into what to them is the fatal trap of an interpersonal relationship with the therapist: because they feel irresistibly drawn into the transference situation, escape into physical symptoms is their only means of preserving their autonomy and their relative independence from what, as experience has taught them, is bound to prove yet another symbiotic and destructive relationship. And as long as the sessions have to be confined to discussion of their grave state of malnutrition, their own secret fears do not have to be brought into the open. . . .

Other patients, fortunately very few in number, will, after a phase of mistrust, enter into a relationship of complete oral dependence on the psychotherapist, interspersed with ambivalent reactions. Since this relationship is bound to be extremely frustrating for them, their physical and mental condition deteriorates dramatically; they 'act out' their aggresssion against the frustrating therapist even while trying to 'possess' him. Such cases cannot be helped in the normal way, but must be seen in a hospital clinic. Since I feel it more useful to mention my failures than to dwell on my successes I shall cite the particularly tragic case of Anna Maria.

Several years ago I imprudently agreed to treat this patient in my consulting rooms, even though I knew that her condition had long since become chronic, that she was poorly educated and in straitened financial circumstances and that she lived outside the city so that each session involved her in the discomfort of a fairly long journey. The patient, whose anorexia had started at the age of fourteen years, had married seven years later, and was twenty-six years old when I first saw her. Her relationship with her husband, a modest bank clerk who declared that curing his wife was to him 'an existential mission', was the exact though veiled replica of her sado-masochistic relationship with her mother.

E

During psychotherapy she regressed to total oral dependence within a few months. Her need for love and mothering, for symbiotic fusion with the therapist was so pressing that she found the reality of the therapeutic situation altogether unbearable. My repeated assurances that I was fully alive to her deepest need served no useful purpose; her condition deteriorated so dramatically that I was forced to advise her admission to a hospital which, for financial reasons, had to be in her home town and hence at some distance from me. For several days practical difficulties (quite apart from my own countertransference) prevented me from visiting her. I did, however, keep regularly in touch with her husband by telephone. After the last of these conversations, the husband (as I learned from him later) told Anna Maria rather sadistically that he had gathered from our brief conversations that I was so dispirited about her that I saw no point in treating her any further. Anna Maria then sent me a laconic note: 'Signora, since you no longer believe in my cure, I have decided to go to my grave.'

As I was hurriedly preparing to leave for her hospital, I received the news of her death.

The husband then came to see me to tell me a secret: Anna Maria had killed herself. At the time she was having a drip of amino-acids, and she had heard the repeated instructions that, because of her precarious state, the flow of liquid must be as slow as possible. On her last day the nurse set the drip at minimum flow. When her husband, who was called to the telephone, returned to her bedside he found that the drip bottle was empty and the valve fully opened. Anna Maria died a few minutes later. Her tragic death drove it home to me how essential it is not to start psychotherapy before weighing up the gravity of every case, one's own availability during moments of crisis and such practical problems as travelling distance, lack of financial resources, etc. Anna Maria's suicide was clearly unconnected with her anorexia as such: her tragic decision to end her life was the direct result of her belief that she had been abandoned by me.

Age of the patient

Some, but few, cases of true anorexia nervosa can be diagnosed at a relatively early age (nine to twelve years). I myself have dealt with a ten-year-old pre-pubertal dizygotic twin, whose anorexia was essentially the expression of a desperate search for identity and autonomy in what was a highly complex relationship with her widowed mother and twin sister. In my view such precocious cases should be isolated from their family and placed into more suitable surroundings. If their condition is not too grave or dramatic, they can, for instance, be boarded out with sympathetic friends who are not too closely involved in the family tensions and conflicts. In graver cases it is best to have such patients admitted to a hospital, preferably one with a special ward in which they can be treated firmly but kindly.

The medical staff must be persuaded to adopt a sympathetic but neutral stance, while making sure they are not manipulated or blackmailed by manœuvres of the kind the patient has found so effective at home. The nurses, too, must be prepared for what is in store for them, lest they repeat the mother's mistake of believing the patient is simply refraining from food because she is wilful and deliberately trying to cause trouble. In particular they must not keep adding that extra mouthful while coaxing the patient with 'Just eat it up as a favour to me, there's a good girl, etc.'

With the change in environment and the elimination of direct pressures, such very young and not yet morbidly structured patients will often pass through an acute crisis and abandon their symptom. Psychotherapy proper can then be safely deferred until the patient is more mature.

Weight

Obviously the most promising cases are stable anorexics who seek psychotherapeutic advice soon after the onset of their illness and are still in a passable physical condition. I am firmly convinced that if all anorexics were treated at an early stage the recovery rate would be almost complete.

Unfortunately the majority of cases only seek psycho-therapeutic help when everything else has failed, by which time their condition has seriously deteriorated. In their case the therapist is faced with a dilemma, for he knows perfectly well that at the start his treatment, far from bringing an immediate improvement, does the precise opposite. He must therefore let

himself be guided by his own feelings and by his other commit-
ments. Thus whenever I meet the parents of anorexics for
discussions I make it a point to take careful note of their
attitude towards the patient and of their general emotional state.
If the results are sufficiently encouraging, I talk about the
expected course of the therapy at some length and stress the
likelihood that the patient's condition will deteriorate further
and that she may have to be hospitalized, but that it is only if
they are prepared to run this risk *with me*, give me time to gain
the patient's confidence, and help me to cushion her against the
shock of her possible hospitalization in a way that she would
feel was neither an imposition nor a punishment, that we can
have any hope of success. This process may be the most time-
consuming for the therapist, but is, in my view, by far the best
for the patient. In some cases, in which I feel I lacked the
necessary time, I advised preliminary hospitalization but
promised to meet and treat the patient after her discharge. In
one very grave case, in which I had to insist on hospitalization
after a few dozen sessions, I found that the psychotherapeutic
relationship had been irredeemably shattered.

Chronic cases

Patients who have been chronically ill for years, have had to
suffer such traumatic experiences as tube-feeding without
psychotherapeutic support, and who, as a result, have adopted
a definite and irreversible anorexic personality as the only means
of preserving their pseudo-autonomy, must, as a rule, be
considered incurable. Psychotherapy can nevertheless be
attempted, but I myself have succeeded in curing no more than
two such cases, and then only after years of hard work and
infinite patience. The best one can normally hope to achieve with
them is to keep their symptoms more or less under control, and
to stabilize them to the level that I like to call the 'magic
weight'. Once the anorexic personality has crystallized out, the
best we can do is to widen the patient's existential horizon and
to help her to express her personality more fully. In fact, rather
than try to effect a true transformation of the ego by breaking
down the patient's defences, the therapist must content himself
with consolidating the existing ego within strictly circumscribed
limits.

Dependence on the parents

The psychotherapy of anorexic patients is generally fraught with the same thorny problems that beset the treatment of all adolescents and calls for the kind of awareness described by Anna Freud, Selma Fraiberg, Lampl de Groot, Peter Blos, Leo Spiegel, Irene Josselyn, Eveline Kestemberg and others. The following facts must be borne in mind especially:

1) The patients are generally minors, and as such economically and otherwise dependent on their parents.

2) The treatment is paid for by the parents, so that the therapist appears a mere hireling of people who often complain of the great expense thus adding to the patient's guilt feelings, or as someone who turns on warmth and sympathy for financial gain.

3) The patients do not themselves choose psychotherapy: generally they submit to it because they think the alternative – hospitalization or tube-feeding – is infinitely worse.

4) At adolescence children attempt to escape from the dominance of their elders, yet paradoxically the psychotherapeutic situation seems to resurrect and, indeed, even to increase their dependence on others.

5) Last but not least, because anorexics are afraid of verbalizing their conflicts and negative feelings they tend to act them out by intensifying their symptom.

The therapist must bear all these points constantly in mind and, during crises, try to draw attention to them in simple and sympathetic ways.

During discussions with the family he must further make it clear that he cannot possibly engage in secret telephone calls or confidential correspondence with them. Nothing must happen without the patient's knowledge; therapy must take place in an atmosphere of absolute trust, not in a conspiratorial climate reminiscent of home. Just how conspiratorial that climate can be was made clear to me by a mother who told me proudly during a preliminary meeting that she had secretly been injecting the stewed prunes that were the only food her daughter would eat with an extract of horse serum and egg yolk. The complicated preparations were all made while the daughter was out, and there was an elaborate system of secret telephone calls from relatives and friends to warn the mother of the girl's imminent return. It is not difficult to see how disastrous the whole atmosphere was for the patient.

As for parental jealousy, one can take it as an axiom that the more indignantly it is denied the fiercer it is. One mother, who had irately 'handed' her only daughter, a fourteen-year-old, over to me for therapy, told me that she was washing her hands of her, and was highly indignant when I suggested in the most tactful way possible that she had come to feel jealous of me. A year later, when her daughter's attachment to me could no longer be glossed over, she told her to keep my fees and to stay away from therapy. This ruse having failed, she went to the girl's teacher and complained that her daughter was trying to kill her by continuing to visit the odious analyst (forgetting that she herself had originally bullied the girl into coming to see me). The neurotic teacher, who immediately identified herself with the irrational mother, then rebuked the poor girl in front of the assembled school. Fortunately my patient had by then developed so positive a relationship with me that she was able to stand the shock of her public humiliation.

During the second year of the treatment, the unhappy mother realized that the child was also developing more positive feelings towards her father, and to squash these she told the patient that, if it was not for her, she would never have come into the world: the father had insisted on an abortion. When the poor girl stammered this revelation out to me between sobs, I let her cry on (while anxiously searching for the appropriate therapeutic response) and then broke my long silence with: 'I think your father was trying to solve a difficult situation in the most realistic way he knew how. He had come to see that he might not make a good father.'

The school problem

Anorexics are intelligent people and set great store by scholastic success. Hence it is a great mistake to take them out of school unless they themselves request it or when their general condition is such as to demand their hospitalization. In some cases, as the therapy progresses, it becomes clear that the only reason why they try to get good marks is that their parents expect it of them, in which case the therapist must help them to discover their real attitude.

The therapist

I am convinced that the therapist treating anorexia nervosa patients must not only be an able physician but must also have a keen *mens medica*, and this despite the fact that he is not dealing with organic problems. In particular he must guard against the temptation to concentrate exclusively on the psyche and to forget that his patients also *have a body and bodily needs*, thus reinforcing the split between body and mind. In fact some of the patients' psychological debilities are the direct consequence of their physical emaciation or of intoxication.

I have sometimes had to rush patients to hospital whose sunken eyes or parched lips suggested acute dehydration or chloropenic hyperazotaemia, only to have my diagnosis confirmed by laboratory tests. Thus, when I started treating a patient with an insistent cough which could easily have been mistaken for repressed aggression, I diagnosed tuberculosis, and called for an X-ray which confirmed my fears. In any case, however sound the therapist's medical training may have been, he must, in all serious cases, enlist the help of a competent physician who can keep an eye on the patient's physical condition without interfering with the therapeutic work. As for non-medical psychotherapists I believe that, in view of the grave physical state of anorexic patients, they are prone to panic at signs of deterioration that would leave the medical man quite unruffled.

The sex of the therapist must also be taken into consideration: some patients find it exceedingly difficult to be open with male analysts. Moreover if he is accepted he may, as the therapy proceeds, become a substitute for a weak and neglectful father figure endowed with negative attributes.

To female therapists, by contrast, the patients will quickly transfer their ambivalent homosexual dependence on the mother. This new tie generally upsets them and may greatly complicate the counter-transference situation. If the therapist is aware of this fact and accepts the relationship *without interpreting it*, it will gradually develop into a symbolic erotic bond between contemporaries (adolescent friendship, small talk, confidences ...) and hence help the patient to achieve greater detachment from her mother and eventually to progress to heterosexuality. One of my sixteen-year-old patients, Sissi, would, during this phase of her treatment, place the photograph or latest letter of a new boy friend on the table between us as a kind of barrier, and then discuss it at length. I would let her rattle on without interruption, and when she eventually dropped the whole charade, I knew her homosexual anxiety had vanished. Quite often, however, the female therapist is seen as a model of complete womanhood with whom the patient can identify herself as an alternative to the mother.

Technical observations

In beginning the treatment of particularly grave and emaciated cases the therapist must be extremely realistic. In particular he must warn the patient that the sessions can only be continued if the weight does not fall below a certain minimum. If it does, the patient will have to be hospitalized, a step it would be very much better to avoid. Having said this, the therapist should abstain from further references to the symptom, or from inquiring into the possible use of emetics, laxatives or enemas, lest he be identified with the patient's parents. Nor should he look suspicious or critical when the patient, as so often happens, asks to go to the lavatory during a session. In this connection Hilde Bruch has spoken of the constructive use of ignorance. I myself strongly disagree with H. Thomä's view that it is best to challenge the patient's resistance directly and to bring into the open all the ruses that serve her as so many defence mechanisms. In this connection I can do no better than mention Liliana's confession at the end of her successful treatment:

I can't tell you how glad I am that you never once harped on the lies and evasions I used at the beginning. Quite frankly, I kept thinking that you must be a bit dim. But then I began to feel an irresistible urge to tell you the truth. Do you remember... one day I came to a session and dumped my enema can on your table. To my surprise, you looked neither triumphant nor indignant. You simply said: 'Let's try to find out why you still seem to need it.' I realize now that you'd known all about it right from the start. But you also knew that, at the time, I had no alternative.

Giving these patients strict orders merely hardens their non-co-operation. Any references to sexual problems not initiated by the patient can also have dire consequences. Moreover the therapist must take care never to volunteer interpretations of emotions or drives the patient himself thinks degrading, for example jealousy, rivalry, aggression, etc.

The parental problem is an extremely delicate one. Some patients will not tolerate the least criticism of their parents, even when they themselves have become increasingly aware of the negative aspects of their home life. In such cases it is always best to sit back while the patient solves the problem at her own pace.

The central approach of the therapist

The treatment of anorexics must be specifically directed at strengthening the patients' egos which they consider totally inadequate and weak. This feeling is masked by a façade of overactivity and diligence. Patients who attend therapeutic sessions for months without removing their overcoats are prime examples of this attitude. No matter what rational justification they may volunteer for their negative behaviour, it invariably serves them as an armour against the encroachments of others. For a long time they feel that all interpretations are so many attempts on the therapist's part to display his own efficiency and superior knowledge and they become even more determined to put him down by taking refuge in their symptom. The omnipotent psychiatrist is the image of the omnipotent parent, an image they are determined to destroy by being 'themselves' – not too deep and not too intelligent.

While anorexics are non-conformists in their diets, they are, by contrast, incredibly rigid and conventional in their general outlook and behaviour. Their rebelliousness is confined to a struggle with their own bodies. They are puritanical, have a horror of sex (in as much as the subject preoccupies them at all), and are hypercritical of their more uninhibited contemporaries.

These attitudes must never be challenged directly. However, their normally flat and sullen recitations may occasionally be interrupted with a humorous remark, or an optimistic reference to existence in general and their personality in particular, or even to the therapist's own experiences – all of which help to improve the atmosphere of the sessions and pave the way for greater confidence.

Many patients will, during the positive stage of therapeutic progress, make friends with someone of the opposite sex and cautiously test the therapist's attitude towards the new relationship. In general these friendships are rather Platonic but occasionally (in my experience only in the gravest cases of bulimic anorexia) there may be sudden outbursts of promiscuity as the only way to release a vague impulse which is, in fact, a mere substitute for the valid interpersonal relationships that elude these patients. I always warn them against such premature experiences, and hold out the promise of more satisfactory relationships when they have reached greater psychological maturity. References to the transference situation are best avoided, not least because the patient finds them too painful. At most there should be fleeting interpretations of such negative transference phenomena as endanger the future of the treatment.

The therapist himself must, however, be constantly aware of his counter-transference. Few patients are better than anorexics at driving him into a corner and at provoking all sorts of reactions.

Their obdurate clinging to their symptom, or indeed their physical deterioration in the face of some psychological progress, can arouse feelings of strong aggression in the therapist, often disguised as therapeutic pessimism, and persuade him to order the patient's hospitalization either as a punishment or else for his own peace of mind. Their overt behaviour, too, is extremely irritating: they either spend large parts of each session in complete silence, or else disguise their fear of a significant encounter by engaging in an incessant stream of childish chatter. Some of them try to annoy the analyst with continuous complaints, even blaming him for the poor weather; others produce nothing but paeans of praise to their parents, and refuse absolutely to admit the pathological nature of their involvement; yet others, and by far the greatest number, keep voicing endless objections against their families, to whom they nevertheless continue to cling like leeches. In all these cases the therapist is tempted to react with aggressive displays of his superior insight, and these invariably have dire consequences.

What the therapist needs above all is inordinate patience, the ability to wait until the patient produces an authentic feeling or positive action, which can then be used to reveal or strengthen the constructive potentiality of his ego. If the patient starts to put on weight (often by nibbling food on the quiet) and to look healthier, the therapist must take care to turn a blind eye or the patient may mistake his satisfaction for the gloating praises she gets from her mother. Generally menstruation will reappear spontaneously just as soon as the patient's weight is back to normal. The therapist must expect that some patients will hide this happy event from him – some will mention it casually long afterwards, and others may never refer to it at all.

The terminal phase

Once the initial problems have been solved and the patient's ego has been sufficiently strengthened, psychoanalysis proper can be begun. However, this happens far too rarely – only one of my successful cases decided to start analysis (under a colleague) with a view to entering our profession. Most of these patients prefer to terminate treatment as soon as their symptom has been cured, certain that they can do the rest by themselves. Often it is best to agree with them and, rather than arouse their hostility and undermine their self-confidence, to express one's faith in their character.

I want to end this chapter by describing the case of Rita, the most serious anorexic I have ever had to treat.

Rita came to me after two painful and humiliating episodes during which she had been force-fed only to relapse soon afterwards. She showed serious disorders of thought and communication of the schizophrenic type and had enormous difficulties in entering into any kind of relationship with me. I worked with her for five years, during which time she suffered two relapses with a dramatic fall in weight from which she nevertheless recovered without hospitalization. These and several less drastic relapses seemed to occur whenever our relationship was about to become more intimate and hence more threatening to her.

However, during the fourth year of treatment, her persistent ambivalence provoked an even more acute crisis: in the course of a mere fortnight her weight dropped to 61 lbs (height 5' 11").

On that occasion she herself asked me to take her to a psychiatric clinic outside the city where she stayed for three months. Her parents, with whom I had maintained friendly relations throughout this difficult period, while in utter despair, once again expressed their full confidence in me. Though her physical needs were being attended to by capable hands, I made it a point to pay her regular visits and to maintain our rapport. One evening, just as I was taking my leave of her, there occurred something that I can only describe as a breakthrough. Rita had come down with me to see me out. The weather was exceptionally bad, and a gust of wind and snow hit us as soon as we opened the front door.

Rita looked silently at my car across the road, and at the puddle separating me from it. As I was shaking her hand, I saw that her expression had changed: she now fixed me with a strange look, that was both tender and terribly sad.

'*Dottoressina*,' she said, shaking her head in anguish, 'I have to get better . . . because you believe I can. . . .'

After her release from hospital, and with the resumption of regular psychotherapeutic treatment, Rita's scholastic and social attainments continued to improve, but her weight remained at the same level it had been on her discharge (88 lbs). This was quite inadequate though no longer dangerous or subject to sudden fluctuations. She had become deeply attached to me as a person, but had begun to show in a host of different ways that she resented my professional role.

She no longer called me Doctor but Madam, and became depressed as soon as I tried, however tactfully, to interpret her attitude or asked why she had missed a session; she claimed that all such approaches were humiliating and made her feel like a puppet. At the start of one session she made an extremely awkward suggestion and insisted on receiving an immediate reply. She said she had thought about it for a long time; she felt that the compulsory aspects of her attendance had become intolerable but that she lacked the courage to break it all off: her parents, who paid for the treatment, were bound to hear about her decision and would have insisted on her returning to me. She therefore begged me to let her parents continue to pay for three sessions a week, and to allow her to attend only when she herself felt like it. No explanations of her absences were to be demanded.

I was suddenly faced with a dramatic and crucial therapeutic decision: either to analyse and interpret the nature of her request in the orthodox manner, or else to offer Rita a chance of discovering the meaning of her choice for herself and to accede to her request.

I made up my mind there and then that the second alternative was by far the better of the two. It was three months before the summer holidays, and during those three months Rita came to see me three times, always towards the end of the hour allocated to her, thus making sure that I was waiting for her and keeping my side of the bargain we had struck.

I also saw her twice in the street. These meetings were certainly not accidental, though Rita pretended that they were, hurrying to embrace me warmly and then rushing off again.

Shortly before the holidays she came to tell me that she had decided to end her therapy. She had turned into a very beautiful and radiant young woman: she was about to go abroad on a two-year scholarship. On that occasion she spoke only of her plans, and said not a word about the past three months. I did not refer to them either, nor did I congratulate her on her appearance – we both felt that no such words were needed.

Rita had decided to take the last steps on her own, and in so doing she had regained her dignity.

18 *The Existentialist Contribution to the Treatment of Anorexia Nervosa*

Unlike classical psychiatry, which describes, catalogues and classifies pathological symptoms or groups of such symptoms 'from the outside', that is investigates pathological deviations from the social norm, existential analysis is a psychopathology 'from the inside': it tries to analyse modes of being a specific person in a psychopathological world, of self-realization through abnormal symptoms. (The concept of self-realization was employed even by Freud, albeit in embryonic form: he considered the neurotic symptom an expression of the patient's desire to realize himself.) The determination of the extent to which man identifies himself with these symptoms in order to realize himself is the very basis of existential analysis and introduces a form of psychotherapy that revolves round the therapist's *participation* in his patient's world.

In fact, though it came into being as a predominantly psychopathological approach, existential analysis has opened up new worlds to psychotherapy, which it has greatly enriched.

In the remarkable case studies published by phenomenologists we notice a deliberate avoidance of the usual clinical arguments. Thus Binswanger's famous account of the case of Ellen West, an anorexic, was in a sense based merely on a retrospective analysis of historical material supplied by the patient herself, by relatives and by the psychoanalysts who had treated her previously. The patient was then seen personally by the author during the few weeks of her last stay in a clinic prior to her return home and eventual suicide.

In Chapter III of his case study Binswanger sets out the theoretical differences between existential analysis and psychoanalysis. In his view psychoanalysis loses the human being in the theoretical 'apparatus' of his psychic mechanisms. This is largely due to Freud's idea of man.

Whereas existential analysis approaches human existence with no other consideration than the uncontestable observation that man is in the world, has a world, and at the same time longs to get beyond the world, Freud approaches man with the (sensualistic-hedonistic) idea of the natural man, the *homo natura*. According to his idea, which is possible only on the basis of a complete taking apart of being-human as such, and a natural-scientific-biological reconstruction of it, psychoanalysis has developed its entire critique and interpretation of the historical experiential material.

However, as Binswanger goes on to explain, 'the real achievement of psychoanalysis, its real genius . . ., like most achievement of genius, is scientifically fruitful only as long as its one-sidedness is recognized and appreciated'.

Existential analysis, for its part, tries to go beyond psychogenesis: it believes firmly that being-human cannot be totally reduced to causal processes. If it could, there would be no such thing as creativity, responsibility or freedom and all life would reduce to predetermined mechanical processes.

Existential analysis, moreover, refuses to treat man's faculties as isolated and abstract functions, but sees them as so many ways of contacting the world. Man acts and moves in a continuous dialectic relationship with his world and seeks to realize himself within it. Individuality, according to Hegel, is being-in-the-world but in a world accepted as one's own. Existential analysis, similarly, refuses to consider even pathological phenomena in the abstract or in isolation, but always treats them as special modes of self-realization in a world of one's own, of coming to terms with that world, and one's own existence in it.

In that sense anorexia nervosa can be called an existential problem by a human being who sees no other means of realizing himself, of being-in-the-world, than starvation and emaciation. *Existential analysis has no wish to usurp the place of psychiatry or of medicine, let alone of psychoanalysis.* Nor does it, for the sole purpose of engaging in brilliant intellectual disquisitions create artificial categories of 'existential' illnesses, as some ill-informed critics have accused it of doing. In fact all human conditions, be they physiological or psychopathological, are modes of men's being-in-the-world, and in that sense they are necessarily existential – none more so perhaps than anorexia nervosa. Existential analysis seeks solely to present a different, wider view of the human person, to depict an anthropocentric world in which the individual, be he healthy or ill, is no longer treated as a mechanism but as a 'subject', as the helmsman of his own existence, however pathological, and in a sense of his own destiny.

Present-day existential analysis is mainly concerned to discover what disturbances in inter-human communication are at work in the genesis of an illness, and hence focuses attention on the I-Thee relationship. Sborowitz, for instance, has remarked that, whereas Freudian psychoanalysis considers psychosexual disturbances the root cause of emotional disturbances, the existential approach takes precisely the opposite view. This explains the fundamental importance existential thinkers, including especially Buber, Jaspers and Heidegger, attach to the *philosophy of communication.* In my view many American psychotherapists, including those who are openly hostile to existential psychiatry (which they accuse of deliberately obfuscating the issues by using grandiloquent and cryptic terms), have in fact tacitly adopted many fundamental tenets of existentialism and, in particular, share its conception of man.

The concepts I have just been outlining, not only help us to a better understanding of all illnesses, but also prove highly rewarding in the therapeutic field. There are in fact many psychological illnesses, including anorexia nervosa, in which the patient's ego is so weak that the analyst must try to share his phenomenal world rather than take him out of it by premature causal interpretations of a psychoanalytical type. Such interpretations may provoke excessive anxiety reaction and a consequent rejection of therapy. Freud himself has said that such patients succeed in keeping the analyst at bay with their icy politeness.

To begin with anorexics are not preoccupied with their own state and hence will never seek out medical, let alone psychoanalytical, help of *their own free will.* This fact alone distinguishes them from the majority of neurotics. Moreover, when they can be persuaded to take Freudian analysis, these patients generally terminate the treatment after only a few sessions: the analyst's silence and non-active participation quickly become unbearable to people who have themselves deliberately taken refuge in silence and are, in any case, incapable of verbalizing their problems.

Moreover the analyst himself, immersed in the rigid walls of his technique, may become covertly aggressive and hyper-critical, blaming his patients for a lack of collaboration that is, in fact, a natural and inevitable concomitant of the anorexic condition. Sometimes the patients will express their hostility to the therapy or the therapist by starving themselves into a state of near collapse, thus bringing the treatment to a temporary or permanent halt.

Gaining their confidence is a very difficult and delicate process. To begin with the analyst must be extremely tactful in any attempts to reveal the psychosexual basis of their illness, lest he upset their low level of tolerance before he is accepted as a genuine friend. Thus when I agreed to treat Liliana, who had been seen by a Freudian analyst for about a year, I deliberately refrained from placing her on a couch, which might have revived painful memories, but sat her in an armchair facing me (which, as I said earlier, is my normal practice with anorexics). Then, after many sessions of friendly conversations, in which I went out of my way to make her feel at home and demanded very little in return, I casually asked her to bring me her album of family snaps. This gave me an opening for a lively, spontan-eous and detailed discussion of her case history. In particular, when she showed me a snap of her classmates and shyly pointed to her best friend, I encouraged her to talk to me about the girl at length, and then spoke warmly of the positive value of adolescent friendships. There was a moment of stunned silence, after which Liliana told me that her former analyst had given her to understand that the relationship had had a homosexual basis. This had so upset her that she had stopped bringing dreams to the analyst and had grown increasingly hostile to him until finally she got rid of him altogether thanks to a dramatic deterioration in her general condition. My positive comment, by contrast, was the prelude to an extremely worthwhile and fruitful psychotherapeutic relationship, during which it became clear that the mother used to disparage that friendship with veiled insinuations, just as her previous analyst had done. Unlike some analytical techniques that try to proffer direct psychosexual

interpretations, existential therapy concentrates on the constructive possibilities of the ego rather than on the libidinal
drives. In the particular case of Liliana her attachment to a
friend, however morbid it may have been, was in fact a step
forward, an attempt to achieve a richer social life, to extend
the limits of her restricted existence, a search for a confederate
in Sullivan's sense. Such friendships are in any case a great
advance over the child's infantile attachment to the mother.
To respect and encourage them rather than criticize their
immature components means helping the ego's spontaneous
attempts to broaden its horizons.

Binswanger in his perceptive analysis of Ellen West, tells us
that, when Ellen was offered the following two 'equations':

1) slender = spiritual (soft, blond, Aryan), fat = Jewish bourgeois;
2) eating = getting fertilized and pregnant;

by her Freudian analyst, she simply rationalized them without
the least therapeutic benefit. In my view the analyst was far too
precipitate in presenting her with an exclusively historical reduction of the pathological phenomena when he ought to have
stayed in the present, in the world of actual phenomena. This is
precisely what an existentialist analyst would have done in his
place.

In that sense the existential comprehension of the patient's
world (or rather of their often irreconcilable worlds) may be
said to differ *substantially* from the psychoanalytical or essential
interpretation. By essential knowledge we refer to that act of
comprehension in which the knower confronts an object; by
existential knowledge to the act of comprehension in which the
knower experiences the known as a partner who can penetrate,
communicate and eventually transform the knower. Hence the
existentialist does not so much offer an analytical interpretation,
but a genuine and true comprehension of a voice calling for
an answer, of a *Wort* demanding an *Antwort*. The result is a
therapeutic dialogue with rich emotional overtones. By way of
illustration let me quote the case of Lena, a grave eighteen-
year-old anorexic. During the third month of her therapy she
produced the following dream, whose existential meaning was
very much greater than any purely analytic interpretation might
have suggested.

On my way from the convent, I stopped outside the hosptial. A woman who had just given birth was being lifted off a stretcher. I was horrified by her swollen and distended stomach. I heard them say that she had been brought to the hospital because her belly was still full of urine.

Lena's associations were few and inhibited: they all hinged round the anatomy charts she had seen in her school. Her infantile juxtaposition of the excretory and genital functions was quite remarkable. At this point I might easily have come up with long and what, in the event, would certainly have been extremely irritating sexual interpretations. Instead I used the occasion to demonstrate to the patient, with obvious sympathy and concern, how incompatible were the two worlds in which she lived and had revealed in her dream: the ethereal world of her ideals and the real world of flesh and blood.

The body, I told her, which generates life is also the site of decay and death, a vessel holding urine and faeces. Life and death, flowering and fading, germination and putrefaction are all inherent aspects of life and existence. The opening up of a flower, and the ripening of the fruit are the starting points of their eventual decay. But it is precisely because it precedes putrefaction that the blossoming of a flower is so beautiful. Similarly, the human condition must be accepted for what it is; we must have the courage to mature to the full and learn to come to terms with our own death. Lena's anguish was the result of her ambivalent fear of life and of death, of her hunger and satiety, her fullness and emptiness – all reflecting the opposing pull of desire and panic. And when Lena, who was highly intelligent, took in what I was telling her, she had an intense emotional reaction. She rightly interpreted my remarks as a sign of my confidence in, and respect for, her, and realized that I was willing to become involved in her adolescent conflicts. My very trust in her convinced her that integration was within her reach and helped her to make a courageous and conscious choice. I add, in passing, that she abandoned her anorexia, which had persisted for three years, after only twenty-seven sessions.

The fact that I did not immediately probe into the psycho-sexual basis of her unhappy experiences and family history, did not, moreover, prevent Lena herself from taking cognizance of that basis in due course and with relative calm. This she could never have done had I followed the opposite course, the less so as her home environment was extremely dull, and as she looked upon her mother – her model of femininity – as someone so steeped in her daily existence as to have lost all touch with the world of ideas and ideals. It is thanks to the participating presence of the therapist that such patients acquire a more positive and meaningful outlook on life and hence learn to look at themselves in the right historical perspective. To reach this objective, the existential analyst makes a less clear-cut, or perhaps less geometrically defined, theoretical distinction than the psychoanalyst between the conscious and the unconscious, and, in a sense, takes a less mechanistic view of the psychothera-peutic process. Every therapist, in fact, observes many inter-mediate stages between his patients' conscious and unconscious, which latter hinges not so much on the bare facts as on their implications. The therapist as a participating presence in the full sense of that term acts almost as a catalyst in the integration and classification of split and obscure meanings.

As Roland Kuhn has put in his interesting 'Zur Daseins-analyse der Anorexia Mentalis':

Existential analysis provides us with new ways of reaching our patients. This special method of integration and engaging in a dialogue suddenly awakens the liveliest interest in them and helps to establish an interhuman relationship that can then be elaborated by psy-chotherapeutic means, the more so as there is never a lack of topics for discussion.

In fact, the cure is the same as that produced by other analytic procedures, but it is preceded by a marked emotional shock.

I would add that this shock is due to two main factors: an appeal to the patient as a whole person rather than a disparate collection of human problems, and the presence of the therapist as the patient's friend and ally.

But paradoxically the contrary is equally true: the cure is not only based on a possible emotional shock, but also on the avoidance of an excessively anxiety-producing and hence, negative impact. The personality of the anorexic adolescent, which makes her appear broody, hypersensitive and prudish, is such as to resent any intimate or other intrusions by a stranger, at least at the beginning of her treatment. Moreover, because she knows that she is weak and easily confused by clever talk, she is chary of those know-alls who try to tell her all sorts of fairy tales in the guise of analytical interpretations. She has had more than enough of people of that ilk, and reacts by absenting herself from sessions, by bottling herself up in obstinate silence or by totally ignoring all interpretations. Psychotherapy can only hope to succeed if it offers her a chance of completely new experience.

'At first, I was afraid that *you too* knew everything there was to know about anorexia,' an anorexic colleague told me after relating a dream in which an authoritarian teacher was seated at a desk near to a meek woman in an apron (the apron was that of her own mother who had died when the patient was five). It was quite clear that the patient was identifying me with both of these dream personages, for I had played each part in turn; but there was also no doubt as to which part she considered the more constructive.

19 *The Experience of Space and Time in Anorexia Nervosa*

Each of us has his own subjective way of experiencing (*erleben*) space and time. This space-time experience is one of the fundamental aspects of individual existence, of our particular life style. There are those who think of space as something to conquer, to explore, or to preserve and defend, and others who merely circumscribe and measure it. Similarly in their subjective experience of time men range from activists who refuse to waste a few moments to those procrastinators who think that there is always plenty of time to perform tasks, especially the unpleasant ones. Between the two extremes lies a vast spectrum of modes of experiencing time and space which are considered normal by different cultures. Psychiatric pathologists of the past few decades, especially those with a phenomenological bent (Minkowski, Strauss, Binswanger, Volkeit and others), have been at great pains to examine the various ways in which mental patients experience the phenomenological categories of space and of time in the particular existential worlds they inhabit. It would take us too far afield to discuss their highly interesting but complex findings however briefly; suffice it to say that some of them, especially Roland Kuhn, have made a special study of the way in which some of their anorexic patients experience spatio-temporal protophenomena.

In my own work I have found that such experiences are articulated most clearly during advanced phases of treatment (though it is highly advisable and fruitful to direct one's own and the patient's attention to these fundamental aspects of their experience from the outset).

In fact, during the advanced phase of psychotherapy, when progress towards full self-awareness enables the patient to attempt a reconstruction of her past experience of space and time, its direct confrontation with her present and new experience often produces the most trenchant insights and novel perspectives.

Such flashes, which are invariably preceded by a slow and laborious process of introspection, often strike our patients like bolts from the blue and give rise to joyous feelings of surprise and astonishment. They have clearly scored a great and quite unexpected victory, and the high price they have had to pay for it suddenly seems to have been fully worthwhile. In this confrontation the patients relive, describe and accurately interpret their past misery, and happily put it behind them.

Let me now quote from recordings that are far more eloquent than any theoretical exposition I could hope to offer. They were all taken during sessions with Liliana, a grave case of anorexia nervosa, after a year of daily sessions. Liliana, who had quite suddenly 'hit' upon the discovery of a new way of existing, spent several sessions speaking incessantly and slowly, trying her utmost to put into words the rush of new insights that kept pouring into her mind.

12 February 19XX

I get up early in the morning though I don't really have to. If I stayed in bed, I should not feel the least bit guilty or inadequate: I get up because I want to do something, that's all. At one time I used to feel that I had to do things no matter what. I had to do them because otherwise I was left with a horrible sense of emptiness. I forced myself to do things in the best way I could, but I always realized that I could never hope to do as well as normal people. Now I do everything quite spontaneously. I put myself into it heart and soul and express my true self. Once upon a time I left things undone out of fear; now I do them without even thinking. I no longer have to do anything to prove that I am not dead. Now I simply exist. . . .

16 February 19XX

I have at last discovered the meaning of days. My days used to end every night; they never continued into the next day. Each morning, I had to start all over again, somehow to purify myself from the 'pollution' of the last day. It was my way of being ready for anything. But in the evening I was oppressed all over again. At night I just had to vomit. Each morning was just one long chore. I had to clean myself all over (baths, enemas), rid myself of the encrusted dirt, of everything that clung to me inside and out, and start from the beginning, all clean. Perhaps I was desperately searching for my true self.

Now I live in time, and make the best of it. I used to be crushed by it, by my efforts *to be ready* for anything. Now I am ready, precisely because I don't have to be. Today blends smoothly into tomorrow. I have lots of time. Tomorrow is another day and even the space round me has grown bigger and I can fill it, too. The whole thing is fantastic! What an enormous discovery!

Liliana's new spatial experiences bore above all on the space of interhuman relationships. Characteristically these experiences were preceded by concrete events to which the patient had responded in an unusual way, and which I must now describe in brief. Old friends from out of town, whom Liliana had not seen since the start of her psychotherapy, paid her a visit during a short holiday. Determined to have a good time and to make their poor sick friend have one as well, and knowing that she was extremely passive, they arranged a whole series of outings and amusements. To their surprise Liliana refused politely but firmly to tag along. One of the friends, who had stood by her during her worst crisis, was so incensed at this that she scolded Liliana. That night Liliana had a most remarkable dream which clearly reflected her discovery of an existential space that, though open to others, was no longer open to their intrusions and browbeatings:

I am at A. in a most beautiful garden. There are many fruit trees laden with peaches and apples. I am sitting between them. A stranger standing next to me asks me how I got in. I say: 'But this garden is mine.'

I can see that the whole garden is surrounded by a mesh and that some distant friends have their faces pressed against it and look at me with amazement. Then two childhood friends, one of whom used to court me, ask me to let them in. I just wait.

Then I see a whole lot of people, including friends of R., and my mother galloping past on horseback. Somebody asks me how it is that my mother is out riding when she is normally such a stick-in-the-mud. I say: 'In our house everybody is mad.' I feel, as I had been feeling throughout the dream, that somebody was about to arrive. And then I see B., smiling and coming down towards me from the top of the garden.

The symbolic meaning of the first part of the dream is too

obvious to need explaining: a garden of one's own laden with fruit, the mesh, the faces of incredulous friends and Liliana's staking out of her own living space, all speak for themselves. But the second part of the dream has an even deeper spatial significance: that of Liliana's entire existence.

During the first years of her illness, Liliana used to be a passionate rider and also attended ballet classes. This excessive display of physical prowess was not only the typical and deliberate attempt of the anorexic to tire herself out so as to lose weight, but also a desperate bid to fill what had become an utterly boring space by fluttering about like an imprisoned butterfly.

It is worth noting that the spatial experience of these patients differs markedly from that of paranoiacs, who project distorted egos defensively into the environment, which then strikes them as restricted and hostile. Anorexics, by contrast, even if their ego distortions are severe, invariably take the blame on themselves: they feel that their own bodies are bloated, sluggish and clumsy, so much so that they come to look upon themselves as degraded 'objects', and accordingly reify their living space as well. Hence their desperate need to leap, fly or gallop on an impossibly wild charger. That is precisely what Liliana meant when, seeing others (and particularly her mother) gallop past in the way she herself used to do, she exclaimed: 'They are all mad'. All her own wild rides had been so many delusive attempts to hide and deny her own incarceration. In the final scene of the dream the spatial motive had become linked to its phenomonic twin: the time motive: 'I feel, as I had been feeling throughout the dream, that somebody was about to arrive. And then I see B., smiling and coming down towards me from the top of the garden.' The person she expects will not knock at the gate, will not have to force his way in. He has been expected with longing all through her life. He is already inside the garden... he is Eros himself. And so chronological time is transformed into waiting time. Though she has lived in a space empty of relationships and in a time without any tomorrows, now that she has become mistress of her garden she realizes at last that she has been waiting all her life long. And in her waiting, in bridging her yesterday with her tomorrow, she has at last learned to project herself towards the future.

This extension of the space-time experience, though rarely expressed with the acute perception of Liliana, a girl who was quite exceptional in many respects, can nevertheless be detected in the conscious and dream material of all anorexics during the positive phase of their therapeutic progress. This development is, to my mind, the most serious argument against the phenomenologist claim that the pathological features of the fundamental phenomenic categories are somehow preformed, that they preexist in the patient's individual history. In that case an inbuilt and psychogenetically obscure structure would determine the individual's relations with the world in which he lives. I myself prefer to think that those space-time experiences which we normally call pathological are the results (and not the causes) of experiential setbacks and especially of unhappy interpersonal relationships during early life. If this were not the case, then such experiences could never be changed by psychotherapeutic intervention, when, as Liliana's case shows only too clearly, they can in fact be altered radically through the new interpersonal relationship into which the patient has entered with her therapist.

20 *The Condemnation and Redemption of the Body*

Anyone familiar with anorexics will sooner or later begin to wonder how their terribly emaciated bodies feel to *them*.

In my view it is essential to gain a phenomenological insight into these patients' body feelings even before attempting a psychogenetic reconstruction of their condition, and more particularly to try and understand why their body should have assumed such negative existential implications at a certain point of their lives.

In this connection it should be stressed that the adolescent is unusually sensitive to certain phenomena, both jointly and severally:

For the first time in his life the adolescent directs his attention to himself and discovers his inner life, that is his ego in its uniqueness and singularity, and experiences his body and sexuality in an entirely new way, almost with a feeling of bewilderment (the particular way in which he experiences his body during this crucial period of transformation and heightened development and in which he interprets the reactions of others to these changes are of crucial importance). He has reached a particularly delicate point in his individuation – the point of self-recognition, self-confrontation and self-differentiation. This is a transitory, and hence necessarily an unstable, phase. (R. Rossini.)

It is during this phase that physiological processes or hostile environmental reactions (critical comments on one's physical appearance) can evoke the most untoward reactions.

That the adolescent is extremely self-conscious and particularly shy of his body even in normal circumstances may be deduced from the general awkwardness and clumsy movements characteristic of that age.

This crisis, initiated by the discovery of her self together with the new, pubertal, experience of her body, faces the anorexic girl with a particularly dramatic challenge and introduces a *split* into her personality.

The result is discontent with her self, a sense of *malaise* and finally the fear – first vague and indistinct, but then more and more pronounced – that there is something radically wrong inside.

For a long time I had the vague feeling that something was amiss in my life and in my relations with others. This went on more or less intensely for many years. In the country village where my sister and I were born and grew up, everybody, including all our friends, thought of us as well-to-do little children, spoiled by their mother and by their aunt who taught them at school. The two of us were inseparable, dressed in the same way, were good at our lessons, but often felt bored. We weren't part of any special gang, and no one ever invited us home. I remember that I used to sit by the window, hidden behind the half-closed shutters, watching all the bigger boys and girls who attended the school in the city come home from the station. I liked to hear them laugh and joke among themselves. I even enjoyed their Sunday promenades along the Corso. . . . I could never go out to join them because we were expected to pore over our homework. . . . I thought what fun it must be to be part of that crowd, and whenever one of them stayed away, I wondered where he might be and what fun he must be having elsewhere. I was still a little girl no more than twelve or thirteen years old. Looking back, I don't think I could have been all that unhappy. I was just resigned to my monotonous life, to being cut off, and to a boring future. I would have become a teacher like my aunt, but I didn't want to remain a spinster like her. I wanted to get married to a good man. We should have owned a little house and I would have cooked away in the kitchen just as my mother always did. . . . I could neither imagine nor did I expect anything else. But just before my fifteenth birthday everything suddenly changed. People started telling me that I was a beautiful girl and paid me all sorts of compliments. I remember them comparing me with my sister. They said that she was gawky and not nearly so pretty, just the type to remain a spinster, but that I would have a much rosier future. At that time my father was transferred and we moved to the city. In the summer, my sister had to study for her matriculation, and I was sent to the seaside with a relative. It was the first time in my life that I had been away from her. I had a wonderful time, with lots of admirers, including the most handsome boy on the whole beach. I had only just shot up, and I knew I had a good face and attractive dark eyes. I was not too satisfied with the rest of my body: my hips were too broad and my ankles not nearly as slim as I would have liked. But I wasn't too worried. I kept telling myself that I ought to slim, but I did nothing about it.

When I returned home, I found my sister looking pale and stodgy, what with the rich food my mother had kept pouring into her. I could hardly recognize her, so ugly had she become.

Full of my own seaside conquests I entered the High School much surer of myself than ever before and determined to be a social success. But to my dismay, none of my classmates really took to me. At first I thought it was because I had the reputation of being a swot. I tried to hide my good marks, and pretended to do very little homework. It was all a waste of time. They kept ignoring me and my disappointment turned into dismay when a new girl, who was not nearly as pretty as me and just as clever at her studies, made an immediate hit with all the boys and girls.

And outside school, though boys kept running after me, invited me to dances or parties, they quickly cooled off again. For as soon as any one of them showed too much interest, I would immediately start flirting with another, and make disparaging remarks about the first. Then I gradually lost my confidence and became more humble. If a boy ran after me I now felt honoured. I also made a few physical concessions just to keep him. In fact, these concessions were just an easy way out, because *I never knew what to say* to either boys or girls. And it was only when boys were kissing and doing other things, too, that I wasn't expected to talk. But it was useless all the same: nobody ever came back and I was feeling more and more depressed.

I started to think hard about what it was everyone disliked about me. I didn't have to look far: it could only be my body. My face was all right and so were my large eyes and my thick black hair, but my hips were really much too broad and my ankles too thick. If I could change that, then I would never be alone again. I suddenly felt a sense of great relief. At last I had hit upon the reason for my loneliness and my despair. And I could do something positive to remedy it. I would go on a *strict diet*. It was like a sudden illumination and I felt perfectly content.

From then I thought of nothing else, remembered nothing at all except my monomaniacal determination to lose weight. People who worried about calorie charts just made me laugh. All that was needed was to eat less and less. I lost all interest in meals. My mother kept pleading with me and dragging me off to doctors. I kept quiet: I only thought of gaining time and of fooling them all.

Rita's story, patiently reconstructed after nearly two years of intensive psychotherapy, is remarkable chiefly for highlighting the sudden change in her feelings that followed her 'great' discovery. Her sense of *malaise*, impotence and failure, all the more painful because it seemed inexplicable, gave way to one of illumination and contentment as soon as she had pinpointed the apparent cause of her misery, and knew what steps were needed to remove it: a strict diet.

Her insistent question about what it was that condemned her to loneliness had received an unequivocal reply that now took complete possession of her ego: 'What is wrong with me is my body.'

One cannot help being struck by the resemblance between these feelings and those that, in schizophrenia, accompany the 'identification' of a concrete persecutor or persecutors. The relief the patients obtain as a result is quite obvious from their unshakeable conviction that, at last, they know who is out to get them. But the anorexic response is infinitely more active.

In schizophrenic paranoia the patient projects the basic disturbance in his interpersonal relationships on to others. But having done so he adopts a passive attitude towards his imagined persecutors, and makes no positive attempts to defend himself against them.

In anorexia nervosa, the disturbance in the interpersonal relationships is projected into the split self, or more precisely into that part of the split personality which is the body, and against which a fierce battle must constantly be waged. Binswanger, in his famous analysis of Ellen West, asked himself at a certain point (*Existence*, pp. 347 f.) whether the obsessive fear of becoming fat should be termed a phobia. His answer was in the negative, since, as he pointed out, in the case of anorexia there is no substitution, in the Freudian sense, no diversion from an authentic content to an unauthentic, phobogenic content. The dread of becoming fat moreover was not in Ellen's case ego-alien – unlike the typical phobic, who, though a slave to his symptom, is 'intellectually' aware that the symptom itself is foolish and contrasensical. At this point I think it would be most helpful to introduce Arieti's concept of *concretization*.

In the Freudian view, phobia is a form of displacement. Thus while little Hans was afraid of his father, his neurosis displaced that fear on to horses. According to Freud, such displacement serves to conceal a sexual threat, and therefore becomes symbolic of what it replaces. Thus the terror of being bitten by a horse replaces the terror of being castrated at one's father's hands. But it is this writer's opinion that the displacement is not necessarily from one object (the father) to another (horse). What happens is not so much a displacement as a concretization. The patient lives in fear of vague and intangible threats that he may find difficult to define or that he refuses to recognize: the father's hostility, the chance of being abandoned by the mother, a baneful or hypercritical family atmosphere, etc. In patients suffering from serious phobias the psychiatrist can easily recognize the concretization of a more general anxiety-producing situation: the fear of sexual relations conceals the greater fear of stable love relationships; the fear of travelling conceals the deeper fear of venturing into life; the fear of a host of small objects commonly conceals a general state of insecurity. Odier had a good inkling of this phenomenon when he wrote that the phobic object conceals a concept, an idea, a vague intuition.

In my view, phobia is the expression of a general psychopathological principle, namely that *whatever cannot be borne abstractly because it generates too much anxiety, or for other reasons, will eventually be concretized.* This concretization of concepts and intuitions is not simply a reduction of the abstract to the concrete level, as Goldstein has described it especially for organic cases, but an active process, i.e. an active translation of the abstract into the concrete.

Applying these comments to Rita's case we find that, once she was forced to recognize the collapse of her narcissistic hopes, and the inadequacy in her interhuman relationships, her character armour prevented her from locating the causes on an abstract or psychological plane, and this for two reasons:

1) because her overprotective upbringing in a well-to-do and conformist home had impeded her personality so as to render her incapable of coping with any but the simplest abstractions; and

2) because blaming her own personality shortcomings for her social failures would have made her intolerably anxious: the requisite psychological changes were quite beyond her. Hence, when she kept wondering what was wrong with her, she eventually came up not with the correct, and to her much too abstract, answer, but with the much simpler concretization: 'I am too fat.'

This flaw was infinitely simpler to cure, and she accordingly seized upon it with alacrity.

The retreat into the body

The result was a retreat into the body coupled to a refusal to exist in it. But it is obvious that the basis of this retreat was prepared at a much earlier stage.

This raises an interesting question, namely that of the nature of the anorexic's body feelings before the sudden onset of the illness. Is she strongly 'embodied', inextricably bound up with her body, its sensations and its limitations, or is she already 'unembodied', that is detached from her body?* My own observations of these patients (whose bio-physical receptivity is similar to that of manic depressives) have convinced me that they are highly 'embodied' from the start and that this very fact is the cause of their unhappiness. In this they are quite unlike schizophrenics, whose body schema is disturbed precisely because they are strongly 'unembodied': they do not experience their body as their own, as something real and finite.

The anorexic feels her body as something omnipresent, something that keeps getting into the way and often gets hurt in the process. I would agree with Sullivan that the anorexic experiences her body as something halfway between the 'bad me' and the 'non-me'. More precisely she experiences her body as her own and as something very real, but hates it for its bulk and dimensions. These make it fall far short of the ideal body, that of a true, autonomous, powerful and capable self. In anorexia nervosa therefore the failure to perceive and recognize body signals, as described by Bruch, is not the primary phenomenon, but is consequent upon the rejection of the body and of its anabolic stimuli. The reader may recall the famous case of Nadia (*Existence*, pp. 331 ff.) which Janet reported under the purely descriptive classification of 'obsession with body-shame'. In fact, in the light of what we now know, we are entitled to say that this case, too, was one of psychopathological concretization: the abstract dislike and rejection of the self had been concretized in the form of body-shame. Since Nadia identified herself completely and consciously with a psychotic ideal of

* For the problem of the embodied and unembodied self, see R. D. Laing, *The Divided Self* (London: Tavistock Publications, 1960).

acorporeality, *she no less than Binswanger's Ellen West did not suffer from obsession or schizophrenia, as their two biographers have claimed, but from anorexia nervosa, a psychosis in its own right.*

These patients blame all their existential failures and all their interpersonal shortcomings on their own bodies, which they deny but to which they nevertheless feel chained as a result of concretization. This introduces the basic materialism of anorexics, spiritual and ascetic though they appear to be.

In fact, they are totally bound up with a parsimonious, mean and materialistically orientated world. . . . The negation of the self, the liberation from the body, ought to lead them away from material concerns, and they do in fact appear to be insensitive to pain, spiritual and asthenic. . . . However, their aesthetic and narcissistic pretensions hide an authentic hunger for life. . . . They act as if they were not hungry, they reject maturity and sexuality, and disparage their feminine and erotic strivings. But their real hunger for love and thirst for life are betrayed by the importance they attach to food in their drawings and dreams, in the way they gulp down scraps from the refrigerator, and in their need to know that food is amply available. (H. Hiltmann.)

It follows that the therapeutic dialogue must be directed at helping these patients to uncover the chained and hidden reality of their existence and the deep contradictions it entails. Psychotherapy must also focus attention on the formal aspects of the anorexic mechanism, and elucidate the process of concretization. The more intelligent patients can, during the advanced phase of therapy, be drawn into a philosophical discussion of their materialistic and deprecatory approach to their own bodies. They can be told they are materialistic precisely because they are spiritually too feeble to grasp any but the most elementary aspects of their body. Instead of thinking topographically – the body is here, and the mind up there – they must be taught to adopt an antidualistic logic, to appreciate that the mind and the body are not two distinct appendages, but that man as a person is spirit and body in one. The body is not given to us as an object, it is not something *we own* – it is what *we are*. It is the significance we ourselves attach to our bodies that either reduces them to the dimension of anatomical objects or else transfigures them into subjects, that is persons. Our body is the measure of our spirit. Even though it has clear limitations, it is our only means of reaching out towards others. The body is our meeting place with others, and its rejection is at one and the same time a rejection of sociability, human solidarity and responsibility. The analysis of daily events in the lives of our patients makes it clear time and again that the contempt they feel for their body, their rejection of it as a clumsy object, is not at all the spiritual choice it purports to be, but a purely materialistic escape mechanism reflecting a kind of social 'absenteeism', and a refusal to become committed to any kind of interhuman relationship. Many concrete events will repeatedly offer the therapist a chance to bring these facts home to his patients, by helping them to experience emotionally what they might otherwise have misunderstood or rationalized. Purely theoretical interpretations must be avoided at all costs, let alone critical or hectoring remarks.

It is thanks to the analysis of concrete events and actions that the therapist can help the patient to open himself to abstract thought – a difficult but indispensable journey if the patient is to resolve the apparent contradiction between his anatomical body or body-object, whose features or imperfections may produce unpleasant feelings even in the healthiest of people, and *the body as a meaningful structure*, in which those very features or imperfections may be accepted for what they really are: hallmarks of man's true personality.

21 *The Reconstruction of Body Feeling*

I mentioned earlier that anorexics seem incapable of introspection, of recognizing not only the unconscious basis of their
own behaviour but also their overt emotions, elementary impulses
and body signals of various kinds. I have mentioned that they
generally adopt a rigid posture during their first session, despite
the obvious inconvenience of that posture. Eissler too has
pointed out that their set expressions and gestures, and their
monotonous tone of voice reflect a general dearth in body
feeling, which sets them off from the psychologically healthy in
which such feelings are the very basis of consciousness and
produce a sense of vitality.

Meng, following Federn, was moreover able to show that their
capacity for feeling (*Gefühlsfähigkeit*) is reduced because libidinal
cathexis has been partially withdrawn from their ego. As a
result the distinction between body and the external world often
becomes blurred, so that man as a total person, living in his
body, feels himself a dead object in an omnipresent and hostile
world.

During interviews these patients are not only inordinately
rigid, but often give one the impression that their negative
armour hides a dispirited feeling of emptiness, a general lack of
clear ideas, of intense feelings and of decisiveness, and a
distressing incapacity to face up to situations and problems.

We know that anorexics suffer from an overwhelming sense
of inadequacy, from a deeply-rooted feeling that nothing they
themselves experience can be legitimate. This, as we saw, applies
even to their most elementary needs. Is it right to be hungry at a
particular moment? And what is the 'right' degree of satiety or
fatigue? When Paola, one of my patients, was sent to a finishing
school and thus separated from her grandmother and elder
sister, she quickly turned podgy and pasty. Her fellow students

were all obsessed with their figures, and their concern weighed increasingly on her mind. What should she do? At home her food had always been served for her – her grandmother had strong views on what was a healthy diet and on everything else as well. Left to her own devices, Paola had no idea of how much she should eat. She had never done anything right at home, so how could she be expected to do the right thing at school?

Her ensuing anorexia was her way of putting herself 'right', with disastrous results.

In her case, too, the inability to produce the correct responses to body signals was a basic element in the pathogenesis of her illness.

But to define anorexia nervosa as coenaesthopathy or coenaesthophrenia explains nothing at all, and, in particular, serves no therapeutic purpose. What we should bear in mind instead is that, even in this particular neurologic and neuro-dynamic sphere, the development of a positive sense of existence depends, above all, on a healthy interpersonal relationship in which the young child's feelings are positively encouraged, and hence correctly conceptualized and integrated in such a way as to further spontaneous and adequate responses (recognition of stimuli and their satisfaction).

It is on these basic and primary experiences that the therapist must base his approach, taking care, as I have stressed before, not to offer premature interpretations of the unconscious meaning of the patient's behaviour (refusal of food as a self-destructive tendency, the secret wish to get even with the family, sexual fears, etc.), for such interpretations can only aggravate the patient's profound feelings of impotence. Here, they will tell themselves, is yet another know-all with the gift of the gab. The first thing the therapist must do, and which according to Hilde Bruch must guide his entire therapeutic attitude, is to make the patient see that she has the capacity to feel, to judge and to act as an individual, and that she has the right to test herself against reality:

Yet without genuine experience of feelings of their own, no true improvement takes place. To achieve true improvement, it became necessary to change the therapeutic approach from a focus on motivation to one on fact-finding, from the inquiry into the why of behaviour to the question of how it had happened that the underlying thinking had developed in this distorted way.

This change-over was not easy. Often the patients were reluctant to give the simpler type of information sought here. Yet in the long run the method proved amazingly effective; and for many patients, it was the first consistent experience where someone had listened to what they had to say and how they had felt, and did not tell them what they were supposed to feel, of 'what must have happened'. In the course of these sober inquiries, it became apparent that many patients used words and concepts, everyday words, not bizarre or schizophrenic expressions, differently from common usage, Over-readiness for interpretation, or stubborn resistance against following the line of an argument, could be traced to such misconceptions or misunderstandings. At times, the writer had called her approach 'doing semantics' or detecting 'counterfeit communication', or simply 'avoiding clichés'.

This she will come to realize first and foremost thanks to the respect with which the therapist treats her, to the help he extends to her as of right, including, if need be, help in maintaining her weight at a level compatible with survival. Once this has been achieved, the therapist can begin to probe cautiously into the psychogenetic problems. The resulting awareness is closely akin to what existentialists call the ontological sense of existence, of the right to be-in-the-world. Such awareness enhances the individual's appreciation of the value of his own existence, regardless of conventional or social barriers. That is precisely why I have bracketed Hilde Bruch with American psychotherapists sympathetic to the existentialist school.

In my own psychotherapeutic work, developed on lines similar to, but independent of, Hilde Bruch, I have often had the experience that the discovery of personal independence and individual worth sometimes comes long before the restoration of the capacity to perceive and recognize the most elementary emotional and bodily stimuli. The assumption of the right, thanks to the therapeutic *relationship*, to hold opinions and to have needs *of one's own*, tends in the long run to eliminate even the most deep-seated perceptive and cognitive blocks, including those that stand in the way of the recognition of elementary body signals.

One day Rita, a patient who, after many months of psychotherapy, was still in a state of semi-emaciation, told me proudly of a crucial event that had occurred since the last session: she

had been able to inform a friend quite calmly that the study pace
the girl had been imposing on her no longer suited her, and that
in future she would work on her own. The possibility of taking
this step, she added, would not even have occurred to her a few
months earlier. Indeed, she would have submitted meekly to
her friend's impossible demands and probably have blamed
herself for her own stupidity and inadequacy. 'If I were to tell
them at home about this victory,' she added, 'they would just
stare at me and wonder what it was I thought so remarkable
about it all.' Obviously the remarkable thing was her spontaneous discovery that she had a personality, needs and rights
of her own. And this she no longer had to express by offensive
reactions, but was able for the first time to assert with the
prudent resolution of the self-aware person.

Another of my chronic patients, Liliana, who had vomited
persistently for years, suddenly stopped doing so after a session
(her 121st) during which she had been led to experience her
autonomy in a *highly emotional way*. It is worth dwelling on the
episode at some length.

This patient, who was living on her own for the first time in
her life – I had persuaded her mother to return home – had
taken up residence in a hotel and had been coming to sessions
with me almost daily. She had a married relative in the city who
invited her round fairly frequently but whose company rather
bored her. One evening she met a young man who escorted her
back to her hotel and then suggested a night on the town.
Liliana was quick to accept and came home very late that
night.

Soon afterwards the young man asked her out again, and
though her relative was expecting her early in the evening, she
nevertheless agreed to accompany the young man. Next day
Liliana spent the greater part of her session wondering aloud
what lies she would have to tell her relative, and what he would
say if the truth came out (the young man had behaved with
perfect correctness). At this point I could contain myself no
longer; I was so irritated that I completely abandoned my
neutral stance and, for the first time in months, asked Liliana
with a trembling voice why on earth a girl of twenty-four should
feel obliged to account for her every action, and moreover try
to camouflage the truth with excuses and lies as if everybody had

the right to order her about. It was time she got it into her head that she was an adult living on her own, and responsible to herself alone.

Liliana listened to my outburst in perfect silence and I, too, made no further contribution for the rest of the session. Next morning I was awakened by a telephone call to be told by Liliana that she had, for the first time in many years, slept like a log without having to get up to vomit. (She never had vomiting fits again.)

I concluded that her vomiting, too, must have been an attempt to gain greater autonomy, though in an ambivalent and con-cretized psychosomatic way.

That distortion became pointless the moment she took cognizance of her own personal rights and the accompanying emotions had grown strong enough to consolidate her self-integration.

Her fear of oral invasion by the 'other' as a threat to her precarious autonomy was also brought home to me by a shrewd observation on the part of her dentist, Dr V. Acht. Throughout his treatment, which was not at all painful but lasted several months, Liliana would take a long time before opening her mouth for dental inspection, explaining that she was not so much afraid of being hurt as of 'being attacked as a defenceless victim'. Obviously this irrational fear was not purely sexual (fear of oral fecundation), but revealed a general personality defect. In my view the sexual fears of anorexic subjects are, in fact, almost invariably the expression of their fear of psychological 'invasion'.

With another patient, Ira, it took four years of psychotherapy before a discovery similar to Liliana's had sunk in sufficiently for her to tell me that, for some time, she had been able to perceive and respond naturally to such elementary body signals as fatigue; she would now lie down quietly and feel a *wonderful sense of drowsiness in all her limbs*. This was an entirely new sensation to a girl who had previously been so compulsively overactive that her mother would often discover her slumped over her desk or curled up on the carpet fast asleep.

But the point that strikes me as being of the utmost clinical importance is that, as a result of psychotherapy, these patients not only learn to recognize body signals but also begin to take pleasure in the sensations of heaviness and relaxation, appreciating them at long last for what they really are: *needs of the whole person.*

However, to achieve this natural state, this ability to *recognize* the signals emitted by one's *own* body and to satisfy the needs they express, is a very much more laborious and difficult process than it appears it be – it is probably the last step along the road to clinical recovery.

22 *Reflections on my own Case Studies*

From 1950 to the date of writing I have examined approximately sixty patients who were referred to me as cases of anorexia nervosa. However, in only thirty of these cases was I able to confirm the original diagnosis and proceed to a study in depth. The rest were either (male and female) cases of pseudo-anorexia or else referred back to other colleagues. (My diagnostic criteria have been set out in an earlier chapter.)

Eight cases, who were also my earliest ones, were examined at the Medical Clinic of the University of Milan. All were in-patients in a grave or terminal condition, and none had received psychotherapeutic treatment. The remaining twenty-two cases had been sent to me as private patients by various hospitals, private clinics or family doctors.

The case histories of the patients I saw in the Medical Clinic were reconstructed carefully from conversations with the patients and their relatives, and the application of such psycho-diagnostic projections as the Rorschach and the Thematic Apperception Test. Before discharging these patients from the clinic, I gave them two or three cautious explanatory talks about the results of their psychodiagnostic tests and also about their emotional state. In addition I saw the relatives during several sessions and advised them about the most positive attitudes they could adopt towards these patients.

Needless to say, I was able to study those cases whom I saw privately at very much greater depth, not least thanks to prolonged contacts with them and the more intimate patient-doctor relationship that can be built up in a non-institutional atmosphere. The resulting situation is admittedly far more risky and unpredictable, but it is also far more spontaneous and less open to friction. In what follows I shall not discuss individual cases in detail, lest minor changes might fail to disguise their identity and cause unnecessary suffering to both them and their families. (Whenever I have mentioned individual cases in previous chapters so as to render the exposition more lively and direct, I have taken special care to change the circumstances beyond recognition.)

As far as the social position of my patients is concerned, the marked prevalence of middle-class girls is in no way significant, since it is obvious that only the economically privileged can afford the luxury of prolonged and expensive private treatment. It is however interesting that both Thomä and Dally, working with hospitalized patients, also found that the great majority of anorexic patients had a middle-class background. In this connection Dally rightly remarked that the recent spread of anorexia from the 'well-to-do' to the less wealthy social classes may well reflect the increased affluence of our society. (In Italy upper-class patients are often sent to expensive sanatoria in Switzerland and other countries, so that the local psychotherapist rarely if ever comes across them.)

As to the size of my patients' families, six of my female cases were only children, thirteen were first-born, eight were second born, two were the youngest of three, and only one was the fifth born of seven children. Such statistics tell us little of importance, except that anorexia is particularly prevalent among small families. But then such families are typical of the middle class.

Of my thirty patients, five had been obese during the premorbid phase: three markedly and two moderatly so.

It is all the more interesting to note that none of my patients who suffered from bouts of bulimia ever exhibited alternating phases of obesity and emaciation. Instead their bouts invariably led to a deterioration in their general condition: food binges were followed by repeated vomiting, the excessive use of laxatives, and an even more restricted diet. I have had occasion to make a brief study of two cases only of alternate obesity and emaciation. These were patients who, on clinical as well as on psychodiagnostic examination, showed clear mental disturbances of a schizophrenic type – one was in a state of temporary psychotic delirium. These two cases are not included in the present report, because I was unable to study them in depth.

The relative absence of oscillations between obesity and

emaciation distinguishes my own experience from that of other, especially American, writers. This might well be the result of cultural differences and thus provide a starting point for trans-cultural research.

All my patients began to menstruate at the age of twelve to thirteen years; the only exception was one girl who came for treatment at a precocious age (ten years). The rest – save for one who had suffered from irregular menstruation even before the onset of her illness – all had regular periods, in rhythm, quantity and duration.

From these data and also from the patients' height and weight during the premorbid phase, I conclude (in agreement with all modern authors) that anorexia nervosa patients seem to have a *perfectly normal physical constitution* in the premorbid phase.

In none of my cases could constitutional hypogonadism be demonstrated. Nor have I, or for that matter any other modern student of anorexia nervosa, been able to find any indication of a special family proneness to mental disease. Dual cases of anorexia nervosa in one and the same family or in monozygotic twins are described in the literature, but these are extremely uncommon and are probably the result of psycho-emotive 'contagion'. One of my young patients did, indeed, swear a solemn 'anorexic oath' with her twin sister at the beginning of her morbid phase, but the twin broke down after a few days and helped herself liberally to food, leaving the patient to fulfil her part of the oath in splendid isolation. Meanwhile the twin kept putting on weight, because she felt that it was only by over-eating that she could induce her sister to take any food at all.

Catamnestic reflections

As I have said in an earlier chapter, I cannot share the prognostic optimism expressed by some writers, or accept the high percentage of recoveries they claim.

In my view, their false optimism has two main causes:
1) common diagnostic errors responsible for the inclusion of cases that do not suffer from true anorexia nervosa (neurotic reactions, depressive conditions);
2) inadequate follow-ups. Temporary improvements followed by relapses are a common feature of anorexia nervosa, so that,

in the absence of long-term follow-ups, chronic cases are often pronounced fully cured.

My own case histories show that anorexia nervosa is a grave illness from which patients rarely if ever recover spontaneously. Thus all the eight cases I saw in the Medical Clinic were extremely serious: two (25 per cent) ended in death, and one turned chronic with extreme loss of weight. Moreover it is worth stressing that, because, at the time, anorexia nervosa was widely confused with hypophysial cachexia, none of these patients was thought to be in need of psychiatric or psychotherapeutic treatment.

One fatal case, whom I examined shortly before her death, had for years been transferred from ward to ward and had, *inter alia*, been subjected to a tonsillectomy in the hope of improving her appetite and general condition. Another seriously emaciated patient (weight: 50 lbs; height: 5' 4"), whose morbid condition had persisted for more than ten years, had previously been treated exclusively and unsuccessfully in a general medical ward.

Of the patients still alive during my last follow-up (October 1968) some were seen by me in person; the mental and physical state of the remainder was ascertained from their family physicians and relatives.

Of the original eight patients two had died and two were chronically ill. Three patients, who had succeeded in stabilizing their weight within tolerable limits and whose menstrual cycle was back to normal, nevertheless continued to suffer from a variety of psychoneurotic disturbances: all but one lived with their families, did no outside work but performed the odd domestic chore, were unmarried and had no wish to find a husband. The one who had married six years earlier had no children, but was gainfully employed and, though frigid, outwardly on good terms with her husband, and greatly esteemed by her professional colleagues. For all that she suffered continually from digestive upsets which, she claimed, forced her to keep to a restricted diet. As a result her weight was still somewhat below the normal.

In passing I must confess that it was my dramatic and frustrating experience with hospitalized anorexics in the University Medical Clinic that persuaded me to give up my idea of becoming a medical consultant and to turn to psychiatry and psychoanalysis. The embarrassing mystery of anorexia had begun to torment me. And I still do not know, and will in fact never be certain, whether it was a genuine desire to help these patients, or rather the need to overcome my own sense of impotence, that drove me to take a step I had never even envisaged.

Let us now look at the case histories of the twenty-two patients I treated privately.

The first problem, as we saw earlier, is that they constituted a heterogeneous group: thirteen were relatively recent cases, and nine had become chronic, and had been made obstinately resistant in the wake of such disastrous experiences as traumatic stays in hospitals and coercive therapies (forced-feeding). Obviously these chronic cases are by far the most difficult to treat.

The second problem is the definition of what constitutes a full recovery. As Searles has argued so convincingly, whenever the psychotherapist looks back on one of his own cases at the end of the treatment he is assailed by guilt feelings:

How many of us can really accept, without guilt, a patient with whom we are no longer working? I cannot, and I feel that my guilt contains not-too-readily-conscious resentment at him for failing to fulfil all my expectations. But again, I surmise that wholehearted acceptance of the patient is another unrealized omnipotent goal. We could unambivalently love and approve of and accept our patient only if he were somehow able to personify our own ego-ideal – and in that impossible eventuality, we would of course feel murderously envious of him, anyway.

Such torturing doubts are the unavoidable consequences of the therapist's emotional entanglement in the appraisal of his own successes and failures. Thus, whom should I consider a greater success, Laura who, having abandoned her anorexic rebellion, now lives an orderly married life, but is utterly indifferent to social problems and completely satisfied with her husband and their little daughter, or Teresa, who left her family and carried her original rebellion into the field to do constructive social work with a volunteer corps, and who lives with a lover?

To avoid such equivocal pronouncements I have adopted Dally's criteria for assessing improvement, namely the patient's weight, menstruation, psychosexual development, degree of independence and mental state. I accordingly consider those patients cured who have recovered their normal or near-normal weight, who menstruate normally and regularly, are contentedly married or have a stable and satisfying love relationship, show a sufficient degree of independence, and do not display neurotic symptoms that require treatment or clearly hamper their existential development.

Of the thirteen patients who came to me at a fairly early stage of the illness, I consider nine fully cured if judged by Dally's criteria. All nine were stable anorexics without appreciable mental disturbances. Of the remaining four, whom I do not consider cured, two showed marked mental disturbances, and tendencies to bulimic attacks. These patients proved extraordinarily resistant to all psychotherapeutic approaches. The ambivalence of one of them was such that, after about three months of treatment, she lost weight so dramatically that I had no alternative but to order her immediate hospitalization, whereupon our psychotherapeutic relationship came to an end. With the other, I myself felt so tortured by her exasperating behaviour and the ambivalent counter-transference it produced in me that I took advantage of one of her long and unjustifiable spells of absence to terminate the treatment.

With the remaining two patients in this group of thirteen who came to me at an early phase of their illness and showed no marked mental disturbances, the unsatisfactory outcome was a direct result of serious errors on my part which led to the premature termination of their treatment. Both patients came to me during the first years of my private practice. I went wrong not only in my psychotherapeutic attitude towards them but also in my relationship with their families, whom I did not treat with sufficient caution, authority and conviction.

Of the nine patients who came to me after years of chronic illness, I can only consider three definitely cured. All were exceedingly difficult cases, involving stormy sessions over long periods and calling for 'heroic' efforts on my part. Such efforts, which are common during the early and most enthusiastic phase of one's professional career, are, in my view, difficult to maintain in the long run.

Of the other six cases, all of them chronic, two, who had been ill for ten and thirteen years respectively and who were not only mentally disturbed but prone to bulimia and toxicomania, deteriorated further under treatment, had to be hospitalized, and eventually died.

A third patient terminated her treatment and developed a form of schizophrenia with persistent deliria. The three remaining patients, though they had been chronically ill for years at the start of their therapy, may be said to have improved in many ways, and quite especially in respect of their work efficiency and social relationships. They nevertheless still have such typical symptoms as vomiting fits, abnormally low weight levels and amenorrrhoea.

From all the above it would appear that most of the cases that proved successful from a psychotherapeutic point of view came from the group of stable or recent anorexics. For these patients the outcome of the treatment depends largely on the therapist himself, or rather on the relationship he is able to establish with them (and their families).

It has to be stressed that psychotherapy is not like a drug whose effects are fairly predictable, but that it involves a strong personal element which, as such, is bound to differ from case to case. Now it was precisely this enormous personal effort (aside from the vast expenditure of time demanded by the psychotherapeutic treatment of many of these patients) when viewed against the paucity of the results, at least in numerical terms, that impelled me to search for new conceptions and new ways of more effective therapeutic intervention. The results of my new orientation are the subject of Part Four.

Appendix to Part Three:
Autobiography of a Patient*

When I think back on my early childhood, I see myself in a small suburban garden staring fixedly across the hedge at a little girl with a beautiful blonde doll. I was standing motionless, struck with an urgent desire to hold the doll in my own arms and to sing her to sleep with a lullaby. Suddenly my mother's voice cut into my daydream, making me jump with fright.

'So there you are, you little wretch, I was wondering where you had got to.'

'Haven't you washed yet, you dirty thing?' added my sister emerging from the door, looking neat and tidy like a real young lady. 'Be quick about it, we are always late at the convent. All I'm short of is a scolding by the nun.' And with a sharp jerk she pulled me indoors and plunged my hands into cold water. A brisk scrubbing, a good rub with the towel and then out again, my head drooping, my eyes filled with resentment.

'Make sure you take good care of that little monkey,' my mother called out as we reached the gate. 'I know I can rely on you.'

'You certainly can,' my sister called back confidently.

'And make her eat her soup!'

'I will.'

And so I followed my sister feeling bitter and cross but too afraid of her to give in to a strong impulse to run away, or to spite her in any way that would have earned her a rebuke from our mother.

* This autobiography is reproduced exactly as it was given to me by a patient, except for changes in names and places.

I hurried at the crossroads and for a moment was lost in the crowd.

'You horrible creature, come back!' My sister's hand reached out, pulled me to her, then landed a slap full in my face. 'The only way to teach you,' she said severely.

And then we were at the nursery school, an old, bleak building. 'Hurry, hurry,' called a nun from the main entrance.

Inside there was a gaggle of little girls, all very correctly turned out and looking so sure of themselves that I felt more lost than ever. I made my way warily towards them and pretended to join them, hoping my sister would leave me alone.

I kept silently to one side because they were all much bigger than me, and refused to let me join in their games. In fact I was only there by courtesy of the nuns, because I was still under the age they usually took children. I spent most of my time there dreaming about the little blonde doll or indulging in all sorts of fantasies, oblivious to everything round me, only too happy to escape into myself. One of the nuns often stood close to me while she supervised the others. Every so often my wondering glance would meet hers, and I would feel an even stronger urge to withdraw into myself – such close scrutiny upset me. 'You are a good little girl,' she would say, patting my head, which would finally droop even lower.

There was always silence at table. Everybody bent quietly over the plates of hot soup. 'Eat up, will you now!' And a side glance from my sister rendered me utterly confused before the bewildering array of spoons and forks. Dispirited but rebellious, I picked up a spoon and plunged it so hard into the soup that the plate overturned. 'There you go again!' My sister's voice was icy. Everyone looked at me, while I remained rooted to the spot, hardly breathing and oblivious to the scalding liquid that was dripping down on to my apron and my knees. 'Well, get out of the way, you idiot' – with a sudden jerk my sister pulled me to my feet, and wiped me down roughly with her hands. A nun appeared. 'So she has thrown away her soup again, has she? Very nice – and to think of all those poor children who die of hunger! You are a naughty little girl. No play for you today.'

I felt humbled and appalled, and retreated still further into my shell. I said nothing at all.

Only later, when everyone was about to be wakened after the afternoon nap, the others to enact a little play, and I to stay behind, did I begin to feel agitated. The nun came up and stood right next to me. Perhaps she had forgotten my terrible crime. I held my breath under the towel with which I had covered my head. I peeked out at her. 'No, not you, you are too naughty.' I could barely keep from bursting into tears, but a threatening glare from my sister made me hold them back. 'And if you are naughty again, you won't watch the play tomorrow either,' continued the nun implacably. Defeated, I lowered my eyes, full of hatred for the receding black figure.

I stayed behind in the silent room, lifting the towel from my head at the slightest noise from the corridor. Finally I threw the towel away and fixed my eyes on the half open door. My heart was aching horribly. Outside little girls dressed in red were passing by with huge white beards – they were playing Snow White and the Seven Dwarfs. Stock still, I looked out at them in wonder. Then suddenly everyone had gone. I cowered away, afraid of the shadows that were cast on the partition walls from time to time. I picked up the towel, closed my eyes and . . . there . . . a huge band of dwarfs, and I was walking way out in front, in a flowing white robe and holding a golden wand in my hand, leading them all.

On and on we marched as the minutes and hours passed by.

I was completely taken aback by the return of the noisy little girls. I pulled the towel abruptly over my head to avoid scoffing looks. 'There she is, the naughty little girl. . . . Oh, you should have seen it. . . . You really wouldn't have been half so naughty if you had known what you were missing. . . .'

I wasn't really sure I had missed anything. I looked at them dreamily and said nothing, enjoying the treasure I had discovered in myself. 'Get up, and tidy yourself, we are going home. Just you wait till I tell Mother. You'll see!' And my sister raised her hand menacingly as, now wide awake, I looked up at her in a panic. My anxiety made me clumsy, and all I could feel was loathing for my sister.

I said nothing at all on the way home, while she kept raising her voice to admonish me every so often, or to mention something or other about the play. But what she was really thinking about was the telling off I would soon be getting from my

mother. At the gate I lowered my eyes, and went into the
house still perfectly silent. I had hardly stepped across the
threshold when Mother asked: 'And how did she get on today?'
At once my sister let fly: 'She threw her soup all over herself
and the sister had to punish her.' I was trembling inside
and looked away, but I could still feel Mother's reproachful
look. Then, quite unexpectedly, Father stepped out of his
study. 'The soup, eh? She threw it away, did she now, the
little devil! Just look at her, she's nothing but skin and bones!
Best to throw her under a tram. What sort of monster have
you brought into the world!' And he raised his arms in a fit
of uncontrollable anger. 'You had best go back to your desk,'
my mother interrupted, and when he had left the room she
gave me four hard slaps. Our maid appeared at the door, and
gave me a friendly smile. 'Do let her be, Madam,' she said.
'Your husband has scolded her from the day she was born. He
was always shouting his head off. To him it was always the
end of the world. Do you remember when we told him that he
had a daughter, not a son? "Nothing but women. A household
of bloody women!" And he slammed the door furiously. And
do you remember when he first saw her? How he said: "She is
utterly disgusting, skinny and ugly." Do you remember, Madam,
he was so eaten up, he couldn't do a stroke of work. Not all
of us can be born saints.' She smiled at me. 'This one gave us
many a sleepless night. She never stopped screaming, and
your husband always said the same thing: "Just throw her
under the tram." But all we need is patience. As the proverb
has it, *sotto i ricci ci sono i capricci* (curls hide many a prank),
and she has curls aplenty. Just look!' And she lovingly lifted
a lock of my fair curly hair. 'She is bound to fill out, you'll
see what a fine young lady she'll turn into!'

'But meanwhile she drives all of us mad,' my mother added,
quite gently, obviously soothed by the maid's kindly words.

I just stood there, confused and silent. 'Under the tram.'
'Screams. . . .' I turned it all over in my mind. Whatever did it
all mean? Still, my terror was slowly going and a sense of
relief crept through me. For all that, I could not shake off the
persistent feeling that I was a stranger in my own home and
that I would never fit in. There was something in me that
resisted their intolerable demands. And whenever I rebelled

against them, I would hear the echo of my father's: 'Just throw her under a tram,' and that phrase, indelibly engraved on my mind, would give me almost a feeling of relief. They didn't really care for me, so I was entitled to do just as I pleased. That phrase excused everything, even my stubbornness when they tried to wheedle me with kindness. I kept opposing them even when I knew they were perfectly right. *I never felt repentant about anything I did, for I was absolutely certain that I owed it to myself to disobey them, for all they wanted was for me to submit to them, to people who would have liked nothing better than to throw me under a tram. And what saved me from them was the world of my dreams in which I discovered everything life had refused me.* Inside it I felt secure. Outside my tantrums continued, and so did the unkindness of the nuns. How many times I was kept in while the others watched plays! How many times was I dragged to the big cupboard in the playroom crammed full of lovely toys, only to be told by a nun: 'Take a good look at them . . . they are meant for the good little girls. But nothing for you!' And she would glare at me in the certain conviction that I would give in sooner or later. But no! I merely stood there aware of the immense distance between me and that cupboard, which was not my fault but that of the wicked nuns. That feeling no longer caused me much pain for I had long since become used to it.

At home I was rarely praised for anything. One day I went into my father's study which was a most mysterious place to me. He was writing at his desk. Suddenly he looked up and smiled: 'Come over here, skinny, let's see if you have grown.' I approached him warily. 'Come along now, lift up your skirts,' he said. I obeyed with a vague feeling of embarrassment, remembering the nun's oft-repeated warnings that little girls who lift their dresses go straight to hell. 'Ah, I see that your little bottom has grown a little fatter,' he said, tapping my bare thigh. 'Come over here, let me give you some caramels.' And he opened the drawer of his desk. I felt deeply ashamed but happy. I took the sweets and went out into the garden. I straightened my skirt properly, lay down on the ground and thought: 'My father and I will both go to hell.' I was certain my father had done me a great injury. I didn't eat the sweets he had given me.

1940

The war had started. My father made arrangements for us to be evacuated to C., where he owned a house. It was a happy time for me. Oblivious as I was to the fears that were gripping thousands of people, the war struck me as a great adventure that was bound to bring glory to many who would otherwise have remained nonentities. When I passed by the nearby barracks, I would stop to admire the faces of the soldiers at the windows. I often recalled my teacher's remark that every one of us must have an aim in life. Those soldiers were happy people: they had found their aim.

I had all sorts of fantasies about their lives, about their dramatic adventures and the heroic exploits in which they conquered the world. And I went off proudly, sharing their glory.

Whenever I saw a mother weeping because her son had been called up, I thought her mean and small-minded. *I, too, would do great things one day and the whole world would have to recognize me at last.*

I spent a great deal of time alone in our garden pursuing my fantasies, and only then did I not feel alone among strangers. This was my own world. Outside a hostile family constantly reproached me for my obstinacy. But the more they thwarted me the more determined I was to have my own way. I would stamp my feet and scream and, as I did so, what might at first have been a mere whim invariably became a matter of the greatest importance for me.

Then came the first day at school. I was only five. I still remember the confusion I felt on stepping into the hall for the first time. All eyes were turned towards me, watching my every move, ready to mock at the first opportunity. The teacher, though, looked at me sympathetically. 'My goodness,' she said very softly, 'how small you are! Why ever are your parents in such a hurry to send you to school?' The shyness that gripped my throat stopped me from answering, but relief surged through me. *I had an advantage over the others: I was only small but I would show them that I was the cleverest of the whole lot.* Once again I was cut off from the rest, but this time I knew what I wanted. From the start I was serious and attentive and did not miss a single word in class. At home my happiest time was spent doing my homework.

And soon I was top of my class. But then I realized that all I had done was to create an even greater gulf between myself and my classmates. They gave me nasty looks, glanced meaningfully at each other and called me 'teacher's pet' under their breath. They shunned my company, didn't let me join in their games, and no one ever confided in me. I was completely shut out, and clung all the more firmly to the kindly teacher. I kept working for her sake, and felt superior to the rest: for once I had an aim in life. But the constant provocation I suffered often made me lose my temper, and that made them even worse. 'Just look, I've got cake, and all you've got is bread and cheese,' a spiteful little girl whispered one day during break, taking a large bite right under my nose. Speechless, I went and sat in a corner and ate my bread there. And from that day on I always did the same.

The time of my first communion drew near. I couldn't wait to put on my white dress. My mother was secretly altering my sister's for me, and when I finally put it on, I felt like one of the heroines in my favourite stories. The church was a blaze of light and flowers. I knelt before the altar, placed my hands over my eyes and tried to concentrate as I had been told to do. Suddenly I was startled by a nudge on my arm, 'Ugh, what an ugly missal you have; it's all in tatters,' the girl kneeling next to me whispered in my ear. I lowered my eyes in embarrassment. It was quite true, that missal belonged to my sister. I was filled with hatred for her and suddenly my eyes were blinded by tears. Then I remembered that hatred was wicked, and tried to think of something else. I would be clever for the Lord's sake and make something out of myself. . . . But I couldn't shake off my deep resentment. I was wearing nothing but cast-offs. I couldn't concentrate on the glorious ceremony or on any of the things I had been told to bear in mind. *At the same time I felt a deep regret that I wasn't as good as Jesus would have liked, that I was anything but the suffering heroine who bears her cross without a murmur.* Still, in the afternoon I would be parading triumphantly through the streets of C., admired by everybody!

And then it started to rain. A gentle, insistent drizzle that seemed as if it would never stop. But I was determined to go out, and said so to my mother. When she would hear nothing of it, I stamped my feet and hurled myself against the door. I was seized by the hair, slapped and flung into my room. The door slammed shut and then silence, an oppressive silence that made me think the whole world was indifferent to my pain. Suddenly the door opened again. Mother came in, took hold of me firmly and before I knew what had happened my dress was undone. I screamed and kicked in despair. My sister hastened to Mother's aid. Together they pulled off my dress and left me seething with helpless rage. Everybody was against me. I stole out of the room on tiptoe: I felt I would suffocate if I stayed there a moment longer. I went downstairs determined to do something that would make them feel sorry for what they had done to me. I stopped at the cellar door. I lay down, curled up in a ball. I was cold. With my tear-stained eyes I spotted a piece of coal. I picked it up, wrote on the stone steps that I wanted to die, and lay there inert, hopeless and alone.

Was this the finest day in my life, the day I had been longing for so much? Then I heard a gasp in the dark. 'Here she is!' My brother had found me, and I allowed myself to be led back into the house. They did not scold me, except for my sister who looked at me with disdain and called me an idiot. All my mother said was: 'You gave me a real scare,' and from her tremulous voice I could hear the relief she felt at finding me safe and sound. I went back silently to my room; I wanted no supper. In the dark, I thought about my classmates. Tomorrow they would boast about their visit to the cinema, and about all the pancakes they had eaten: 'You should have seen the sugared almonds' . . . , 'I this' and 'I that', all of them laughing gaily and full of happy memories. I felt that I was choking.

Then I had a sudden flash of inspiration. 'I'll tell them I went to my grandmother's far away, they won't know what really happened!' And in the end I felt quite light-headed, though some of the bitterness remained.

I was pleased with the shadows that grew longer and darker all around me. Everything must come to an end. For me and for everyone else. Tomorrow. . . .

And the war went on. C. was now in danger, and my father decided to send us to S., a small village clinging to the mountains and dominated by their sheer peaks. The local people were hardy, abysmally poor and totally ignorant. I noticed that the little girls looked at my faded old dress with obvious envy. At school I was a long way ahead of the rest, and soon they all came to me whenever the teacher's inadequate explanations went over their heads. Everyone kept saying 'She knows much more than the teacher,' and, basking in their admiration, I quickly made this new world of mine a haven of refuge from the baneful existence I had to live at home. Then they discovered that my sister was good at arithmetic, and all of them, especially the boys, turned to her for help with their sums. I started to neglect the subject, which I had never liked in any case. I even let her help me and felt no resentment at all.

During playtime I became a kind of ringleader. I would invent nonsense rhymes which we all sang while dancing rounds or while walking across the fields in search of flowers, and I made up one sad story after another. I could never remember them for even while I was telling one, the next was already flooding through my mind. This was my main trump: the little girls gazed at me with enraptured eyes as, deeply moved, they laughed and cried with me. 'Wherever did you read these beautiful stories?' they would ask. 'Oh, in a book as big as that,' and I would raise my arms to show them just how big. 'But how do you manage to read all that?' 'Well . . .' and my lips would close in mysterious silence. I knew I must never let on that I had made up these stories for, if I did, they would immediately have found fault with them. As it was, I was able to give full rein to my fantasies, creating countless characters, all stumbling about an unknown world in search of the happiness they had never known. *They were all little boys and girls whom nobody loved, who were beaten and tortured, and then ran away to make their fortunes across the mountains and valleys, meeting monsters and obstacles of every kind. They were all of them great heroes who finally returned home in triumph. Everybody had to bow to them,* deeply ashamed of all the suffering they had caused them in the past.

I revelled in the way my companions hung on my every word – their enthusiasm for my heroic characters seemed almost directed at myself. This was my world, my victory.

Between me and my sister there was an enormous gulf. She

was in the top class, consisting mainly of boys, a compact group that preferred noisy ball games, or played 'hide and seek' in the attic, the cellar or between the woodpiles. I kept well away, for I sensed that their games had ugly and sinful undertones. And my vague suspicions were confirmed when my mother scolded my sister one day for having done something that was never actually specified, though, judging from her mysterious hints, was obviously a horrible sin. Luckily I had nothing to do with my sister's gang. I felt superior, and was quite certain that I would never be so vulgar as to keep company with boys. But though my sister had received a scolding, she was still in the saddle. If any heavy job had to be done it was always she who was called upon to do it. We had an outhouse with rabbits and some goats, and my sister was responsible for feeding the animals. I always tagged behind, carrying the grass and twigs she had picked and generally doing as she ordered. She was the leader and I the follower. True, because I was so frail I wasn't expected to do too much, but whenever my latent rebellion got the better of me and I refused to do what she told me, I would get a slap across my obstinate face.

Back home she would complain that she didn't want me with her, that I only got in her way and was good for nothing. My mother would look at me as at something totally useless, and say to my sister: 'Why don't you just ignore her? Can't you see that she'll never amount to anything? Surely, you are big enough to understand.' It was worse than a slap in the face. I wanted to shout out that I wasn't useless at all, and that I had been more than willing to help, but I would choke with resentment and suppressed sobs. And then my sister would round on me with: 'Just look at that cry-baby, whenever she is put in the wrong, she just bursts into tears.' And her voice would show her complete contempt. She herself never cried, she declared triumphantly. I would run off and hide myself in my favourite little corner in the loft. There I had a beautiful dolls' house. I had built it myself using all my ingenuity, and, when I had finished it to my satisfaction, had put in several dolls, most of which had some part missing, an arm, a leg or their hair. *I had done my utmost to cover or disguise their defects.* I loved these dolls with desperate passion. Woe betide anyone who tried to touch them. I comforted them, rocked them tenderly and tried to fill them with warmth. I placed them in their beds in the calm of the setting sun after putting them through the arduous tasks of a busy day. In the twilight they came back home to their gentle and sympathetic mother who dried their tears and lulled them to sleep. And as they closed their eyes, their tears became iridescent pearls: they were suddenly happy and safe in their cosy little shelter.

I would sing to them and go on singing until my own sobs were stilled by the new sweetness and warmth that welled up within me. Here was my other kingdom: inviolate and closed to all others. My sister sneered at it, but I didn't mind, for I knew that she didn't understand. In fact I didn't quite understand it myself, except that I could rid myself of all my bitterness up there, and become strong enough to be my real self. Still, there were also a few moments when I felt quite cheerful and confident downstairs, when I really enjoyed doing such little things as arranging flowers, laying the table or darning. My mother would let me get on with them, for she knew that I was good at these chores, and I would go about my business full of enthusiasm, dreaming that I was a delicate and elegant lady. And I was even praised. My sister despised such tasks and kept well out of the way. In my heart of hearts I thought of her as a crude lout, particularly when she said: 'You and your flowers! Can you eat them? What you need is some hard work, not all this messing about with bits of flowers!'

I didn't mind eating, but I felt that I was cut out for far better things, things that could not be bought in the market place and that only the vulgar did without.

And I slowly grew more and more contemptuous of humdrum work, including mathematics which was only for those who wanted to make money and nothing more. Still, I continued to tag behind my sister gathering food for our animals, and as I bent over the grass in the fields I was always lost in my dreams and fantasies. I pulled the grass up, and as it came away, my mind changed it into magic with profound and hidden meanings.

In the woods, while my sister cut down the twigs, I would curl up on the moss, listen to the birds and hear in the rustling of the leaves messages from an enchanted world. 'Get moving, pick up those sticks,' my sister would shout, trying to bring me back to earth. But by then I didn't really mind, for even while my hands were gathering up the twigs, my dreams were still weaving their invisible plots. And so my life continued. Only now and then there would be a welcome change: a letter from Father who was still working in the city. I listened open-mouthed to his description of life in a city at war, though some of the words Mother was reading seemed quite meaningless to me.

But I filled the emptiness of those sentences with my own fantasies. Rising above the ruins of the town, I could see my father waging a heroic struggle and during the short visits he paid to S., I tried to keep myself at his disposal, showering him with small attentions, happy to serve so important a personage. Oh, how wounded I was when my mother or my sister told him of my lapses, and when he invariably replied: 'But what do you expect, she is such a little thing!' It would have been a thousand times better had he stayed in the city, where I could spin all sorts of dreams about him. I would write him long letters and hint at my love for him by sending him the first violet to open on the little wall in our orchard, the last cyclamen sered by the first cold wind, or a little bit of earth from the cemetery where our grandmother was buried, and to whom I knew he was deeply attached.

I would decorate these letters with little drawings and post them to him secretly. And his replies would fill me with joy. And I withdrew more and more into myself, afraid that the others would scoff at my feelings and wound their delicate substance. I became increasingly secretive and taciturn. The world outside was hostile, and the less I had to do with it, the better.

The war was over, and we would soon be returning to X. Our house had been destroyed, but Father was looking for a new apartment. Back in S. we drew up plan after plan; I shut myself up in my world of day-dreams and conjured up an enchanting house, full of atmosphere.

Then the great day arrived. There were no regrets at all as the coach took us down to the valley. Away from that miserable village, away to a much bigger world full of exciting new things! But my enthusiasm quickly vanished when I found myself wedged in a lorry between the backs of two upturned armchairs. I hated lorries. In S. their deafening din on the dusty main road had always filled me with a sense of desolation and vague fear. I would look at their huge wheels and see myself lying prostrate under their weight. Even now that my father and sister were near me I could not get rid of that feeling; at every lurch of the lorry I could see myself being hurled under the wheels. The hours passed, and then, at long last, the dawn. I could see roofs, big buildings, broken walls, tarmac roads. 'We are home,' Father announced. I looked around me in complete bewilderment: I felt we were in a wasteland inhabited by animated puppets totally remote from me. I was a stranger in an unknown world. When the lorry finally came to a halt, I felt a tremendous sense of relief at being able to get out. Looking around, I found myself standing on a neglected pavement, which ran in front of a large gateway.

A group of curious boys were watching me with interest from a short distance away. They were giggling, and whispered jeering observations in my direction. I could hear the rumbling of trams, and suddenly I remembered the kindly face of our maid: 'Your husband always used the same phrase: "Just throw her under the tram." Do you remember, Signora?' The recollection was like a blinding flash of light. I felt like hiding away in some corner. We went up the stone stairs. On the floor I saw pieces of plaster and some tools the workmen had left behind. We stopped on the second floor and went through a door. The rooms were bare and newly whitewashed. I felt bitterly alone and tears welled up in my eyes. Suddenly I felt cold, and curled up on a case in a corner, rolling myself tightly into a ball. 'Are you hungry? Here, have something to eat!' My father handed me a piece of cheese and half a loaf of bread. I had no wish to eat like that. I could see my sister tucking in with relish. I followed suit, but reluctantly and with bad grace.

A few days later the apartment was tidy. There were few rooms and a great deal of furniture, all very functional but not very pleasing, merely hiding the bare surroundings. I went out of my way to put a few ornaments and to fill a few vases with flowers. At noon, when my father saw what I was doing, he said with a look of cold disgust: 'Get rid of all that rubbish. It just clutters the place up. What we need here is a typewriter, and there I shall put my T-squares. . . .' 'But,' I broke in with dismay, 'this is the dining-room.' My father looked at me as at a simpleton. 'Remember that this is first of all my work room, my study. I have to work if you want to eat. You can give thanks to the Almighty that I have found this apartment.' I said nothing. In the afternoon I took down all the ornaments, put them into a box and carried them down to the cellar. That night I fell exhausted on to my divan, and cried for a long time under the blankets. All my dreams had vanished into thin air.

And then back to school, to Form Ia. In the large playground there was a continuous toing and froing and friendly exchanges of smiles and greetings, as boys and girls carrying their satchels milled around each other. I felt completely lost and ill at ease with their uninhibited antics. Now and then I would cast a furtive glance at the large building looming overhead. It seemed a barracks run on unfamiliar lines.

I clung to my sister who seemed quite unruffled by all the confusion. I felt her strong hand in mine with relief, and tagged meekly behind her. In the classroom I rushed to the bench she had picked for herself and sat down next to her. Suddenly the whole class fell silent. A pale-faced lady dressed in black had come in. She stepped on to the platform. A quick glance at the class, and then she looked down at the floor. She started to speak, slowly, with few pauses, as if she were reading from an invisible book. But what was she talking about? *Lacune?* What were they? *Sofisticata?* What did that mean? So many incomprehensible words I had never heard before, and I was supposed to be good at Italian. I felt more and more depressed. Then a nudge from my sister startled me. 'Whatever is she saying?' I whispered. 'I can't understand a word myself,' she confessed, shrugging her shoulders. At last the teacher stopped talking. I sighed with relief. My classmates rose with a clatter and we all went home, I myself clinging to my sister's arm, glad I was out of that prison.

The days passed. I had no friends at school or at home. I lived in a world that I did not understand, and that gave me the creeps. One morning a thin young woman entered the classroom, a sardonic smile on her heavily painted lips. I heard whispers that she was to be our maths teacher, and my heart started pounding. The teacher gave us all a searching look and finally her eyes came to rest on me. 'Why are you back in the fourth row? You're a little one, you ought to be sitting right in front.' My whole body froze. But then my sister rose to her feet: 'She is my sister and we have to share our books,' she explained. The teacher looked at us for a moment, and then said: 'Very well, I shall keep my eye on you two.' I breathed a sigh of relief, though I still felt deeply anxious. Her 'I shall keep my eye on you' had been a severe blow. I would never again be able to copy my sister's maths homework. I was lost. I hated the subject. I would never work at it, never. I clenched my fists. But at least she had not separated us, and I would still be able to help my sister with her Italian. The Italian teacher was much nicer. My sister always got the best of every bargain, I thought.

A month went by and I grew more and more confused. I wasn't clear about anything I had been taught: it was all a mass of obscure ideas that made no sense to me at all. Then came the first Italian composition. I felt greatly relieved. Now I would show them. I wrote a long essay and let myself go as I always did. Soon afterwards my essay was returned to me in a deathly hush. The paper was full of corrections in red and blue, and at the bottom was an ominous four out of ten, with the following comment: 'The treatment is far too elementary, and there are far too many grammatical errors.' And that was that. I could feel a tear roll down my cheek. I peered across at my sister's essay: it had earned her three out of ten. She seemed quite happy about it. 'It just shows she doesn't like the way I write,' she whispered, passing me her handkerchief: 'Don't show them that you are crying, you goose!' Bewildered and hurt, I held back the tears that were choking me. A girl sitting in front of me raised her paper, and I could see that she had nine out of ten. I gasped, and looked her over carefully. She was rather short but slim, and her hair was pulled back and fastened at the neck with a clasp. She wore a short fringe on her high forehead, and had large mischievous dark eyes. Her face was thin and pale. I was filled with profound jealousy. Her self-assurance made me feel clumsy and inadequate. I looked from her slender arms to my own which were rather plump. *For the first time in my life I felt gross, oppressed by the great weight that was pulling me down.*

I looked at the rest of the class, and tried to recall what I had felt like back in S. when I, too, used to get nine or even ten out of ten. But that was when I was merely competing against ignorant peasant girls, not against so much learning. I suddenly longed for *the glorious freedom of my mountains*, far away. Instead I would have to listen contritely to my father's bitter reproaches. The exercise would have to be signed by him, back at home with its bare and cold walls, in that confusion of objects and furniture. And back home I went, dragged along by my sister as always. It was just another humiliation. My father shook his head in sorrow and then went to speak to the teacher. 'They still have a long way to go before they can catch up with the rest...,' he was told, and there seemed to be many other complaints as well. I listened in silence. I realized that she was quite right. My education was full of 'lacunae'. That word tormented me and I kept harking back to it. In bed that night, just before falling asleep, my eyes fixed to the wall, I made up mind to study as I had never done before. My father's ironical words over supper were still hammering away in my head. 'Lacunae, lacunae . . . nothing but two stupid geese!' And he had opened his mouth wide while hooting *qua, qua, qua* in imitation, before stuffing himself greedily with food as he always did. I couldn't stand it any more: I left everything on my plate and ran off to bed. In the darkness, the cruelty of his remarks struck me with renewed force. I tossed about for a long time until finally I could hear my father snoring in the room next door. Quietly I put on the light, opened a book and began to swot. *Rosa, rosam, rosae. . . .* I kept at it, rubbing my tired eyes every so often. In the end I fell asleep with the book open. In the morning I woke at first light, saw the book and started to study again. I remembered everything I had learned during the night, but my whole body was sagging with fatigue. I refused to give in. Whenever my tired eyelids drooped, I would imagine that brilliant girl sitting on a golden throne in all her slender beauty. In a flash my eyes would clear, and in the dim light I would bend again over the book. And the clock which was ticking out the seconds had only one sound! *Qua, qua, qua. . . .*

I had to succeed, I just had to. I would become like that girl – perhaps even better. To begin with, I would have to

change my hairstyle to one that made me look less childish. . . .
I would have to get rid of that unruly lock . . . draw it back
off my face as she did. And I might even have a fringe. No, no,
not that, my forehead was too low. My face would look much
too fat. If only I looked like her! I was bloated. I shook my
head sadly, re-read the last paragraph, and again became
immersed in my studies. 'Whatever are you up to? Usually
it takes ages to get you to wake up. . . .' My sister's voice
brought me back to earth. 'I am studying,' I said shortly.
'Yes, I had better get down to it as well.' And she too picked
up a book. And so it went on every night and morning – a
ruthless contest between us.

As for my classmates, I always kept my distance from them,
afraid they would take me for a country bumpkin as soon as
I opened my mouth. But I listened attentively to everything
they said, memorizing and repeating to myself many of their
brilliant turns of phrase until I, too, could produce them at
will. I knew that they often visited one another to do their
homework together and that they had lots of fun. I would
have loved to join them but I noted with bitterness that they
seemed only too glad to ignore me: I was at the bottom of
the class, a useless little girl. I would have liked to ask them
home, but that would only have made things worse. They
would have laughed at our ugly house and the untidy clutter.
No, the only thing to do was to study alone until I was clever
enough to keep up with them.

When evening classes started at the local church I joined
with enthusiasm. The teachers were gifted, and slowly the
clouds started to clear; my mind was illuminated with a new
light. I started to get six out of ten at school, but I wasn't
satisfied: I had to catch up with the slim girl at the top. She
was for ever in my thoughts, a continuous challenge. I had
also begun to detest my country dresses, and kept complaining
about them at home. At first my mother was disconcerted.
'Whatever has got into you? You never used to bother about
such trifles . . . ,' she would say, as I kept pressing her. I felt
that *all my family were common people concerned only with
stuffing themselves and nothing else.* My father was worst of
all. 'You have had it too good, you have. If you had suffered
hunger as I did during the war . . . ,' he repeated time and

again. Yes, he had suffered hunger, but that was as far as his heroism had gone, I thought with contempt.

And when I saw that I could get nowhere with him, I turned increasingly to my mother. She understood me much better. And sometimes, on the quiet, she would buy some lovely material for me, though when it came to the actual dressmaking we had unending quarrels. 'I want the waist taken in,' I would say, 'quite a bit.' 'And who will wear it next year when you fill out? Just throw it away, eh? So much money down the drain,' she would complain. 'I don't want to look even fatter than I am!' 'But in a year's time. . . .' And so it would go on. Another year, always another year. When I would fill out. But as it was, I looked like a whale. What did she want me to turn into? And all because of money. I hated it. It was so vulgar; and she lived for it, for nothing else. How many arguments didn't we all have over money!

'Peel those potatoes properly,' my father would snap out when he happened to come into the kitchen whilst my mother was preparing the vegetables. 'But I am peeling them as thin as I can . . . ,' my mother said. 'Seems thin to you, does it? You are living off the fat of the land, if you ask me. I sweat my guts out for my family, while you idle your life away in comfort. It would do you the world of good if you had to work in an office or go on night shift. . . .' 'So, I do nothing, is that it? I suppose the home and the children look after themselves. Who does all the washing, the mending and the cooking, I would like to know? . . . And on top of that I have to be the dressmaker as well. You're on to a good thing, a good thing. . . .' 'No it's you who is on to a good thing. You ought to have married a peasant not an engineer. It's more your level. . . .' 'Me, a peasant? . . .' And my mother threatened him with the ladle. 'If anyone is like a peasant, it's you, you ignorant so and so. You've obviously forgotten where you came from.' 'And you don't seem to know whom you are talking to.' And he hit her hard in the face. Purple with rage, my mother turned to belabour him furiously with the ladle. There was a confusion of flailing arms and upturned chairs, and then my mother's desperate wail: 'He's done for me at last.' And all the while I cowered in a corner, hating my father with an unspeakable loathing. Occasionally I made attempts to place myself between

G

them, only to get blows from both sides. Then my father slammed the door and went off to sulk in his room. In tears, I meanwhile tried to comfort my mother, gently stroking her shoulders. She sobbed convulsively while stammering out such things as: 'I've done everything I can to . . . to protect you, . . . oh, if it weren't for me, you would see . . . what . . . sort of a dance he . . . would lead you. You would all be walking about in rags and tatters . . . like beggars.' I heated up something for her to drink, all the while stroking and caressing her. 'Don't worry, Mother, we are with you.' 'Just wait till I'm grown up,' my sister added.

Little by little we managed to calm her. Father re-appeared for supper, looking furious and not saying a word. Mother turned her back on him, refusing to eat. And all of us went to bed in silence. I curled myself up into a ball under the blankets, an icy feeling in my heart. My father was a brute. I remembered the little things my classmates had let drop about the happy lives their parents led, and also the many love scenes I had seen in the cinema. God, were my parents really so different from everyone else?

I lay there motionless, tears rolling down my cheeks. And then suddenly I could hear their bed creaking next door. Over and over. I clenched my fists and stopped up my ears. Not that again, for Heaven's sake! But I couldn't keep still. I felt weighed down by an intolerable burden that I had to shake off. In the end I couldn't stand any more and jumped out of bed. Thoughts flashed through my mind; I remembered the times when I was still very little and sharing my parents' bedroom. Father would suddenly fling himself on to my mother, crushing her until she groaned with pain. And I remembered the lewd remarks of some of the older girls. Everything suddenly came together, and I felt sick to my stomach. Then a turn of the latch; someone was going to the bathroom. The tap was turned on, water splashed and then silence. I stood motionless for a long time, hating my father from the bottom of my heart. He was a brute, a swine, who treated women like dirt, both during the day and at night as well. All he could think of was his vile pleasure, no matter at what cost to poor Mother. But she bore part of the blame, for she put up with it. I would never have let him. You had to stand up for yourself with all your strength. In any case the whole business was sinful, as the confirmation class teacher had told us. Sinful and vile.

I was choking with rage when I eventually went back to bed. I tossed and turned and finally dropped off to sleep. In the morning peace reigned supreme in the house. Mother and Father were talking to each other as if nothing at all had happened the day before. I lowered my head and gritted my teeth. So that was why Mother had given herself to him during the night! Just to make peace, to buy it with her body. A filthy business! If only I could get away from it all! And I would pore over my books almost blind with suppressed fury. If only I could forget and somehow find a ray of hope in all that gloom!

The days passed, and slowly I calmed down. But then another row would blow up, over nothing at all, and I was overcome with anguish as I thought of the nightly goings on that were bound to follow. All that shouting was just a cheap excuse for what they were about to do. I gritted my teeth. I would make absolutely certain that if they had to fight it wouldn't ever again be over me. But invariably it was I who, without meaning to and in all innocence, caused the rows to begin. And slowly I began to feel guilt-ridden. I simply had to get away, Mother must not be allowed to keep sacrificing herself for me. I loathed my father. I had to study, make my own way, and never, never allow myself to become like them.

And, in fact, my marks were getting better all the time, to the surprise of the teachers and my classmates. The only subject I was still bad at was mathematics, in which I relied increasingly on my sister. Certain that I would never be able to make sense of it, I had come to loathe the whole subject, and on the few occasions that I forced myself to do sums I did them regretfully and with great difficulty. In Italian I went on from triumph to triumph, and was the envy of the whole class. Girls would increasingly invite me to their homes, and I would visit them as often as I could and stay as long as possible, far from the turmoil of my own home. I would make myself comfortable in their plush armchairs, book in hand, near a well-stocked bookcase and lose myself in the kingdom of fantasy, fired on by nineteenth century novels, in which the pale heroine, though disliked at first, came through to triumph in the end, revealing her prodigious worth to an amazed world.

Sometimes I read romantic love stories, in which the hero was a kind nobleman who showed his beloved every possible consideration and was to all a perfect gentleman.

The true lover was one who revered and respected the woman he had chosen. And my own father did anything but that.

I devoured these books in quietly elegant surroundings, where every object was in its proper place, in perfect harmony with the rest. The considerate way in which all the girls' mothers treated their husbands and children, first overwhelmed me and then filled me with envy. If only our own life were like that!

I would return home increasingly embittered by the contrast I found there. To my frequent complaints, my mother would generally reply: 'Whatever are you going on about? Your father and me, we are as we are and so we shall remain. Not even the Almighty can change us. And anyway,' she would add with a touch of malice, 'don't think that it's all a bed of roses for them. They are just better at hiding their feelings. Believe me! Some people may appear all very nice on the surface, but you just peer beneath their skin. . . .' And she would look meaningfully at me. Yes, she might be right. I knew that the mother of one of my friends was separated from her husband. But then she was an exception. I felt sure that kindness and tact would enable a woman to keep any good man. And I was not like my parents! I felt deeply rebellious towards them, said harsh things, answered them back, slammed doors and locked myself in my room more and more often.

I would never be like Mother! A woman tied to her kitchen stove, with no greater concern than to fill her husband's belly, completely uninterested in his work or aspirations, petty-minded, without a will of her own or any kind of ambition for herself. A woman who had gone to seed and had grown fat.

I was determined to be different, to make something of my life. And so I studied like one possessed, and became increasingly disgusted when I saw my father stuffing himself at table or even talking about food. 'Ah, eating is one of the few great pleasures,' he would say as he indulged himself at length. I, for my part, would never linger over my food: my only wish was to get down from the table and back to my work. My father's chatter became an intolerable nuisance.

The school leaving exams were not far off. 'You know they

are giving each pupil a separate desk,' I heard one of my friends whisper one day. I trembled with fear. I was done. I would not be able to crib from my sister's maths paper, as I had always done. I thought about it day and night, but there was no way out. I felt totally lost, and all because of those dreadful sums. I would have to hand in a near blank paper. I shuddered at the thought.

The days went by, each hotter and more oppressive than the one before. At last the great day came. I felt feverish and quite ill.

For the Italian exams they had left us together, but then it was impossible to cheat with essays.

We were allowed to sit in our usual places for the other exams as well, and when the maths teacher came in, I tried to make myself as small as possible to become invisible. She read out the problems and I wrote them down with a shaking hand. I kept my head well down. Nothing at all came to me as the minutes ticked by.

Nothing. And meanwhile my sister scribbled away for all she was worth, looking perfectly content and confident. But I was afraid to look at her paper; I was certain I would be disqualified – the teacher seemed to keep her eyes on me all the time. And so I just sat. At long last my sister stopped writing. She must have finished and my paper was still blank! Suddenly there was the creak of a chair. The teacher had got up and was moving towards the door. 'Hurry!' My sister passed her paper to me and then sat still with her hands on her forehead in a thoughtful pose. I copied her figures feverishly. My hand was trembling. Nobody had seen. Standing at the door, the teacher was looking down the corridor. I never stopped writing until I was finished. Ages seemed to have passed. I read my paper over, checking everything carefully. I looked up for a fraction of a second, and then I slipped my sister's paper back to her. I was saved.

I now made a few minor improvements, rubbing out and re-writing some figures that weren't legible enough. I hesitated a little longer, handed the paper in and left the room. The whole corridor was flooded in sunlight. It was spring, and I felt joyful and happy. I could see the meadows and mountain slopes of S. in my mind's eye.

Suddenly I was filled with nostalgia, but then I thought that

I would soon be going back there for my holidays. I ran down the road feeling exhilarated. I did not go straight home, but wandered about, revelling in dreams of glory, and feeling terribly strong within myself.

In the summer we all went back to S. Now I had started eating, and was putting on weight to my parents' obvious delight. My father seemed particularly pleased with me. I had asked a very clever schoolfriend to join us, but I felt rather ashamed of our poor house, and right from the start made a point of doing all the tidying up so that the place would not look too shabby.

But my friend seemed to grow more and more uneasy. She would withdraw into herself, speak very little and eat even less. I would keep her company in silence. One day she suddenly asked me: 'What have you decided to do this autumn?' It came to me as a shock. I hadn't given it a thought until then, still glorying in the triumph at my exams. Without waiting for my reply, she continued: 'I shall take science at night school. My parents cannot afford the fees, and I shall have to work during the day.' I looked at her in amazement, full of admiration. But I also felt deeply envious. 'I . . . ,' I hesitated for a moment, 'I shall go to the Teachers' Training College.' 'Do you really want to be a teacher?' she asked. I knew that I didn't, but what was the alternative? 'My sister,' I said, 'has decided to do accountancy. But my maths being what they are. . . .' 'But why not read classics,' she broke in. 'Classics? Well . . . I don't know. It takes too long. And then you have to take your degree . . . I really want to do something else.' But I didn't know just what. I had vague visions of elementary school teachers who had risen from nothing, like the tenacious Ada Negri. I could see her, and many others like her, walking across green meadows, while keeping watch over their young wards, especially those who had been ill-treated, mocked and neglected. They were loyal to these poor children and so would I be . . . a strong shoulder on which they could all lean. My friend kept silent. Perhaps she, too, was weaving dreams.

'What matters is not to allow yourself to become bogged down in the petty details of a humdrum life. To work for some end,' she said eventually. 'That's what matters.' And I suddenly felt very close to her.

At supper that night I refused to eat more than she did. My mother was surprised. 'What does this mean? Only a few days ago you were eating like a horse. You have put on weight at last. . . .' And she looked angrily at my friend. 'You are just a copy cat,' she spat at me. I was furious with her. There it was: all she cared about was fattening me up. But that was the last thing I myself wanted. Had I really been putting on weight? Well, yes, that was quite true. I had grown much too fat. *Suddenly it seemed to me that I had always been too fat.* I saw myself swaddled in all those baggy clothes, like a wretched peasant woman. *It just couldn't go on. And next day I ate even less. They gave me castor oil. It didn't do anything. My friend went. I was left to wage my tremendous struggle all on my own. I knew now what I would have to do. And dieting was the first step.*

My mother sighed with relief: 'At last she has gone,' she said. 'Now you will eat properly again.' But that made me even more determined to keep away from food. Irritated by the fuss they made about my eating, I started to use all sorts of ruses. I held the food in my mouth, I would hide it, and use all my wits and cunning to outsmart them. If they told me that a particular dish was good for me, I immediately got rid of it. It was branded for ever. I would never eat it again. My mother became more and more obsessed with making me eat, and I intensified my angry efforts to hide the food. One day, worn out by all the rows we had had, I decided to take no more meals with them, on the pretext that I couldn't stand being watched. I now ate in my own room and felt a great sense of relief. Now I could get rid of the lot. *I only took fruit: I had been told that you couldn't possibly grow fat on it. And as I got thinner it seemed to me that my dream was coming true; I could see the slender face of the top girl of the class – I would be just like her at college.* Without my sister's help. *A shudder passed through me as I felt the new me stirring deep down.*

From time to time one of our neighbours would exclaim: 'My goodness, how thin you have grown. And to think that you used to be just like your mother!' That was enough. I intensified my efforts. My mother was now so upset that she even took me to a fortune teller. 'Won't you please tell me why you have stopped eating,' she implored me time and again.

'But I do eat,' I said angrily. 'Then why are you so thin? You look a proper fright.' 'No, I don't; it's just that I have lost some useless fat. I work, you know, and I have a lot of worries.' And in fact I often lost myself in vague reveries and was moved by visions of people who suffered spiritually, who tortured themselves to reach a secret objective. I no longer felt any hunger pangs; what little fruit I took seemed excessive. I was eating much too much, just like my father, and I often despised myself for it.

We returned to the city. The new term was about to start. I felt confident. My father shook his head and muttered: 'You used to be so pretty, and now you look like a scarecrow!' 'Pretty, was I? You just like fat women. Of course you do, you can do what you please with them. And I know what pleases you most.'

He took me to see a doctor. I was given drugs, and pretended to take them. He took me to another doctor. And yet another. None of them realized that I was perfectly healthy, and that I was eating all I needed. . . .

In the end one doctor sent me to a hospital. In despair I realized that all my dreams were about to evaporate. I shouted, I begged my father to take me out of the place. Oh, I would eat as much as they liked, but only at home. And all the time I was filled with bitter hatred of all my family.

PART FOUR

23 *Family Psychotherapy as a New Orientation*

It was not until 1965 that I began to make a thorough study of the copious literature on the subject of family research and family psychotherapy. Many of the most important of these papers are chiefly concerned with the families of schizophrenics. I was particularly struck by the fact that, as early as 1959, J. Haley had pointed out that the psychiatric approach to schizophrenia was being radically transformed: the old idea that the family disturbance was chiefly caused by the schizophrenic member was making way for the view that most of these families included a pathogenic mother and that the father was inadequate to the pathological system of interaction in which all family members are involved.

Since this is what happens with schizophrenics, it seemed quite natural to ask whether the same situation might not exist in families with an anorexic member, the more so as the most authoritative workers in the field had been able to state categorically that, if we take a transpersonal view of the family, *all forms of mental illness must be considered logical adaptations to a deviant and illogical transpersonal system.*

Was anorexia nervosa, too, the only possible adaptation by a *given* subject to a *given* type of family functioning?

Even the earliest students had felt some dissatisfaction with the common practice of labelling people as 'normal', 'neurotic' or 'psychotic', on the grounds that these labels should far more appropriately be attached to their particular situations. And when they began working with families they did, in fact, discover that a so-called neurotic only behaves *differently* from a so-called normal person because he is reacting to a *different* situation. Similarly, the behaviour of a *psychotic* becomes more comprehensible the moment that his *psychotic* situation is taken into account.

This fundamental observation demanded the rejection of the old model imported into psychiatry from general medicine, that is, that mental patients pose purely medical problems. Once accepted, the fundamental idea that every human problem is interpersonal, and that it *invariably* involves several people, demands a shift of observation from the individual to increasingly wide systems of relationships.

In particular it became increasingly clear that what persuades the 'patient' to behave in a particular way is not something that primarily occurs within him, and which appears in the form of 'symptoms' considered as expressions of his intrapsychic disorder. If the observation is shifted to more than one person and the medical model is discarded, then psychiatric problems become problems of transactional disorders.

Today we see that the shift from the individual unit posited in psychiatry is but one aspect of a universal cultural shift (in biology, economics, ethology, ecology, etc.), or rather of a new overall orientation calling for the rejection of the study of isolated phenomena in favour of the broader natural context in which these phenomena occur.

Psychiatry, for one, can certainly not escape from this new shift. In proceeding by steps, as scientific disciplines do, psychiatry is inevitably brought face to face with the family as a universal institution in which the individual develops as a social being, thanks to the interactional patterns characteristic of this group. It was in the 1950s that some psychotherapists, working mostly in isolation, first made the attempt to help their patients by treating them in conjunction with their families. Observing the interactions of the various family members, they discovered many phenomena whose existence they had never even suspected. In fact it is impossible to make any discoveries in the absence of situations specially structured to that end.

With the shift from the monad to the dyad and triad and to even larger groups, the traditional psychological vocabulary and psychoanalytical models have proved quite inadequate. In fact, as we pass on to triads, we can already speak of alliances or coalitions of two against the third, which calls for new concepts different from those appropriate to the dyadic model. There is also the important leadership problem which is fundamental to the nuclear family consisting of two generations. The problem becomes more complicated still when the observational field is enlarged to comprise the interactions of the nuclear with the extended family and with the various social institutions with which the family interacts as a sub-system.

In opting for the new approach I had first to solve a crucial methodological problem. As Haley has pointed out, the problem is no longer how to characterize and classify individuals: it is how to describe and classify the habitual patterns of responsive behaviour exchanged by intimates. I shall try to show briefly how this turning point was reached, and examine the underlying theoretical assumptions.

Family research faces the psychotherapist with problems that cannot possibly be solved in the conceptual framework elaborated during work with artificially isolated individuals. As the observational field has expanded, the conceptual instruments have had to be changed.

A phenomenon remains unexplainable as long as the range of observation is not wide enough to include the *context* in which the phenomenon occurs. Failure to realize the intricacies of the relationship between an event and the matrix in which it takes place, between an organism and its environment, either confronts the observer with something 'mysterious' or induces him to attribute to his object of study certain properties the object may not possess. Compared with the wide acceptance of this fact in biology, the behavioural sciences seem still to base themselves to a large extent on a monadic view of the individual and on the time-honoured method of isolating variables. This becomes particularly obvious when the object of study is disturbed behaviour. If a person exhibiting disturbed behaviour (psychopathology) is studied in isolation, then the inquiry must be concerned with the *nature* of the condition and, in a wider sense, with the nature of the human mind. If the limits of the inquiry are extended to include the effects of this behaviour on others, their reactions to it, and the context in which all of this takes place, the focus shifts from the artificially isolated monad to the relationship between the parts of a wider system. The observer of human behaviour then turns from an inferential study of the mind to the study of the observable manifestations of relationship. (Watzlawick *et al.*)

For that very reason the conceptual instruments of psychoanalysis cannot cope with the type of interchange that occurs in the family and constitutes its special mode of interaction. We refer to that mode as a *system*, because it appears regularly whenever a group of people share their lives over any length of time, and develop characteristic interpersonal behaviour patterns.

A system (for instance a family from a system point of view) is characterized by three things:

1) Wholeness, in the sense that the system is not only more than the sum of its parts, but is *independent* of its parts. What is primary is the arrangement between the elements, not the elements; system parameters will predominate over initial conditions. The relationships have an objective, independent existence in the changing organization of interaction.

2) Self-regulatory processes (cybernetics): a family is a rule-governed system, which tends to constancy within a defined range (homeostasis). All families that stay together must have a certain degree of negative feedback, that is resistance to change, in order to withstand the stresses imposed by the environment and the individual members. This resistance to change is organized into *rules* that are often neither conscious nor explicit. Of these rules, the most universal is what I would call the 'rule of rules', that is the rule that it is forbidden to make comments, or to metacommunicate, about the rules. Disturbed families are peculiarly refractory to change and demonstrate a remarkable ability to maintain the *status quo*, often ensnaring the therapist in rules which, in fact, he ought to be trying to change.

3) Transformation. A family is a system of transformations. As Rabkin has put it so well: the best example of a family as a system of transformations comes from myths. When the princess kisses the frog, she *transforms* him into a prince. Marriage is also a powerful transformation. Suddenly, if the formula is pronounced correctly, you are husband and wife and possibly transformed from a frog to a prince, or from a prince to a frog.

The study of the family system in action shows first of all that only the analysis of communication can reveal what type of interchange is capable of defining the functioning of the system. In this connection I can do no better than give the reader a brief account of the contribution by the discipline known as the 'pragmatics of human communication' (Watzlawick *et al.*), and in particular of its three basic axioms. The first axiom states that it is impossible not to communicate because all behaviour is communication. Thus, when someone asks me to communicate with him and I remain silent, it is not that I am not communicating – I am, in fact, telling him that I do not wish to communicate with him at this moment.

The second axiom states that every communication takes place on two levels, a content level that is usually verbal, and a second level that is more often non-verbal, and by which the transmitter of the message communicates to the recipient in what way the message should be interpreted in the context of their particular relationship and at that particular moment.

Let me give you an example. One person may say to another: 'I hate you' (content level), and at the same time show by his angry expression, the tone of his voice, his red face and his gestures (second level: the definition of the relationship) that this message is meant seriously, and that the transmitter is defining his relationship to the other as one of hatred. In other cases, however, the identical content ('I hate you') may be disqualified by a certain tone of voice or by a certain look and gesture that communicates the contrary. This may perplex the recipient of the message, who is often unable to tell on which of the two levels he should interpret it. In the case of the congruency of the two levels, the recipient can respond in three ways, viz. he can (1) confirm, (2) reject, and (3) disconfirm the message.

While the confirmation of coherent messages is an essential aspect of human communication, so, within certain limits, is their rejection. In other words some alternation between these two types of response is a *sine qua non* of healthy communication. However, the rejection of messages becomes pathogenic when it is systematic or predominant. This is typical of what we call a 'rigidly symmetrical relationship' (see below).

The disconfirmation of messages, by contrast, is invariably pathogenic. It is a modality we encounter with great frequency in seriously disturbed systems, for example families with a schizophrenic member. In this case the recipient of the message behaves in so cryptic and tangential a way that he communicates neither a confirmation nor an outright rejection of the other's definition of the relationship – he simply conveys the message 'You do not exist'.

There can be little doubt that this situation tends to lead the other into a 'loss of identity', that is into alienation.

The third axiom, which is very important to the understanding of my own research, states that all communicational interchanges are either symmetrical or complementary, depending on whether they are based on equality or difference:

In the first case the partners tend to mirror each other's behaviour, and thus their interaction can be termed symmetrical. Weakness or strength, goodness or badness, are not relevant here, for equality can be maintained in any of these areas. In the second case one partner's behaviour complements that of the other, forming a different sort of behavioural *Gestalt*, and is called complementary. Symmetrical interaction, then, is characterized by equality and the minimization of difference, while complementary interaction is based on the maximization of difference.

There are two different positions in a complementary relationship. One partner occupies what has been variously described as the superior, primary, or 'one-up' position, and the other the corresponding inferior, secondary, or 'one-down' position. These terms are quite useful as long as they are not equated with 'good' or 'bad', 'strong' or 'weak'. A complementary relationship may be set by the social or cultural context (as in the cases of mother and infant, doctor and patient, or teacher and student), or it may be the idiosyncratic relationship style of a particular dyad. In either case, it is important to emphasize the interlocking nature of the relationship, in which dissimilar but fitted behaviours evoke each other. One partner does not impose a complementary relationship on the other, but rather each behaves in a manner which presupposes, while at the same time providing reasons for, the behaviour of the other: their definitions of the relationship fit. (Watzlawick *et al.*)

Let me finally describe yet another characteristic family interaction: inter-family communication often strikes the observer as being cryptic, precisely because prior relational messages have established fixed transactional rules. When we observe such exchanges between family members, we are struck by the fact that the recipient of a message will unhesitatingly choose one particular meaning from a host of possible ones. In other words, the exchange spiral seems to be one-directional in as much as we can repeatedly observe the exclusion of alternative meanings as so many redundancies. The message has ceased to be polyvalent. Now the outside observer, though a participant in the conversation, may not be aware of this particular function of the system, in which case he is forced to decode the message by observing its *effects* on the family member or members to whom it has been addressed (pragmatic analysis of communication).

To that end he may have to intervene by asking: 'What precise effect has your husband's (or your wife's) words (or action) had on you?' Only members of the system can clarify the meaning of messages exchanged within the system – unlike the therapist, they have participated in the elaboration of the system from the outset, and hence hold the key to it.

We may therefore postulate that the elements of the system constitute the 'signs' of a particular relationship from which alone they derive their meaning. Precise modalities of functional integration thus ensure a particular position in the system to every member, and also preside over a series of rules that govern and maintain the homeostasis of all family interrelations. However, because only some of the personal characteristics of the elements are fully absorbed and utilized by the system, *others remain available and can be put to use in constructing a working family system, for instance when the equilibrium of the old has been destroyed.* This fact seems to me to be of central importance because it relates to the system as a system of transformations. It is only on this basis that it is meaningful to call a therapeutic intervention a 'change-inducing' operation. Inasmuch as they are active and directive, the therapeutic moves are so many attempts to produce transformations within a structure having cybernetic properties. If we change the rules, we change the organization and thus pave the way for a sudden jump towards a new organization. The latter enables the components to recover some of the interactional characteristics that used to be blocked through the exigencies of the earlier organizations. It should, moreover, be stressed that this interaction does not demand hard and protracted work on the part of the therapist but only the ability to seize the right moment at the right time. Hence it takes no miracle to see just what Rabkin saw, namely the transformation of princes into frogs and *vice versa*.

To sum up: in my recent work I have tried to investigate whether or not a family with a member diagnosed as an anorexia nervosa patient constitutes a typical system. Before I could do so, I had first to adopt an appropriate methodology.

After a few short attempts based on psychoanalytical techniques, I decided to apply various conceptual tools drawn from cybernetics, general system theory and the pragmatic study of human communication to the task in hand, that is the analysis, not of the intrapsychic structure of every family member considered separately, but of the observable transactional patterns in the here and now of family psychotherapy. The more poorly a family functions, the more rigidly it tends to repeat its peculiar interactional modality; hence it is important to identify that modality with a view to changing it by therapeutic intervention. In other words, adopting the cybernetic view that the family is a self-regulating system based on certain rules, the therapist must do his utmost to unearth the secret rules (often unconscious and unverbalized) by which the family perpetuates its own malfunction. His aim will then be to change these rules, and hence the functional modality of the system. Therapy is an effort to induce a transformation in a structure that has cybernetic properties.

The tools used by various authorities for family research can be divided into three groups:
1) family interviews or questionnaires;
2) observation of family interactions in standardized experimental situations: the performance of fixed family tasks; reactions to collectively administered psychodiagnostic tests, etc. (direct observations should be complemented with [video] tape recordings and films);
3) psychotherapeutic treatment of the entire family group including the anorexic member (here, too, [video] tape recordings should be regularly employed, and carefully analysed by the whole research team).

Being a therapist, but not only for that reason, I believe that the therapeutic context is the best possible way of observing transactional patterns which, in the case in point, also include the therapist(s). Far from being an obstacle, this becomes a positive advantage (a research instrument), provided only that the therapists, though close observers and participants, do not

become involved in the system as such, which would render them totally impotent.

Only by avoiding this pitfall can they become agents of therapeutic change, and at the same time further scientific research. As K. Lewin has put it so well, to understand how anything works, we must first try to change its function.

24 *The Family of the Anorexic Patient: a Model System*

In 1968–9 I made a number of preliminary studies, based on:
1) work with the parents of an anorexic patient, their only child, who had been treated by a colleague;
2) work with the parents of an anorexic patient (Azzurra, see p. 64) whose eventual cure after four years of psychotherapy had caused a grave crisis in the parents' relationship to each other, for which they sought help;
3) work with a young couple, the female partner of which had been a bulimic anorexic since adolescence and who had also become a dypsomaniac after her marriage.

These investigations, the results of which were published in 1970 as part of *The Child in his Family*, revealed the existence of an *intrapsychic* dynamic. At the time I was still using the old approach I had been taught during my own psychoanalytical training, and still lacked the courage to draw the whole family into the psychotherapeutic situation.

However, I was then able to join the Milan Centre of Family Studies and undertake work in a team with the family therapists Luigi Boscolo MD, Gianfranco Cecchin MD and Guiliana Prata MD. The next three chapters are devoted to the preliminary results of our study, and in Chapter 27 I relate them to a wider social context.

The idea of doing research into whether or not the families of anorexics show characteristic behaviour patterns was suggested to us by J. Haley's 'The family of the schizophrenic: a model system'. In this article Haley, basing himself on a study of fifteen families with a schizophrenic member (the study began in 1953 and formed part of the Bateson research project at Palo Alto), put forward a theoretical model designed to describe the family as a unit.

The best method of studying the system of family interaction is to interview the whole family together, and to observe them over a fairly extended period of time, in a structured therapeutic context.

From a methodological point of view families with an anorexic member seemed more satisfactory than families with a schizophrenic. This was because schizophrenia, as L. Wynne has shown, covers a wide spectrum: from transitory catatonic blocks to persistent and organized paranoid delirium and extreme disorganization of a precocious hebephrenic type. It is only recently that Wynne and his collaborators have tried to impose some sort of order into the subject by classifying the various clinical categories on the basis of thought disorders and breakdowns in family communication. Their research has shown that communication disorders in families with a fragmented way of thinking are quite distinct from those found in families with an amorphous way of thinking. The two types of families also seem to differ in internal organization and role allocation, in their ability to communicate and in their openness to therapeutic help.

By contrast anorexia nervosa, as first described with surprising clinical accuracy precisely one hundred years ago by Gull and Lasègue, is characterized by the appearance of constant symptoms at, or shortly prior to, puberty, generally in girls.

In the psychiatric literature there is wide disagreement as to whether or not the rare cases of male anorexia should be considered authentic instances of anorexia nervosa.

Because we ourselves have only had occasion to study a single family with a male anorexic, we have decided to treat it as an exception, and to defer any discussion of our findings until such time as we have been able to study a representative number of such families.

In family therapy we are not so much interested in the nosographic description of the individual patient as in the diagnosis of the family as a total system, including the therapist. However, since we are still a long way from a satisfactory system of family diagnostics, we continue to classify families in terms of the patient's nosography.

To introduce some order and method, we have based our research on Haley's model, that is on the following pragmatic axioms of human communication:
1) that it is impossible not to communicate and not to respond to a communication, and
2) that every communication involves at least two levels (a level of content and a level of relationship definition.)
We set out to investigate:
1) how the family members qualify their own communications in the particular context of family therapy;
2) how they qualify the communications of other members, and in what circumstances;
3) the problem of leadership in the family;
4) the problem of coalitions;
5) the problem of acceptance, rejection or shifting of blame among family members when something goes wrong;
6) the problem of the interaction patterns of the parental couple.

The research was based on the psychotherapeutic study of twelve families. According to our standard practice, all interviews were handled by one male and one female therapist. The interviews were recorded and monitored by other members of the team who, if necessary, suggested alternative strategies.

Our data should be considered preliminary, both because of the smallness of our sample and also because four families have not yet completed their treatment.

Generally families with anorexic members have a capacity for communication, for focusing their attention, for carrying an argument to its conclusion and for conveying coherent meanings which is macroscopically superior to that of families with a schizophrenic member.

With a few exceptions, which I shall specify below, our families did not straightaway evince the sense of discouragement, futility, meaninglessness and chaos that is so characteristic of the families of schizophrenics, nor did they have the fatuous 'drawing room' attitude so often exhibited by such families. *Instead there was a clear display of drama and suffering.* The parents made it clear that they were prepared to do anything they could to help the patient, though they often withheld important information in order to maintain a respectable front to which they seemed to attach excessive importance.

How the family members qualify their own communications

The members of the family of an anorexic patient generally qualify their own communication coherently, verbally no less than non-verbally. They seem to be sure enough of what they say, and of their right to say it, to feel justified in imposing rules on the relationship. The exceptions were some families who, even during relatively relaxed interviews, disqualified their own communications by their concomitant behaviour and verbal messages. These were families of anorexic patients whose symptoms had been complicated by violent behaviour towards other members of the family (blows, over-feeding of another member, strange or unjustified demands, shouting) or by bouts of bulimia. This would tend to corroborate my Rorschach findings with individual patients. In particular I found that patients suffering from severe bulimic crises displayed thought and communication disorders not present in patients who keep strictly to their reduced diets. Family observations also seem to suggest that major bouts of bulimia go hand in hand with psychotic confusion, violence and a complete breakdown of family communication.

How the family members qualify the communications of other members

The *rejection* of messages sent by others is extremely common in families with an anorexic patient. Very rarely will one member bear out what another has said, particularly about how he defines himself in the relationship. Contradiction is common. This type of rejection, therefore, does not concern the general invitation to communicate (Axiom 1), which is accepted and reciprocated, but the two levels of the message as such (Axiom 2). In fact it is as if each member of the family reacted to the other's message in the following way:

'I reject the content of what you say, even though I acknowledge your right to say it. And I also reject your definition of yourself (and myself) in our relationship.'

Here I can do no better than report a series of brief and typical interactions during an interview of a family of six.

Identified patient: 'Our trip to Rome convinced me that I can never have any relationship with my sister, because she does not want it.'

Sister: 'It's not true that I don't want it, I do everything I can to make it better.'

I. p.: 'How can you get on with people if you are not sincere. In Rome you never said anything about my vomiting, but when we got back home you told Mother all about it.'

Sister: 'Well, I was being sincere, at least when we got back. It's you who are never sincere, because you never mention your vomiting to anyone.'

Therapist: 'Why don't you admit that you vomit up every meal?'

I. p.: 'Because I don't vomit up every meal.'

Therapist: 'Nearly every meal.'

I. p.: 'Because, to talk about certain things, you need someone who is prepared to meet you half-way. But you [to her sister] aren't prepared to. In Rome you sulked all the time.'

Sister: 'No, that's not true, I wasn't sulking. I simply said that I wasn't enjoying myself, and then *you* began to sulk. But when I said I wasn't enjoying myself I was simply being sincere, and whenever I'm sincere you get offended.'

Mother: 'I, too, am at my wits' end with her. If I scold her she says, "You see, Mother, you've ganged up with the others." If I'm kind to her, she says, "You see, Mother, you're handling me with kid gloves, you're not sincere, you've put on your mask again." But she has never been sincere with me.'

I. p.: 'You see, Mother, you too keep attacking me.'

Mother: 'That's not true.'

This brief excerpt is typical of the rejection of messages. The rejection, moreover, was undisguised and left no doubt about the position of the speakers *vis-à-vis* one another, and was, in itself, a means of communication or rather of metacommunication.

There are, however, exceptions to this rule. In families with communication disorders more closely related to schizophrenia, there is a much greater tendency to disqualify or even disconfirm the messages of others. This tendency is particularly marked in certain parents to whom it is a matter of great importance to stress the patient's 'pathological' state of mind. They tend to discount any messages and even to ignore evident improvements in the patient's behaviour or physical health. Thus the parents of one family with whom it had proved quite impossible to communicate during the first four interviews because the daughter kept shouting and being generally aggressive, failed by mutual agreement to acknowledge the subsequent improvement in their daughter's behaviour, even when her shouting and aggression had stopped completely. Moreover, at the slightest sign of impatience on their daughter's part, the parents made a great point of expressing their despair to the therapists, implying that she had not really improved. If the daughter herself referred to her changed behaviour, they immediately discounted her remarks by reminding her of her abnormal eating habits, and whenever she pointed out that she was eating more, they immediately criticized her general behaviour at home.

In such cases communication is of the psychotic type and confusion between past and present is the rule. Thus the parents may preserve absurd forms of behaviour on the grounds that they are afraid of triggering off reactions that the daughter has, in fact, long since abandoned.

In another case the patient missed several interviews during which the parents expressed their deep anxiety about their daughter's inadequate diet. The therapists were all the more surprised to find that, on her return to the interviews, the daughter's physical condition had greatly improved. In yet another case the family therapy started after the patient had resumed normal eating habits (she was, in fact, rather obese) only to develop catatonoid symptoms. When we eventually succeeded in reducing these symptoms, the parents put through a highly dramatic telephone call to inform us that their daughter had reverted to a grave form of anorexic behaviour, though its consequences proved to be absolutely invisible. What had happened was that the girl was no longer prepared to let them stuff her with food, and had decided to eat what and when she liked.

These extreme forms of behaviour are, in any case, characteristic of families with marked communication disorders, in which the anorexic symptoms of the patient, as I have already explained, are complicated by such other symptoms as violent forms of behaviour and bouts of bulimia.

The problem of leadership

One characteristic of these parents, that has also been noted by other authors, including particularly Minuchin and Barcai, is their reluctance to assume personal leadership of the family. In particular each of the parents feels a need to blame his or her decision on others. Here are a few examples:

Mother: 'I don't let her wear miniskirts because I know her father doesn't like them.'
Father: 'I have always backed my wife up. I feel it would be wrong to contradict her.'

Mother: 'My husband had decided to spend his holiday by himself in our country cottage [a place she loved herself] but I was simply forced to follow with the whole family and my old parents *on account of my father.* You see, Father wasn't well and he had to be near a doctor [her husband was a doctor].'
Father: 'My wife and I never went out because Angela [their elder daughter] protested. Now we have Anna [the i. p.]. How can we even feel like going out?'

The arguments used in the following two examples are even more intricate.

Mother: 'Angela came back from school with a peculiar look in her eyes. "What's wrong with your eyes?" I asked. "Did you get hit?" She told me that a school-friend had applied some brown eye-shadow. "Ugh!" I said, "how can you put on brown eye-shadow? What horrible taste!..."'
Therapist: 'Were you disgusted by the brown colour? Would blue have been all right?'
Mother: 'Well . . . the fact is that my husband cannot stand girls who look like painted hussies.'

The same mother also produced another gem. Her husband had

accused her of living like a recluse. It appeared that the patient, Anna, had for some years been friends with a classmate, Patrizia, and that the two families knew each other.

Father: 'But *whom* are *you* friends with? With no one. You have even stopped seeing Patrizia's mother.'
Mother: 'Well, how could I be friends with Patrizia's mother? You know perfectly well that Angela [the elder daughter] can't stand Patrizia's father.'

So the actions of each member are never attributed to personal preferences but to the needs of another member; all decisions are for the good of someone else. This rule applies to the patient's behaviour as well, except that her symptoms are so overpowering that she cannot be expected to spare the family. 'It is something that happened to her, nothing can be done about it.' *The result is a form of family leadership that is only acceptable because it is pathological. Its subject is not the patient, but the illness.*

The problem of coalitions

In my view the system of alliances constitutes the central and most serious problem facing the families of anorexic patients. It is the basis of a large number of secret rules that must never be mentioned or even hinted at, and that give rise to a whole series of distorted behaviour patterns. However, as we shall see, it may be used to good effect by the therapist. As a typical example I shall now quote the case of a family whom I shall call Bianchi.

The family was made up of the father, a forty-five-year-old clerk; the mother, a forty-two-year-old housewife; Flavia, the seventeen-year-old patient; and Claudio, her eight-year-old and obese little brother. Claudio was obese because his sister forced him to eat enormous meals which she herself prepared for him. In the course of the interviews the behaviour of the various members of the family exemplified the taboo against open bipartisan alliances within the family. Thus it appeared that the mother had confided to Flavia that she had only stayed and put up with her husband for Flavia's sake (who consequently owed her a tremendous debt of gratitude). But whenever Flavia herself (often egged on by her mother) dared to criticize her father during the interviews, the mother would immediately rebuke her, which exasperated Flavia and put her even more against her father. When the quarrel between daughter and father had reached its height, the mother, who was sitting beside her husband, would pat his hand in a friendly manner. At this point the whole interaction would come to an end, with the father murmuring, 'Let's drop it,' and with Flavia bursting into tears. The husband's behaviour towards the wife was similar. Whenever he criticized her in the presence of the rest of the family and found someone to back him up, he immediately began to look at his wife affectionately and, at the end of the interview, would help her with her coat (which he did not do normally), thus showing that he had not really meant to run her down.

Again the mother had apparently entered into a secret coalition with Claudio so as to protect him against the enormous amounts of food that Flavia expected him to eat. Thus when she took him to school she would throw away the snacks Flavia had put into his satchel. At the table, on the other hand, she urged him to eat up all the food that Flavia put on his plate, 'so as not to make your sister suffer'. In the course of the tenth interview the family discussed the arrangements for Claudio's summer holidays. The father said that he was sure Claudio would enjoy himself at a camp with other children. It appeared that the idea had been suggested by Flavia; the mother was convinced that Claudio would be very unhappy and was only prepared to send him to camp 'for Flavia's sake . . .'. Flavia then burst into tears, saying that everyone thought her wicked for wishing her brother out of the way. But all she was thinking of was his own good; the boy had to become more independent or else he would end up like her.

The only one not to have been consulted at all was Claudio. Asked by one of the therapists how he felt about going to camp, he promptly gave his mother a questioning look.

Clearly the members of the family behave as if an alliance between any two is a betrayal of the third. They seem to have great difficulty in entering into a two-person relationship; the exclusion of the third strikes them as a grave threat to their pseudo-solidarity – only in the absence of all open alliances can this threat apparently be averted.

Alliance phenomena in families of three are much easier to study than alliance phenomena in larger families, and illustrate the *modus operandi* of the taboo against bipartisan coalitions particularly well. The patient is forced into an impossible position; she is continuously invited to ally herself with the father against the mother and *vice versa*. Worse still, each of the parents, deeply disillusioned with their partner, secretly encourages *the patient to make up for the partner's shortcomings*. As a result the patient finds herself playing the role of secret husband and secret wife all at once, dividing her sympathy equally between her parents.

An excellent example of this situation was provided by Chiara, the only child of a man with refined artistic tastes and an ignorant and loquacious mother. From early childhood Chiara's father had tried to imbue her with a love of art; on Sundays he would take her to visit old churches and museums, while the mother stayed in the car reading the papers. 'You for one appreciate beautiful things,' her father would say to her, clearly venting his dissatisfaction with his wife. But as soon as Chiara was alone with her mother, she had to fill in all the details of the day's events to make up for the silences of the sullen husband, immersed as he was in his books or his music.

Much the same thing happened to Rosella, the idealized child of a father whose hobbies were sport and ecology. She was invited to join him in the country for horse rides, but also had to take his 'place' in bed by the side of her mother, a depressed and drab housewife who shared none of her husband's interests and was far too often left alone.

In the peculiar arrangement, which we have called 'three-way matrimony', each member of the family is married to two persons: the mother to her husband and her daughter, the father to his wife and his daughter, the daughter to her mother and father.

The arrangement works fairly well for the parents but not for the daughter, who is expected to share out her attention as fairly as possible, and consequently has no means, or energy, to build up a life of her own, or to risk open rebellion on reaching adolescence. Indeed we observed that the daughter generally accepts the role she is expected to play to the point of developing her symptoms precisely when the system is threatened by changes.

Thus, in the two families in which the patient was an only daughter, the symptoms set in shortly after the father, until then fairly detached from the life of his family, made his presence more obviously felt, in one case due to a serious illness, in the other as the result of his disillusionment with politics. The return of the father had quite obviously upset the old equilibrium.

In families with two, three or four children the critical factors are much more difficult to identify. However, in a number of families we found that the symptoms appeared after a change in the old system of secret alliances. In some cases, as one of the brothers (or sisters) grew older, he changed his relationship with one or both parents, thus threatening the family equilibrium and the patient's presumed privileges.

However, during the first family session, the interview invariably shows that the patient starts the therapy in a state of isolation from her brothers and sisters; far from being allied to any one, she is secretly detested by all thanks to the privileged position she is rightly or wrongly believed to enjoy in the household thanks to her illness. Here again the patient's fatal loyalty to the older generation not only makes her a stranger to her contemporaries but also makes her play the role of a sort of extra parent, resented by her siblings.

Two-person alliances outside the family are equally frowned upon. Thus when one of our thirteen-year-old patients made friends with a girl of the same age, Patrizia, and invited her home, the patient's eight-year-old sister immediately set out to turn the relationship into a threesome, and succeeded in making friends with Patrizia despite their considerable age difference. The patient found the strain so great that she abandoned Patrizia soon afterwards. In other cases friendships, far from being incorporated into the group, are criticized, often for being too intimate or morbid. There are also cases in which the patient tries to 'save herself' by imposing the impossible role of saviour on some boy or girl. In several cases the predictable failure of this attempt directly preceded the onset of the symptoms, thus triggering off a family crisis.

The problem of blame-shifting

Precisely because every family member 'effaces' himself for the sake of the rest, no one member is really prepared to assume responsibility when something goes wrong. The mothers may blame themselves for their daughter's illness but they promptly invalidate this self-accusation by explaining that they only acted as they did through excess of zeal and devotion (for which they cannot be blamed). If, on the other hand, they are criticized on any concrete point, they either defend themselves hotly or, alternatively, get depressed and declare that they are prepared to leave home if that will improve their daughter's chances of getting better. This apparent spirit of self-sacrifice is a veiled threat to the other members and makes them feel guilty, with the result that they stop voicing any criticisms.

The fathers characteristically speak of themselves as people whose only possible fault may have been to put up with too much for the sake of peace. They consider themselves rational and well-balanced persons, and regret that they have never succeeded in making these qualities prevail over their wives' irrational behaviour. When one gets down to particulars, however, it always becomes clear that they have so blinded themselves with self-pity as to be totally unaware that their daughter, too, was having difficulties in her relationship with her mother. They seem never to have taken their daughter's part in anything like a courageous or emphatic manner. As for the patient, her attitude, once the symptoms have appeared, is that she can do nothing about them. She realizes that her parents are worried, and wishes they were not. But she is now in the grip of an illness that is quite beyond her control, and for which she can in no way be held responsible.

The interaction patterns of the parental couple

Behind the façade of respectability and marital unity the parents generally conceal a deep disillusionment with each other that they are quite unable to acknowledge, let alone resolve.

This failure reflects their ambiguous view of their marriage: while they welcome its gratifying aspects, they deeply resent its compulsory elements. In all the families we have treated to date, the fathers' and mothers' respective view of themselves in the relationship seems to be identical. The mothers see themselves as 'Ladies Bountiful', completely dedicated to the good of others. Their rectitude and avowed generosity preclude any criticism of their constant encroachments. They attack anyone who refuses to view them as benefactresses. The fathers, for their part, invariably see themselves as essentially good and decent men. Nothing would induce them to think otherwise. Hence, while the mothers occasionally round on the therapists, the fathers remain respectful at all times. If they are asked to do something, they will do it conscientiously, as if it were homework.

Their blame-transfer manœuvres in the interpersonal relationship are much more subtle than those of their wives: their sad silences are so many fingers pointed at those of whose injustice and lack of comprehension they are the innocent butts. Two moralistic people who both consider themselves the victims of a compulsory relationship will inevitably compete with each other for moral superiority, and the simplest way to do this is to appear to be the victim. Their position in the relationship is therefore of a symmetrical type, but what we have here is a peculiar symmetry: in it one-upmanship serves to prove that one has made greater sacrifices in the cause of duty, respectability and marital stability than the other. We call this 'symmetry through sacrificial escalation'.

It is a well-known fact that two marital partners who maintain a rigid symmetrical position in their relationship normally go in search of allies: first of all among their own relatives, and next among friends, advisers or priests, who are asked to take sides, to act as referees in the conjugal jousts and to intervene during moments of crisis. *But this does not happen in the case of our couple which engages in sacrificial escalation in complete secrecy*, because the rule of respectability requires that they appear as an exemplary couple to the outside world. The secret has to be kept from relatives and, *a fortiori*, from social acquaintances, contact with whom is confined to the exchange of conventional courtesies. As a result the system of alliances and the search for an arbitrator are kept within the family and focused especially on the patient, who is secretly encouraged to side with the more persecuted of her two parents. But since each of the parents sees himself in that role, and since the patient depends on them both, she occupies an extremely ambiguous position in the system. This ambiguity is complicated further by the fact that, though the two parents vie for her support, neither is prepared to enter into an open alliance with her since, paradoxically, that alliance would detract from their professed roles of being the more downtrodden of the conjugal pair. In other words the parent who succeeds in winning the alliance of the daughter drops behind in the sacrificial escalation race, and hence loses his moral superiority. For this very reason both parents show striking contradictions in their behaviour during interviews. Each seeks the compassion of the daughter and, failing to obtain it, expresses his or her disillusionment, but nevertheless is pained and even indignant if the daughter is too critical of, or aggressive towards, the other.

We have observed this phenomenon time and again. Let me quote just one example: during one family interview, the mother burst into tears while trying to explain her difficulty in communicating with her husband who was always working in his office, even on Sundays and holidays. Exasperated by the old excuse that he had a lot of professional engagements, she finally said, between sobs: 'In that case put a notice on your office door to tell your clients what your working hours are. Then at least I'd know where I stand.' Throughout the argument the patient had maintained a detached silence, careful not to side with either parent. At the end of the interview the therapists asked the father to dine alone with his daughter for a certain time, but did not explain the reason for this request. At the next interview the daughter, when describing her meals with her father, mentioned the same painful silences and sense of emotional detachment that her mother had complained of. She did this very delicately, indicating that she did not blame him in any way. The mother at once rose to her husband's defence – her daughter, she said, was expecting much too much, whereas she herself had always been content with what little affection she got. In another family the father suddenly expressed anxiety about his wife's long-standing hypertension. 'From now on,' he said, 'she must not be allowed to suffer the least strain.' This happened after an interview in which the daughter, with visible anguish, had for the first time succeeded in describing some particularly painful aspects of her relationship with her mother.

H

The 'go-between' of couples of this type, that is the patient, thus seems quite satisfied to assume a role that is much too difficult for her to play. If she attempts to engage in a real dialogue with her father, he will reject her out of fear, while her mother will reject her out of jealousy. If she gives in to her mother, she is taken over completely as if she were still a baby, and hence rejected as a person; at the same time the father will rebuff her because of her infantile behaviour. If she attacks either of her parents, the other immediately rejects her by rushing to his (or her) defence. If, finally, she attempts to abandon the unequal struggle and tries to stand on her own feet, she will, for the first time in her life, find herself opposed by a *united couple*, determined to reject her bid for independence. *In a system where every communication has so high a probability of being rejected, the rejection of food seems to be in full keeping with the interactional style of the family.* In particular it is in perfect tune with the sacrificial attitude of the group, in which suffering is the best move in the one-upmanship game.

25 *The Use of Therapeutic Interventions*

At this point we think it is opportune to give a brief, preliminary description of some forms of therapeutic intervention that have led to positive changes in the family system of communication and hence in the patient's physical health. Admittedly we have been using these techniques for a relatively short period of time so that no follow-up has been completed. (We are at present drafting a programme for the regular follow-up of the families we have treated, and consider such follow-ups essential to the accurate appraisal of our therapeutic techniques. With the last five families we have treated, the system was successfully changed and the anorexic symptom eliminated in less than ten sessions.)

On the other hand we think that by describing even these preliminary attempts to change the system we may help to shed fresh light on a number of important problems. J. Haley, in a chapter of his book entitled 'Approaches to family therapy', states explicitly that the fundamental problem of family therapy is one of method. He adds that whereas a beginner would feel happier with a rule of thumb, the experienced therapist realizes that this would, in fact, be a handicap.

Every family has a specific problem that may need a specific therapeutic approach. Hence, rather than try to fit the family to the method, the experienced therapist will seek to devise a method suited to the particular needs of the family. Thus instead of insisting that the whole family attend every session, he may, if he thinks it a tactical advantage, decide to divide the family into sub-groups. Some cases may benefit from frequent but short interviews, others from less frequent but longer interviews.

What little experience we ourselves have accumulated in this field leads us to agree whole-heartedly with Haley. In particular, when treating families with an anorexic patient, we have sought to devise modes of therapeutic intervention that take the special characteristics of such families fully into account. Our main aim has been to devise modes of therapeutic intervention that do not depend too much on the imagination, personality or experience of the therapist. Once we are familiar with the peculiar mode of functioning of this type of family (usually dissimulated and difficult to detect) we are on the look-out for certain patterns and hence in a better position to devise techniques for transforming them.

In particular we have found that with greater experience we have come to intervene much earlier than we used to. We have in fact learned from a host of errors that the state of grace the therapist enjoys in family therapy is rather short-lived. Thus if he fails to fathom certain secret rules of the system, for instance by paying insufficient heed to behavioural redundancies, and hence being unable to change them by concrete directives, he himself may be incorporated into the system and rendered impotent. It is for this very reason that in November 1971 we initiated a research project centred on 'short-term family therapy'. We now believe that the therapeutic cycle should be completed in no more than twenty sessions and even less when it proves easier to obtain a substantial change in the family system and to eliminate the anorexic symptom. The family are, however, told that, they have a 'credit' of so-and-so many sessions, which they may or may not use at their discretion in the future.

In our opinion this approach (though still subject to review) goes a long way towards assuaging the family's understandable fears that they will be drawn into protracted treatment with an unpredictable outcome. Moreover, by setting a time limit, we force them to behave responsibly and not with passive acquiescence. The therapists, too, are put on their mettle: they cannot afford to let their attention slip when time hangs over them like the sword of Damocles.

As for the interval between sessions, which was originally fixed at one week precisely, we have since seen fit to vary it as the situation demands. In particular we now tend to lengthen the interval, especially after we have made good contact – we have found that a concrete instruction has a much greater effect if it is left to sink in. The main problem is to set the correct interval for each particular case.

The family members are informed of our technique during the first meeting; they are told that we tape all our transactions, that we work in a team and that we use a one-way mirror.

The therapeutic observers never intervene personally during the sessions though, when things go terribly wrong, they knock on the door, call one of the 'active' therapists out and suggest a different approach. Strategic decisions are, however, invariably taken by the team as a whole, generally before the session but, in particularly difficult situations, towards the end. In such cases the session is briefly interrupted, while the therapists in charge go into conference with their colleagues. The family is told from the outset that, in the course of the treatment, they will receive a number of directives, and that the success of the entire therapy hinges on their implementation.

We invariably see the family as a whole, but may from time to time split them up into different groups, the better to provoke meaningful responses and to stabilize the generation barrier which is usually confused or non-existent.

Let me now specify some of our techniques that have proved particularly effective.

Interventions to change the qualification of communications by other family members

To cope with the highly repetitive pattern of the rejection of messages, we have, as I pointed out earlier, made it a standard practice to work in heterosexual pairs. This calls for a word of explanation. Sometimes one of the two therapists will join the fray while the other plays the part of the silent observer. After some time the first may find himself reduced to impotence in the face of a whole series of rejections. At this point the second therapist, instead of speaking up in defence of his partner, will continue to play the part of the impartial observer, while 'metacommunicating' with his colleague about what is going on. The two therapists eventually agree, taking care to give the behaviour of the family a positive interpretation, by arguing that, if every member of the family finds it so difficult to confirm what the therapists say, there must be a good reason for it, and no attempt need be made to change it. On other, more difficult, occasions, we carry this tactic or ploy even further. Thus it has sometimes happened that one of the therapists has been driven by the system into adopting a sharply critical attitude towards one member of the family. It is then observed that the member under attack will defend himself either by rejecting the criticism out of hand or else by making such remarks as: 'I must be stupid; I just don't understand.' At this point one or several of the other members of the family will often look pleased. The purpose of the whole manœuvre is to convince the therapist that with someone so stupid, it is clearly impossible to change the family system. To dramatize the situation the second therapist, who has kept silent until then, now asks his colleague to join him outside for a private talk. After a while the two return. The second therapist now does all the talking. Very calmly he expresses his disagreement with his colleague, and explicitly allies himself with the member of the family under attack. The *rejected* therapist looks duly contrite and, by acknowledging his error, *confirms* his colleague's message. A tactic of this sort has invariably proved highly effective. Not only does it deliver a powerful blow to the system, but it also shows that a couple can peacefully change their respective 'one-up' or 'one-down' position in the relationship. I might add that in our dramatizations the final 'one-up' position has always fallen to the male therapist. This, we think, is therapeutically constructive, not so much on account of the prevailing cultural stereotypes or the fact that we are working with a certain type of family, but by virtue of certain phylogenetic constants from which the distinct gender-roles seem to derive their universal validity. This point, however, requires further investigation and discussion.

In the rarer cases, in which the entire family group tries to protect the *status quo* by employing disqualifying communications, we have recourse to other tactics. I shall cite the case of a family, which we shall call Crippa, consisting of the parents, both university graduates in their fifties, and four children. The patient, Emilia, was the eldest child. She suffered from chronic anorexia and was extremely emaciated. The crucial intervention occurred at a relatively late stage in the therapy (thirteenth interview), when the therapeutic team at last cottoned on to the defence mechanism used by that family; humour, intelligent, witty exchanges and funny faces. This evasive manœuvre was performed with such subtlety, and with so much apparent goodwill, that it escaped detection for a number of interviews. It was only during a team discussion, in a cheerful and pleasant atmosphere, that one of the therapists, clearly irritated, put his finger on the real problem when he said: 'To tell you the truth, I find these interviews awfully boring. I keep asking myself how it is that so intelligent, pleasant and perceptive a family should have a daughter who is still starving herself to death.' This comment led us to identify the secret weapon with which the family had so skilfully been confusing us, and we decided to disarm it during the next interview.

That session was opened by the patient, who told the therapists of a trip she had taken a few days before with Gianna, her younger sister. She described how disastrous their outing had been and how much she had missed her mother's presence. She said that her sister had been very off-hand with her, which was not surprising seeing that 'they had set her up on a pedestal and treated her as a model of intelligence and beauty' (from the tape recording).

Therapist: 'Who set Gianna up on a pedestal?'

Emilia: 'Everyone . . . Granny . . . and . . . Mother . . .'

Therapist: 'Tell me, Emilia, what did your mother and your grandmother think of you when you were Gianna's age?'

Emilia: 'That nothing . . . absolutely nothing about me was right.'

Father: 'Not even her beauty, and believe me, Emilia *was* beautiful!' (He sniggers as if her present condition were a joke.)

Emilia: 'Nothing was right. They used to say that my body was mis-shapen . . . [she sits on the edge of her chair and imitates a puppet, looking grotesque because of her extreme emaciation] . . . I had flat feet pointing inwards . . . [to her mother] . . . When I was small you did your best to get me to have . . . ugly knees . . . legs like a football player's . . . a bottom that touched the ground . . . quite frightful . . . and a bust . . . that absolutely defied any bra [gesture].'

(They all laugh at Emilia's funny antics, and egg her on.)

Brother: (grinning) 'And what about your nose?'

Emilia: 'Ah yes, an enormously thick nose, and my teeth . . . I had a very small palate and I always slept with my mouth open so that I dribbled all over my pillows. . . . My hair, thin and mousy . . . absolutely ghastly. . . .'

Brother: 'You forgot your low forehead. . . .'

Emilia: 'Yes, that too . . . good for nothing . . . at school I did get top marks, but then I had to swot for it all day . . . and all that time I spent in church. . . .'

Mother: (speaking in dialect, evidently imitating her own mother, and laughing) 'An old bigot just like her father.'

(Emilia follows her mother's unspoken command and also breaks into dialect, imitating her maternal grandmother in an obvious attempt to divert attention to that [absent] person. Throughout the entire farce everyone keeps laughing, as if they were discussing happy memories of bygone days. The therapist does not join in the general merriment but grows visibly sadder; at long last he cuts into the transaction and addresses the patient in stern tones.)

Therapist: 'Emilia, in these distressing circumstances I can't see how you could possibly have loved your mother so much, or why you should have missed her on your recent trip to Rome. How can you miss someone who had such a low opinion of you and said all these horrible things about you. . . . I should have felt terribly resentful in your place.'

(Everybody, including Emilia, falls into an icy silence.)

Emilia: (plaintively) 'But I thought it was all Granny's fault. . . .'

Mother: 'Everyone knew what Granny was like . . . no one took her seriously. . . . Emilia, you weren't meant to believe her. . . .'

Therapist: 'How could Emilia fail to believe her? [turning to the patient]. . . . And how did your mother react to Granny's remarks?'

Emilia: 'She just laughed. . . .'

Therapist: 'Well? Didn't that make it even worse?'

Emilia: (sobbing) 'But how could I possibly hate my own mother?'

Therapist: 'Whom did you hate?'

Emilia: 'Myself! [long pause] I won't be parted from her – if I'd hated her I would have left – but I didn't . . . I believed every word she said, I talked like her, I was like her, even at school. . . .'

Therapist: 'How can you call this love . . . you keep clinging to her and speak of anger and rebellion as if it were love. . . .'

Brother: 'That's because *their* family expected one to call it love' (by 'their family' he was referring to his mother's family, and, at the same time, betraying a secret rule).

In this transaction we can see clearly that the rejection (clown-ish antics, laughter) of the dramatic content of the communica-tion was shared by the whole group, including the patient. The therapist's intervention cut short these antics and revealed the true drama they were meant to hide. This kind of intervention is far more beneficial than stopping the entire transaction so as to point out the incoherence of the two levels of communi-cation. In the present case this would have meant robbing a crucial moment of its therapeutic potential.

(It is important to note that in subsequent interviews the family never again displayed this type of behaviour so that it became possible to collaborate with them more constructively.)

Interventions into the problem of leadership

When each member of the family finds it difficult to state in the first person what he wants or does not want, one method of intervention is to metacommunicate the therapist's own observa-tions. In so doing we take care to emphasize the right of each member to have desires of his own and to express them frankly. Experience has shown that interventions of this type, far from being rejected, very often cause astonishment: no one had realized that he or she was engaging in secret and deceptive manœuvres. On occasion we have asked that, during the interval before the next session, each member of the family should always state what he wants or does not want in the first person, and that one member keep written notes of any failures to observe this rule (his own included). This forces the family to 'metacommunicate' continually even between interviews and thus to reduce obscurity and confusion. Asking family members to state their likes and dislikes in the first person sometimes drives the patient into a paradoxical situation from which she can only escape in one of two ways: by abandoning her symptoms or by coming into the open. In the second case it becomes clear that her use of the symptoms was a form of blackmail and not a frank expression of her own desires.

Interventions into the problem of coalitions

The problem of coalitions is undoubtedly one of the most important in family psychotherapy. Failure to grasp the necessity of intervening into the system of coalitions has caused us quite a few failures, especially during our initial period. Essentially, this type of intervention calls for the invention of tactics designed to draw father and daughter into a constructive alliance. *This alliance, however, should only be temporary, and great care should be taken that it is not destructive to the mother*, who will otherwise feel excluded and may become depressed or hostile. *The ultimate purpose of this type of intervention is to open the generation gap, so that the daughter may at long last start living her own life.*

This procedure, though easy to explain, is difficult to put into practice. To begin with the system often succeeds in convincing the therapists that the father is in fact totally unreliable. The mother misses no chance to point out her husband's inadequacies where family problems are concerned, and the husband's behaviour confirms this view. Moreover, because the daughter often evinces hostility and impatience or expresses fears that it will never be possible to have a meaningful dialogue with him, he, in turn, becomes increasingly reluctant to enter into a bipartisan relationship with her.

In order to surmount these difficulties we have used a variety of tactics and prescriptions, some of which I shall now mention in brief.

In one case, in which the daughter's physical condition was extremely grave and the problem of getting her to eat devolved exclusively on the mother, we thought it essential to compel her detached and Olympian father to become emotionally involved with his daughter. Ostensibly so as to avoid the imminent tragedy of hospitalization, we solemnly proposed that the father alone should take charge of his daughter's meals for some time and that he should eat with her in her room. He was to have the same amount of food as his daughter and to leave whatever she left. Thanks to his extreme self-control, he lost several kilograms before hunger and exasperation finally drove him to have a violent scene with her. The girl had at last got the better of him and had for the first time in her life received a clear and coherent message from him. (Immediately afterwards, she abandoned her symptoms.)

In another case, taking a sympathetic view of the great suffering the patient's refusal to eat caused her mother, we suggested that the mother make the great sacrifice (she was totally 'dedicated' to the good of others) of leaving home for a fortnight's holiday. Father and daughter, in their turn, were to make the 'sacrifice' of looking after themselves during her absence. By this device we were able to clarify the real nature of the relationship between father and daughter without putting the blame on anyone.

In families with sons and daughters we tried more complex alliance tactics which, however, proved to be of purely marginal effect unless they went hand in hand with the consolidation of the father's position. When this strategy is successful we invariably end up with intelligent, effectual fathers. *This suggests strongly that the so-called ineffectual father is a product of co-operation between all the members of the system and not an intrapsychic fact.* In this regard I must mention that in one such family the system misled us into writing the father off and conferring his role on one of the sons, in the belief that he would provide a more reliable ally for the patient. We had to acknowledge that this was a further humiliation of the father (required by the system in order to avoid changes).

I should like to add that whenever a temporary alliance between father and daughter is expressly advised by the therapists or tolerated as the unavoidable result of some instruction, the purpose must always be to bring the existence of perverse triangles into the open the better to combat it.

By perverse triangles I refer to *secret* coalitions between one generation and the next against one of the peers. Such coalitions are never acknowledged, and whenever the behaviour of the two is such as to betray their secret compact,

the betrayal is immediately washed over by metacommunications. The pathogenic structure of the perverse triangle,
therefore, does not so much lie in the coalition itself as in the
simultaneous denial of its existence and that of the generation
gap.

In other words, 'there is a certain behaviour which indicates
a coalition, which, when it is queried, will be denied as a
coalition. More formally, the behaviour at one level which
indicates that there is a coalition is qualified by metacommuni-
cative behaviour indicating that there is not.' (Haley.)

I use the term 'coalition' in Haley's sense. By coalition I
refer to that process of joint action which is directed *against*
a third person, in contrast to an alliance in which two out of
three people may openly make common cause.

There is, of course, no reason at all why one of the parents,
in our case the father, should not have a close emotional
relationship with his daughter, or even declare that he has
entered into a temporary alliance with her against certain of
his wife's more intolerable incursions. However he must guard
against the temptation to ignore the generation gap by putting
the daughter in his wife's place. Whenever he enters into alliance
with her, he must do so for rational and explicit ends.

I would also like to add that, in some cases, our instructions,
aimed at bringing father and daughter face to face, far from
resulting in a closer emotional relationship, have led to the
exposure and elimination of a pathologically ambiguous situation. In all these cases the father, manifestly dissatisfied with
his wife, was in the habit of sending his daughter subtle messages, generally of an unspoken kind. It takes an attentive
therapist to observe the furtive exchange of ironical glances
or the sighs that occur whenever the wife voices one of her
usual grievances. It is with the help of such secret messages –
so many redundancies – that the father reinforces the daughter's
hostility to the mother, insinuating that, if only the mother
were not in the way, they would share heaven knows what
wonderful mystical experiences. (In this connection I might
point out that none of our anorexic patients has ever selected a
chair near her father – they usually sit next to the mother or
away from the whole group.) In two such cases we issued
instructions, without further explanations, that entailed face-

to-face encounters between father and daughter long enough to provoke clarifying reactions. Now in both cases our orders were greeted with ill-concealed delight by the daughter who was no doubt hoping that her father would at last make good the promise of his glances with some sort of beatific dialogue. What happened was the precise opposite.

One of the two fathers, who found himself trapped with his daughter in a small seaside flat for a whole week, shut up like a clam except to break the silence from time to time with: 'Wouldn't it be lovely if Mummy were here with us!' and scotched any attempt on his daughter's part to get him to join her in various activities. Everything would have to be deferred until that glorious moment when Mummy would join them!...

The other father, who had proved even more underhand in his secret communications with his daughter, was filled with immediate panic by our instructions. As soon as the much maligned wife, whom he had called a simpleton and a gossip, returned home after her prescribed holiday, he burst into tears like a baby (he was the efficient manager of a large business!). In his daughter's presence he pulled his wife close to him and implored her with further tears never to abandon him again; never to make him suffer as he had suffered during her two weeks' absence. During the session following this dramatic scene, we observed that the meaningful glances between father and daughter had come to an end. The father, clinging to his 'legal' wife like a drowning man, shouted at the daughter to leave them in peace and to get on with her own life. The wife, so unexpectedly showered with appreciation, rallied to his side, and the daughter, incensed as only a woman can be who has for years been fooled by the wrong man, was for the first time in her life confronted by a fully united couple and made to realize that she could no longer importune them with her own problems.

Such observations are, of course, not new to psychiatry, for they can also be made during individual therapy, and quite especially in the analysis of transference phenomena. What is new, however, is the strategy of trying to bring matters quickly into the open without having to put them into words.

In fact, once we accept a cybernetic definition of the family, that is once we see it as 'a self-regulating system obeying certain rules', we are immediately in possession of quite novel therapeutic instruments.

In the two cases I have just described it did not take the therapists long to realize that one of the unspoken rules of the system was *the taboo against seeing the relationship between father and daughter in its true light, and hence against metacommunications about this topic.* Now, had the therapists been imprudent enough to reveal the obvious redundancies in the behaviour of father and daughter, and had they metacommunicated these observations to them, they would have been greeted with a series of disqualifications or blunt denials. Nor is that all. Because of our moralistic cultural background, such revelations, though expressed with neutral benevolence, are bound to be treated as so many accusations. The inevitable feedbacks are totally counter-productive and impede therapeutic progress.

Hence therapists and observers must keep their own counsel about their observations and use them to devise an appropriate intervention strategy, that is a set of *concrete* directives intended to explode one of the secret rules responsible for the malfunction of the system as a homeostatic unit. Only when this has been achieved can the therapist begin to intercommunicate about it meaningfully and hope to have his observations confirmed.

Interventions into the problem of blame-shifting

In all our interventions we take great care not to accuse anybody, however, indirectly, and least of all the parents. Even when exceptional circumstances (that are becoming rarer) have forced us to expose a particularly dramatic situation, we have confined our attempts to revealing certain secret rules that stand in the way of honest communication and perpetuate ambiguities and confusion (as when Emilia described her bitter resentment as 'love'). Experience has taught us to rely increasingly on the method of *positive connotation*, that is to attribute constructive intentions to the kind of interpersonal behaviour that is commonly described as destructive or injurious. We realize that in using the term 'positive' we fall into a linguistic trap, since such antinomies as good–bad, positive–negative, etc. have no place in our cybernetic model. But such is the moralistic climate of our age that, to make ourselves understood, we have, for lack of anything better, to continue using the old terms.

To clarify this point I can do no better than mention an actual example of positive connotation which helped us, *inter alia*, to thwart a dangerous manœuvre on the part of one of our patients.

The reader may have gathered by now that anorexic patients (and not they alone!) are extremely skilful in presenting their parents in the worst possible light. They often do this by inciting them to act in ways that are bound to be disapproved of by others. If the therapists allow themselves to be caught in this trap, they may seriously endanger the further course of the treatment.

Thus, during the first family interview, one patient skilfully brought the discussion round to her premorbid phase, and quickly succeeded in getting her parents to express antiquated and repressive views on sexual matters that showed them up as old fogeys united only in their determination to thwart their daughter's nascent sexuality. The therapists, far from swallowing the bait, proceeded to make favourable comments on the parents' obvious fascination with their daughter's feminine charms, and on the way in which they had succeeded in driving these charms home to the patient herself. They would certainly not have acted in the way they did had they thought her anything but highly desirable. In fact their assessment of the situation was one with which the patient must have been in full agreement. Why else had she always been so loyal to them and never used even the slightest subterfuge to defy their prohibitions?

As a result of such interventions all members of the family are put on a single plane. This enables the therapist to fit their interactions into the model, which automatically excludes all arbitrary causal punctuations. In fact, in the present case, who is to say which member of the family 'caused' the actual situation? Did the parents impede their daughter's sexual development with their fears? Or did the daughter herself start the whole process by signalling her own fears to them in one way or another? The only thing we can see, and quite clearly so, in the here and now of our family sessions, is that the entire family collaborates in maintaining the *status quo*, notwithstanding their accusations and counter-accusations which merely serve to harden self-defensive and rigid attitudes (including the depressive manœuvre, especially on the part of the parents, of throwing up their hands in despair so as to convince the therapists that it is quite impossible to change people as set in their ways as they are).

Positive connotation of transactional behaviour is to us the golden road for entering, and being freely admitted into, the system, *and changing it in due course. This is no less true of the system as a whole than it is of the patient's symptom.* For it is impossible to prescribe what has previously been criticized. Thus treating the anorexic symptom as a deliberate display of 'badness' can only lead to immediate disqualification – the patient will always insist that it is not that she does not *want* to eat but that she simply *cannot*. If, by contrast, we give a positive connotation to the symptom and, in each case, stress the 'good' intentions with the help of the particular material offered during the session, we are preparing the way for the paradoxical *prescription of the symptom*. Thus in the case we have been describing we were able, at the end of the very first session, to recommend that the patient (who, in our presence and without being asked to do so, had promised her parents a rapid improvement during her impending Christmas vacation) be extremely cautious in putting on weight. Her emaciation, we explained, was an extremely important protection against a host of fears and dangers with which we fully sympathized. In this way we set up a therapeutic double bind from which the patient could extricate herself only by rebelling against us, which, in the event, meant abandoning her symptom.

This subject of positive connotation is still one to which we have to devote a great deal of further thinking and experimentation, the more so as what is involved is not merely a tactical ploy but also what may turn out to be an important move from a bad to a better epistemology, one that may take us to the very heart of interhuman behaviour. We shall deal with the problem in more detail in the following chapter, see pp. 234–39.

26 *The Cybernetics of Anorexia Nervosa*

Having discussed the analytic approach to families with an anorexic patient, we can now take the final step: a theoretical synthesis based on the cybernetic model.

In systems theory, the family is treated as a whole that cannot be reduced to the sum of the characteristics of its members. What characterizes the family as a system is rather the specific transactional patterns it reflects.

Every family, considered as a transactional system, tends to repeat these patterns with a high frequency and consequently gives rise to redundancies. The latter enable the observer to deduce the rules, often secret and generally implicit, governing the functioning of a given family at a given moment and helping to maintain its stability.

If we define the family as a self-governing system based on rules established through a series of trials and errors, then *its members become so many elements of a circuit in which no one element can be in unilateral control over the rest*. In other words, if the behaviour of any one family member exerts an undue influence on the behaviour of others, it would be an epistemological error to maintain that his behaviour is the *cause* of theirs; rather must we say that his behaviour is the *effect* of past interaction patterns. The study of this type of family transaction is therefore the study of fixed behavioural responses and of their repercussions.

We have spoken of an epistemological error; the latter results from the arbitrary separation of a given behavioural pattern from the pragmatic context of the preceding patterns with which it forms an infinite series.

When I speak of 'epistemology' I am not referring to an esoteric discipline reserved for professional philosophers. Every one of us, by his very being in a world he has to share with others, is bound to take a stand *vis-à-vis* his particular mode of existence, and hence to adopt a certain epistemology.

Again, when I speak of epistemological errors or bad faith, I am referring explicitly to a common error of modern Western culture (and hence of psychiatry): the idea that there is a 'Self' capable of transcending the system of relationships of which it forms a part, and hence of being in unilateral control of the system. For a more detailed analysis, see 'The Cybernetics of "Self": A theory of alcoholism', in G. Bateson (1972).

It follows that even such behaviour patterns as reduce the ostensible victim to impotence are not so much stimuli as responses. In other words both partners in the transaction are mistaken – the manipulator who believes in his omnipotence no less than his apparently powerless victim.

But if both are mistaken, where does the real power lie? It lies in the rules of the game played in the pragmatic context of the behavioural responses of *all* the protagonists, none of whom is capable of changing the rules from the inside.

By defining the patient as a pseudo-victim, we are avoiding the blind alley of moralistic psychiatry. It would appear that R. D. Laing and his school, precisely because they have adopted Sartre's distinction between *praxis* and *process*, have fallen into just this moralistic trap. By contrast, if we treat the family as a system in which no one member can hold unilateral sway over the rest, then praxis and process become synonymous. 'Persecutor' and 'victim' become so many moves in one and the same game, the rules of which neither one can alter from within – all changes depend on strategic interventions from without.

In the particular case of a family with an anorexic patient, we find that the epistemological error of the whole group is that all of them believe that the patient, *because* of her symptom, wields power over the rest and renders them helpless. If we were to take a snapshot during the very first therapeutic session, we should see an anguished expression on the parents' faces, the patient sitting apart from the rest, straight as a statue, pallid and detached, her face showing utter indifference to the others' distress. Her behaviour is a clear message, not least to the therapist: 'If you think you can get me to break my fast, you'll have to think again. Just look at me: I am nothing but skin and bones and I might easily die. And if death is the price I have to pay for *my power*, then I shall willingly pay it.'

This shows that the patient completely misjudges her own situation. To begin with, she is prey to a most disastrous Cartesian dichotomy: *she believes that her mind transcends her body* and that it grants her unlimited power over her own behaviour and that of others. The result is a reification of the 'self' and the mistaken belief that the patient is engaged in a victorious battle on two fronts, namely against:
1) her body, and
2) the family system.

Now this error could not be called a mental illness, were the patient to adopt it voluntarily and were she to declare quite openly that she will take no food until she gets what she wants. This would constitute a rational choice on her part, not a 'mental condition'. Instead the anorexic sticks rigidly to the family rule that *no one member may assume leadership in his own name*. That is precisely why she derives her powers from an abstraction: her illness. It is the latter which wields power, afflicts her own body and makes others suffer for it. Like every mental symptom, the 'anorexic' symptom, too, is a paradox oscillating between two illusory poles: spontaneity and coercion.

This raises the following problem: does the symptom indicate that the patient does not *want* to eat (spontaneity) or does it rather show that she *cannot* (coercion)? If we take the epistemological view we have just adumbrated, then we must answer both questions in the affirmative. The anorexic herself, however, insists that only the second alternative is correct, that is that she really *cannot* eat.

In dealing with such patients, the psychotherapist must therefore pay careful heed to:
1) the false epistemology shared by all the family members, that the patient is in unilateral control of the whole system;
2) the patient's belief that her *self* (or *mind*) transcends her body and the system, and that she can wage a successful battle on two fronts;
3) the fact that this battle is never waged in the first person, but in the name of an abstraction: the disease for which the patient cannot be held responsible;

4) that this abstraction is considered 'evil' because it inflicts suffering on all concerned.

The therapist must devise his strategies accordingly and, in particular, he must aim at correcting the false epistemology underlying all these phenomena. But how is he to do that? By academic discussions, by communicating his insights or by critical remarks? If he takes any of these courses, he will, as we have found to our cost, be sent away with a flea in his ear. What he must rather do is, first of all, reduce all members of the system to the same level, that is assign them symmetrical places in the system. Having observed the prevailing communication patterns, and avoiding the temptation of participating in any of the mutual recriminations, he will make it a point, and one that never fails, to approve unreservedly of all transactional behaviour patterns he observes. We refer to this type of intervention as 'positive connotation', and the therapist must extend it to even those forms of behaviour that traditional psychiatry or psychoanalysis pillories as destructive or harmful. Irritated though he may be by overprotectiveness, encroachment, parental fear of filial autonomy, he must always describe them as expressions of love, or of the understandable desire to maintain the unity of a family exposed to so much stress and the threat of dissolution.

In much the same way he must also lend a positive connotation to the patient's symptom. To that end, he will use what material he has collected to prove that the patient keeps sacrificing herself, albeit unwittingly, for a completely unselfish end: the cause of family unity.

This first and fundamental step in the practice of *positive connotation* is full of implicit messages:
1) The therapist ensures or consolidates his superior position on the hierarchial scale. This is because, in Western culture at least, a disapproving authority casts doubts on its self-assurance (as witness those pseudo-authorities who dispense punishments and prohibitions for the sole purpose of making their presence felt). An approving authority, by contrast, and one, moreover, that explains the motives of its approbation, is clearly one that has no doubts about its rationality.
2) The therapist shows that the entire group is engaged in a single pursuit, namely the preservation of the unity and stability

of the family. This connotation, however, introduces an implicit absurdity: how can something so wonderful and normal as family unity exact so abnormally high a price as anorexia?

3) The therapist gently displaces the patient from her customary position to one that is complementary in the game, and, in so doing, alters the respective roles of all the members: he shows that the patient is so sensitive and generous that she *cannot help* sacrificing herself for her family, much as the others *cannot help* sacrificing themselves for the same ends.

4) The therapist keeps stressing the compulsive nature of the symptom ('the patient cannot help sacrificing herself') but takes care to underplay the 'harmful' aspect by defining the symptom as something 'beneficial' to the whole system. At the same time he also defines as 'symptoms' the behaviour patterns of the other family members (they, too, 'cannot help themselves' if the family is to stay together) and gives these 'symptoms' the same positive connotation.

The way is now open for the decisive therapeutic step: the therapeutic paradox. The symptom, defined as essential to family stability, is *prescribed* to the patient by the therapist, who advises her to continue limiting her food intake, at least for the time being. The relatives, for their part, are also instructed to persist in their customary behaviour patterns.

The result is a situation that is paradoxical in several respects, the first of which is quite obvious: the family has consulted the therapist and is paying him for the sole purpose of ridding the patient of her symptom, and all he apparently does in return is not only to approve of this symptom but actually to prescribe it!

Moreover the therapist, by prescribing the symptom, implicitly rejects it as such. Instead, he prescribes it as a spontaneous action which the patient cannot, however, perform spontaneously, and this precisely because it has been prescribed. Hence the patient is driven into a corner from which she can only escape by rebelling against the therapist, that is by abandoning her symptom. In that case she may return to her next session looking better, only to find that the therapist fails to reprove her – yet another paradox.

A series of such moves proved so successful with three patients during the very first session, that they soon afterwards dropped their symptom. In general, however, we prefer to hasten more

slowly. Active tactical interventions designed quite specifically
to elicit significant responses from the family have been described
in the last chapter, but as our work has advanced, and with it
our understanding of the epistemological error responsible for
the malfunctioning of such families, we have gone on to devise
other tactics.

The most important and effective of these is the one that
follows the cybernetic model more closely. It calls for the
prescription of family rituals. Let me mention two concrete
examples.

The first family to whom we applied the new strategy was not
one with an anorexic member, but one with a six-and-a-half-
year-old son whose aggressive behaviour bordered on the
psychotic. I mention it here because it is so clear-cut.

The child, whose EEG had shown minimal brain damage,
was brought to family therapy when a child psychoanalyst
refused to continue his treatment. The child seemed totally
inaccessible to psychoanalytic approaches and, moreover,
intolerably hostile. After four sessions with the parents, two
in the presence of the child, the therapists realized that, apart
from being exposed to intense interparental conflicts, the child
had been forced into a double bind situation from which he
could not extricate himself. Labelled 'sick' by the neurologists
and having been doctored with massive doses of sedatives, he
was treated like a maniac at home and hence allowed to behave in a way that no parents would have taken from normal
children: vicious kicks at the mother's face as she bent down
to tie his shoelaces; lunges with the table-knife; plates of soup
over the mother's dress, etc. By contrast he was invariably
treated to long sermons and reproaches about his past misdeeds
whenever he behaved like a normal child of his age. The therapists saw quickly that their first move must be the eradication
of this double bind situation, and this by destroying the parents'
conviction that their child was 'mental'. But they also realized
that they could not achieve this end by verbal explanations,
which would have been disqualified there and then. Instead
they decided to prescribe the following family ritual: that same
evening, after supper, the entire family, consisting of the father,
the mother, the patient, his little sister and the maternal
grandmother, would go in procession to the bathroom, the

father carrying all the child's medicine bottles and solemnly addressing the following words to his son: 'Today we were told by the doctors that we must throw all these medicines away because you are perfectly well. All you are is a naughty child, and we simply won't take any more of your nonsense.' Thereupon he would pour the contents of the bottles, one by one and with great ceremony, down the lavatory, all the time repeating: 'You are perfectly well.' This ritual proved so effective (notwithstanding the mother's fears that the child would kill her without his sedatives) that it led to the disappearance of the aggressive behaviour and, soon afterwards, to an amicable solution of the secret interparental conflicts (ten sessions).

Another ritual, this time repetitive, was prescribed to a family with a grave anorexic patient, whom we shall call Nora, and who, during the course of family therapy, had tried to commit suicide so effectively that she had to be resuscitated. This attempt showed that her therapists had made a serious miscalculation: they had focused attention so exclusively on her nuclear family as to miss the secret rule that nothing but good must be spoken of any members of Nora's extended family, a close-knit and powerful clan. It was only during the dramatic session following Nora's suicide attempt that her elder sister dropped some vague remarks about Nora's particularly 'difficult' relations with one of her female cousins. Apparently the latter, backed by her mother, and envious of Nora's undoubted good looks, treated Nora with a mixture of affection and great cruelty. Both parents immediately hastened to repair the damage by harping at length on the angelic goodness of the cousin, 'a real sister to our Nora'. This caused Nora, who had never before mentioned the cousin to us, to speak of her throughout the rest of the session. She had clearly come to distrust her own feelings: if the cousin seemed spiteful and nasty, it was, no doubt, because she, Nora, was herself spiteful, envious and bad.

In their meeting after the session, the therapists decided to keep their new knowledge to themselves, and not to engage in what were bound to be futile discussions. Instead they decided to prescribe the following ritual.

In the fortnight before the next session, Nora's family would lock the front door immediately after dinner on alternate days, and sit round the table for an hour. A clock would be placed in the middle of the table, and every family member, in order of seniority, would have fifteen minutes to vent his own feelings and views, not least about other members of the clan. While any one was speaking the rest must not interrupt, let alone contradict. Moreover, whatever was said at the table must not be discussed outside the fixed ritual hour.

In this case, too, the ritual proved so effective that the treatment could be terminated in a total of fifteen sessions.

We can now explain what precisely we mean by family ritual.

From a *formal* point of view, a family ritual is an action, or a series of actions, accompanied by verbal formulae and involving the entire family. Like every ritual it must consist of a regular sequence of steps taken at the right time and in the right place.

Ritualization may smack of the magical or the religious, but this is not necessarily a disadvantage. It should, however, be stressed that the idea of prescribing a ritual was originally suggested by ethology, and quite particularly by certain intraspecific submission rituals whose sole purpose it is to convey placatory messages. The primary *aim* is to cure the patient with the help of a group engaged in a common task, that is the performance of the ritual.

We have found that the physical enactment of a ritual is infinitely more productive of positive change than any form of verbalization can hope to be. To return to one of our examples, had we merely told the parents of our little 'maniac' that their son was not really ill, and that they must not treat him as an invalid, we should never have effected so rapid a cure. But by uniting the whole family in a carefully prescribed ritual, culminating in the destruction of the child's medicines, to the repeated cry of 'You are perfectly well', we were able to introduce a powerful collective motive and hence a new *normative system*. In that sense the ritual may be said to work because it persuades the whole group to strive towards a common goal.

In this connection I must stress the widespread use of rituals in modern China. These do not consist of verbal formulae and slogans to which the individual can turn a deaf ear through selective inattention, but try to foster the idea of social and family co-operation by means of dances, plays and other public entertainments including, paradoxically enough, a whole range of competitive sports.

The 'invention' of a family ritual invariably calls for a great creative effort on the part of the therapist and often, if I may say so, for flashes of genius, if only because a ritual that has proved effective in one family is unlikely to prove equally effective in another. This is because every family follows special *rules* and plays special *games*. In particular, *a ritual is not a form of metacommunication about these rules, let alone about these games; rather it is a kind of counter-game* which, once played, destroys the original game. In other words it leads to the replacement of an unhealthy and epistemologically false rite (for example the anorexic symptom) by one that is healthy and epistemologically sound.

I am absolutely convinced that mental 'symptoms' arise in rigid homeostatic systems, and that they are the more intense the more secret is the cold war waged by the sub-system (parent–child coalitions). We know that such pathological systems are governed by secret rules that shun the light of day and bind the family together with pathological ties.

In other words psychiatric 'symptoms' tend to develop in family systems threatened with collapse; in such systems they play the same part as submission rites play in the animal kingdom: they help to ward off aggression from one's own kind. There is just this tragic difference: the specific human rite, called 'illness', acquires its *normative* function from the very malfunction it is trying to eliminate.

At this point I feel that I ought to summarize the central conceptions guiding our recent research, the better to bring out the difference between it and my earlier approach.

We have tried to establish whether or not families with an anorexic patient function as a typical model system that, at a given moment, gives the patient no choice but to take refuge in her anorexic symptom.

As described in Chapter 24 our research had a number of objectives and motives including:
1) shift of the psychiatric focus of attention from the artificially isolated individual to the wider context of the institutional relationship in which he is involved;

2) my special concern with the problem of anorexia nervosa, thanks to which my services have been sought by a very large number of families with an anorexic member and which has enabled me to accumulate a very considerable body of data;

3) The extremely monotonous clinical picture of anorexia nervosa, which suggested that it ought to be possible to find variables less complex and less numerous than those associated with other psychiatric syndromes, for example the schizophrenic.

It was mainly the well-known work of J. Haley with schizophrenic families that provided us with a methodological research model, or, more preciesly, with parameters more suited to describing the family as an interactional system. These parameters are derived from systems theory, the pragmatics of human communication and cybernetics.

At the Milan Family Study Centre our team has been able to study twelve families with an anorexic member, treating each family as a single unit functioning as a system in which:

1) there is a willingness to communicate;

2) every member of the system generally defines himself in the relationship in a coherent manner;

3) every member rejects the messages of others (either on the content or the relationship level) with a high frequency. The rejection of food, which the patient finally expresses in her symptoms, seems to be specifically adapted to the interactional modality prevalent in her family: the symptom seems moreover to be specifically attuned not only to the repeated act of rejection, which thus constitutes one 'redundancy', but also to another. During the sessions we usually observe that the parents will insist on defining the relationship to their daughter as one between 'feeders' and 'fed'. The daughter, by contrast, will define the relationship in the opposite way, and this precisely through her anorexic behaviour which helps her to gain the upper hand in the fundamental human problem of who defines the relationship for whom. This redefinition is not made by using the first person singular, but in the name of the illness, that is of a condition that is shrewdly presented in the customary moralistic and sacrificial tone of the family group. This explains why these patients so regularly make it their business to cook for the rest of the family, thus presenting themselves as 'feeders';

4) all family members have great difficulty in playing the role of leader overtly:

5) all open alliances of any two againstthe third are proscribed;

6) no one member will take the blame for anything.

As for the peculiar interactional modality of the parental couple, we have defined it as one of 'symmetry through sacrificial escalation'.

In chapter 25, devoted to the therapeutic method, we have given a brief account of the techniques designed to change the mode in which anorexic families function. The parameters we have chosen to define the system have also suggested the best tactics for changing it.

The results have proved to be much more rapid and encouraging than those obtained through individual treatment: in the twelve families we have treated, five patients abandoned their symptoms within less than ten sessions; four in less than twenty sessions; and three broke off their treatment because of grave errors on our part.

Not only did the patients abandon their systems, but their families began to function in a new way.

Of course these conclusions are tentative, since only follow-ups can tell us whether the improvements are either lasting or, as we hope, stepping stones on the road to further progress.

With two families we were brought face to face with the problem of a pathogenic interaction between the nuclear and the extended family. In both cases we found it necessary to devise intervention tactics designed to break this pathogenic pattern.

This opens up a new vista based on Watzlawick's claim that 'a phenomenon remains unexplainable as long as the range of observation is not wide enough to include the context in which the phenomenon occurs'. In other words family therapy is the starting point for the study of ever wider social units.

27 *The Family of the Anorexic and the Social Environment*

Our twelve families all shared one major characteristic: they tried to preserve agricultural-patriarchal values, roles, rules and taboos in an urban-industrial setting.

According to this particular ethos the greatest of all qualities is self-sacrifice: the more self-effacement and self-denial an action demands, the more praiseworthy it must be. Conversely, any form of self-indulgence is considered reprehensible. The family is conceived as a unit for survival, both individual and collective, a conception akin to that of the so-called 'exclusive' family still found in some agricultural and pastoral areas of Sardinia.

The collective sense of the family is so pronounced that the individual is pushed into the backgorund. There is a tendency to stick together like a brood of ducklings. Enjoyment is acceptable so long as no one is excluded: the suffering of any one imposes sadness and mortification on the others. Yet of the twelve families in question only one had an authentic agricultural-patriarchal background. The parents had lived in the Tuscan Maremma and the father kept a tight feudal rein over his five married sons, daughters-in-law and numerous grand-children like the traditional *capoccia* he was. The sons had to marry in order of age; their choice of a wife had to be approved; precedence among the wives depended on how long they had been members of the family. The youngest son married a seamstress from the nearby town whose life was one long martyrdom; she came last in the hierarchy of her 'predecessors', and was completely incapable of rebelling against the iron laws of the clan. During the agricultural crisis that followed the

Second World War, and after the death of the old *capoccia*, the family left the countryside and moved to the city, where the five brothers set up a small construction company. They all lived in the same house, though in separate apartments. The two daughters of the youngest son both developed anorexia on reaching adolescence. The remaining eleven families we treated had spent their entire lives in industrial areas, and so had their parents.

These twelve families had the following socio-economic background: one, as we saw, was of peasant stock; another was working-class with lower middle-class aspirations; four were lower middle-class (office workers, craftsmen), six were middle-class (professional men, company directors, small manufacturers). On marriage, ten of the wives withdrew from all outside activities, even though two were university graduates and some of the others held diplomas. Two continued to work outside the home, for which they were criticized by their husbands, children and extended families; as a result they both went to exaggerated lengths to make up for the 'sin' of not being full-time housewives. The fact that they were gainfully employed, when there was no financial need to be so, apparently deprived them of any right to enjoy themselves in their spare time. All the fathers stated explicitly that in their opinion a 'real' wife must dedicate all her time to her husband, children and the well-being of the family. They also showed a common tendency to minimize the difficulties and monotony of housework, made it clear that their wives were economically dependent on them, and kept them in line by the infallible method of conveying their dissatisfaction as often as possible. The wives revealed three types of attitude to their roles:

1) reluctant adaptation, based on fear of blame, and reflected in anxiety about the performance of their chores, which, however, were never openly said to be intolerable;

2) martyr-like adaptation, based on secret resentment and expressed through gross inefficiency, refusal to accept even the smallest responsibility, physical complaints, depressive states and excessive spending, not on themselves but on the children (medicines, clothes);

3) total dedication, reflected in intolerance, perfectionism and rituals (meals, order, punctuality, manners).

These attitudes by husbands and wives alike seem to reflect the mores of a changing culture. The battle of the sexes has been joined, but the two contenders are still a long way from being able to discuss their differences frankly and fearlessly and reaching an explicit and mutually satisfactory compromise. The parents of all our families were rooted in the old ways, and deeply attached to their original families and to their mothers in particular. In fact, in nine cases out of the twelve, the grandmothers played some part, or even the major part, in the family disorder. Since the fathers were unsure of themselves and afraid of independent women, they mostly chose wives from respectable families, attached or submissive to their own parents, conservative, and often reactionary. In this way they obtained partners of whom they had no reason to feel afraid, but who had numerous shortcomings. Intelligence, adaptability, culture, imagination, interests, were so many qualities that undoubtedly appealed to the fathers but were unlikely to be found in women of the type they had married. And it was only after marriage that they first became painfully aware of defects that ought to have struck them right from the start. The mothers, too, had a low opinion of themselves, which induced them to seek a higher social status and a valid identity in marriage and in the traditional role of wife and mother. They paid no heed to the clamour for women's liberation, the agitation against the humiliation of unpaid household drudgery, and so on, that is, to the woman's right to a status of her own, parallel to, but not strictly identical with, her husband's. According to the patriarchal code, the family is the main, or even the only, means of survival, and therefore has to be both powerful and stable. This calls for a strict division of labour, with husband and wife occupying the one-up and one-down positions respectively. A series of generally accepted rules is applied to the few situations and areas of activity in which the switching of roles is permissible. (*I libri della Famiglia*, written by the fifteenth century humanist Leon Battista Alberti, attributes the one-up position to women only in respect of the early upbringing of the children.) These rules have been handed down from generation to generation in a cultural environment whose political and social changes have left the traditional model of family organization largely untouched.

In pre-industrial society the fundamental structure was the extended or patriarchal family: human existence was generally confined to a small local circle, in which the individual had a precise social status determined by his birth and the position of his family. This in turn had an authoritarian structure headed by the eldest son, on whom wife, children, sons- and daughters-in-law, grandchildren, collaterals, etc., all depended.

The socio-cultural training of the individual was, in the great majority of cases, entrusted entirely and solely to the family, much as roles and functions were assigned in accordance with the structure of the family group. Generally, all members of the family lived together, and developed their working skills – agriculture, handicrafts, commerce, etc. – within the family. The family thus constituted the framework in which the individual acquired his social status, education and social training, did his work, and spent his leisure. Social relations were confined to a fairly small social unit (pre-industrial towns, villages) and consisted mainly of contacts with neighbouring families, and family property and wealth were the keys to power in these relationships. From the bonds between ruling families down to the bonds between the humblest village families, the family constituted the connective tissue of society, and this was so even during the early phase of industrialization, when the ownership and management of factories (though not the industrial labour) were still provided by the family.

In these circumstances, it is obvious that great trouble had to be taken to preserve the maximum strength, continuity and integration of the family, even at the cost of individual liberty. The rights of inheritance and primo-geniture, the authoritarian relationship between parents and children, the subordination of women, sexual ethics, and professional rules all served to ensure that the family functioned as smoothly as possible, thus guaranteeing the solidity and harmony of the social order. (F. Crespi)

But with the advent of the industrial age, radical socio-economic changes took their toll of the patriarchal family and, *inter alia*, began to bring the battle of the sexes into the open. This phenomenon first entered Western Europe, the cradle of industrial civilization, towards the middle of the nineteenth century. Significantly enough the earliest clinically impeccable accounts of that typically feminine illness, anorexia nervosa, appeared in 1873, from the pens of Gull and Lasègue, who worked in London and Paris respectively, two cities in the grip of a cultural crisis. It should also be remembered that the

patients of Gull and Lasègue were drawn from the relatively
well-to-do (it is unlikely that this type of illness would have
affected people living below the breadline). By 1873 the fem-
inist movement had already proclaimed that women were an
exploited social class and was making significant progress.
During the French Revolution Olympe de Gouges had founded
two Women's Clubs and had submitted a 'Declaration of
Women's Rights' to the Constituent Assembly. (She was, however, bitterly opposed by Robespierre and executed in 1793.)
In England, women won the right to vote in municipal elections
in 1869; by 1873 they were already fighting for universal
suffrage. The conviction that women had a natural right to
participate in public life spread so swiftly that in 1903 Emme-
line Pankhurst was able to found the 'Women's Social and
Political Union', which vigorously campaigned for, and finally
achieved, women's suffrage. During this transitional period it
was inevitable that the traditional roles of men and women
should be called into question, especially by the new middle
class, in which women were enjoying an increasingly higher
level of education.

While agricultural families continued for decades to be
oblivious to these changes, families living in industrial towns
were confronted with a host of new difficulties. As so often
happens, artists and novelists preceded psychiatrists and sociologists in providing shrewd and skilful descriptions of family
life in a changing society. I need only mention Thomas Mann's
first novel, *Buddenbrooks*, the story of a leading merchant
family during the second half of the nineteenth century,
every member of which was a pathetic victim of radical changes
he vaguely sensed all around him but could not even begin
to understand.

Since then the crisis has become more acute and at the same
time more extensive, involving increasingly larger sectors of
Western culture. The status of women has improved and in so
doing has changed that of men. But every such change produces
resistance and nostalgia for the 'good old days', causing a
widespread *malaise* in both men and women. Catherine Valabrègue, in a recent article entitled 'Freeing women means
freeing men', had this to say:

Why does female emancipation cause so much disquiet among men?

There must be good reasons why men should fear it and try to halt it with a series of taboos and traditional notions. Here are some of them. Woman have hitherto been considered chiefly in relation to men, but society is rapidly moving towards a reversal of their respective roles. Men did not take the initiative in emancipating women, and hence view this situation as an attack on the traditional concept of virility. Like 'the new woman', man lacks the appropriate images or models, and it will be some generations before there is a change in our conception of virility and femininity.

Only after we have come to realize that a woman remains a woman, and a man a man, even when their behaviour differs from the traditional models, will it be possible to establish a lucid and fraternal dialogue between them. And finally, man has not yet recognized the advantages that will accrue to him from everything that contributes to the betterment of the lot of women. And are women themselves ready for the independence that many of them demand? Are they ready to live with a 'liberated' man and to share with him all the responsibilities that he has always borne, in political, economic, professional and family life? Few of them are. Women must still learn what freedom really means, just as men must learn to change, to accept a new type of relationship with women. No change or progress is ever free of risk. But perhaps this is one risk worth taking.

Catherine Valabrègue is perfectly right, of course, but I should like to complement her remarks with my own findings. The essence of the matter is not that the risk is 'worth taking', but that it is the only way of survival. Let me try to make this point clear. The family system, like every natural system, tends towards homeostasis. However, no living system can survive unless it is free to evolve, to change when conditions change. In the family this evolution is the result of stimuli from within (individual members or alliances of members) or from without (changes in the social environment). To take some simple examples: a family system can be stimulated to change from within when a child reaches adolescence and demands new modes of family interaction. It can be stimulated from without by the economic activity of women. A family system becomes moribund if it has so rigid a homeostatic tendency as to preclude even the slightest positive feedback of stimuli from within or without (rigidly morphostatic family system). On the other hand it will cease to exist (as a system)

I

if it allows itself to be drawn into indiscriminate changes to the point of losing its *raison d'être* (dissolution of the family). The danger of such dissolution in the wake of indiscriminate acceptance of change stimuli (even if they are valid) is particularly great in revolutionary movements. To be creative a revolution must be selective. Its leaders must be able to rely on certain homeostatic components of the system or else court total chaos. Thus Olympe de Gouges' 'Declaration of Women's Rights' came at an inopportune moment, since it threatened a 'revolution within a revolution', thus weakening indispensable homeostatic components (the traditional subordination of women).

Finally a family, like any natural group, can conserve its homeostatic tendency and yet be pliable enough to open itself gradually to stimuli that permit it to evolve without carrying it over the brink of dissolution (morphogenetic system). Only in this way can the system hope to continue, which would seem to bear out my contention that the risks involved are not simply 'worth taking' but essential if the family is to survive. Yet throughout history the family has always served as a homeostatic barrier against social change, and never before has it had to face more rapid and radical changes than today. Hence the universal feeling of *malaise* with which modern family life is suffused.

This power of the family to serve as a homeostatic barrier is one of which all revolutionists have always been aware and the reason why they rely so strongly on the young in their attempts to change family and social conditions. J. Haley, in his 'The Power and Tactics of Jesus Christ' (1969), mentions this as one of Christ's own tactics. Haley considers Christ the great precursor and teacher of all leaders of mass movements. On the role played by the family he had this to say:

The conservative force of the family is an impediment to any mass movement, and only after becoming the establishment does a revolutionary group call for family solidity. The precedent for twentieth century movements' separating the follower from his family resides in the statement of Jesus when he says: 'Think not that I am come to send peace on earth: I came not to send peace, but a sword. For I am come to set a man at variance against his father, and the daughter against her mother, and the daughter-in-law against her

mother-in-law. And a man's foes shall be they of his own household.' (Matt. 10:4–36.) And Jesus also said: 'He that loveth father or mother more than me is not worthy of me: and he that loveth son or daughter more than me is not worthy of me.' (Matt. 10:37)

Our research has shown that families with anorexic patients have a particularly stubborn resistance to change, regardless of whether the stimuli come from within the family or from without. The anorexic patient seems to be a tragically ambiguous emitter of interfamilial change stimuli. On the one hand her symptoms represent an 'invocation' of a change in the relationship but, on the other hand, that 'invocation' is expressed in the elusive language of analogic communication. The illness is, in fact, an all-embracing message involving a series of contradictions. The patient:

1) rebels without appearing to be rebellious;
2) revenges herself without appearing to be vengeful;
3) punishes without appearing to punish;
4) does not explicity state that her parents are responsible for her condition but allows it to be vaguely suspected;
5) causes a crisis in the family system by placing it in a situation from which there is no escape, thus encouraging homeostasis;
6) papers over the cracks in her parents' relationship by compelling them to join forces to deal with her illness;
7) protects herself against any risk of changes in herself.

We are therefore entitled to ask whether anorexia nervosa may not be considered a social illness in the sense that it is specifically bound up with certain socio-cultural situations. To give a reasoned answer to this question we should first have to make a systematic survey of a number of factors, for example the relative incidence of anorexia nervosa in urban and rural, in industrial and non-industrial and developed or underdeveloped regions, and of the social class of the patient herself and her parents and grandparents. In addition we should have to express the frequency of anorexia in a particular region as a percentage of the total female population of that region, and again of the eleven-to-twenty-five-years age group.

How can these data be obtained? The admission records of psychiatric and general hospitals cannot form the basis of such a survey because they are difficult to check, and because a very large number of patients are treated at home.

In my own case it might very well be that the increase in the number of anorexia nervosa patients I myself have been seeing is due simply to the fact that I have specialized in that illness.

But I hasten to add that, while I used to think that the prevalence of families with anorexic patients treated at our Centre was due to the reputation I had acquired in this field, the increase in the variety of psychiatric illnesses that the Centre is asked to treat rather suggests that families with an anorexic patient are more inclined to seek therapeutic help and to persevere in it than families with patients showing different symptoms, for example infantile neuroses, and schizophrenic or characteropathic syndromes. This might be due to the high blame-conferring power of a symptom that can lead to death, the more so as it is a well-known fact that hospitalization rarely brings more than temporary, if any, relief, and generally tends to cause a deterioration in the anorexic's state. The hospitalized schizophrenic patient, on the other hand, poses a far less serious threat to the family system, which promptly adapts itself to a situation that does not involve the drama of death. In Italy at least it would thus seem that, in the present cultural climate of prejudice against family therapy, it is the anorexic patient who has the greatest power to induce her family to undergo therapy. It should also be remembered that this type of family has a more pronounced 'sacrifical' tendency.

In addition I have a number of interesting outside observations which, however, need still to be checked. An academic psychologist, who spent a year at a Psychopedagogic Centre which screens practically all cases of mental disturbance reported by secondary schools (eleven to fifteen years) in the province of Bergamo, told me she had not encountered a single case of anorexia nervosa during her term of office. This is a highly interesting observation since in Bergamo agricultural-patriarchal family patterns are still the general rule, and the children are given a traditional religious education that tends to identify the role of women with family and household work.

On the other hand a lady who has taught for twenty-two years in a secretarial school in Milan has told me that cases of extreme 'slimming mania' are rapidly increasing in number.

During the last three years, in addition to a large number of relatively mild cases (but in which the exaggerated weight control went hand in hand with obvious psychic disorders), she has encountered five evident cases of grave anorexia nervosa in a total of about 120 pupils. My own impression is that anorexia nervosa is on the increase in Italy and that it is spreading from the North to the Central South, and from the middle- to the urban lower-middle and working-classes. This is corroborated by our twelve families who, though drawn from different social strata, all reflected the contradictions and conflicts of a changing society. *However, this concomitance does not necessarily imply the existence of a causal relationship.* The same could be said of another phenomenon which is highly indicative of the contradictions of modern culture: the fact that the affluent society discourages women from satisfying their appetites, holds up a kind of unisex body as a model, and forces them to make complicated dietetic calculations and to engage in undesirable ascetic practices.

In these circumstances it is surprising that only a very small minority of girls who adopt such practices should develop anorexia nervosa. At the 1965 World Congress on Anorexia Nervosa held at Giessen (Germany), M. Pflanz, Professor of Statistical Documentation and Epidemiology in the University of Giessen, had this to say after an analysis of the socio-anthropological aspects of the illness:

While, as we say, there are no broad social structures that specifically induce anorexia nervosa, the same can certainly not be said about the structure of the family. Psychoanalysis has not yet proved that it can grapple with that structure: it has concentrated on the mother–daughter relationship and has neglected the father, the brothers and sisters, and the relatives. Even social family research has failed to develop methods for dealing with all aspects of the family structure that may throw light on the development of anorexia.

I fully agree with this statement – I started family research precisely so as to bridge the gap between sociology and psychiatry. I fully realize that our current practice of treating the family as a sub-system in relative isolation is a heuristic artifice. This is a shortcoming which, for the time being, I have no means of remedying.

The field of investigation and intervention will undoubtedly have to be enlarged. As J. Haley has put it:

There is an increasing awareness that psychiatric problems are social problems which involve the total ecological system. There is a concern with, and an attempt to change, what happens with the family and also the interlocking systems of the family and the social institutions in which the family is embedded. The fragmentation of the individual into parts or the family into parts is being abandoned, and there is a growing consensus that a new ecological framework *defines problems in new ways and calls for new ways in therapy.* (My italics.)

Bibliography

Accornero, F., 'L'anoressia mentale. Una priorità italiana e l'osservazione di 4 casi', *Riv. sper. fren.*, 67, 447 (1943).

Acht, B., 'Titubanza psichica nella chiusura della bocca', *Min stom.*, 2 (1955).

Adams, J., 'Letter to editor', *Lancet*, 1, 597 (1888).

Aggeler, P. M., Lucia, S. P. and Fishbon, H. M., 'Purpura due to vitamin K deficiency in anorexia nervosa', *Am. J. Digest. Dis.* 9, 227 (1942).

Alberti, L. B., *I libri della famiglia* (Turin: Einaudi 1969).

Aldrich, C. A., 'A type of anorexia seen in runabout children', *Bull. Menninger Clin.*, 8, 185 (1944).

Alexander, F., 'Influence of psychologic factors upon gastrointestinal disturbances, A symposium' *Psychoanal. Quart.*, 3, 501 (1934).

Alexander, G. H., 'Anorexia nervosa', *Rhode Island Med. J.*, 22, 189 (1939).

Alliez, I., Cadaccioni, J. L. and Gomila, L., 'Anorexies mentales masculines', *Ann. méd. Psychol.* 2, 697 (1954).

Allison, R. S. and Davies, R. P., 'Treatment of functional anorexia', *Lancet*, 1, 902 (1931).

— 'Anorexia', *Nutrition Reviews* 271 (11–19 September 1953).

Altschule, M. D., 'Adrenocortical function in anorexia nervosa before and after lobotomy', *New England J. Med.*, 248, 808 (1953).

Amelung, W. and Brandt, A., 'Voraussetzungen und Möglichkeiten der Behandlung hypophysärer Kachexie und verwandter Zustände von Magersucht (Inkretorische Margersucht)', *Ergebn. phys. diät. Ther.*, 2, 45 (1943).

Anand, B. K. and Brobeck, J. R., *J. Neurophysiol.*, 15, 421 (1952).

André-Thomas, 'Anorexie mentale', *La Clinique*, 4, 33 (1909).

Arieti, S., 'The two aspects of schizophrenia', *Psychiat. Quart.* 31, 403 (1947).

Appelstatt, J. C., *De anorexia* (Lugd. Bat. 1686).

— 'The functional psychoses', in *Am. Handbook of Psychiatry* (New York: Basic Books 1959).

Appelstatt, J. C., 'Schizophrenia: the manifest symptomatology, the psychodynamic and formal mechanism', in *Am. Handbook of Psychiatry* (New York: Basic Books 1959).
— 'Recent conceptions and misconceptions of schizophrenia', *Am. J. Psychoth.*, 14, 3 (1960).
— 'A re-examination of the phobic symptom and of symbolism in psychopathology', *Am. J. Psychiat.*, 118, 2 (1961).
Arnhold, M. B., 'Physiological differentiation of emotional states', *Psychol. Rev.*, 52, 35 (1945).
Astles, H. E., 'Anorexia in young girls unaccompanied with visceral disease', *Brit. Med. A. Proc.* (South Australian Branch (1882) p. 31.
Aubry, Thiodet, Raynaud and Odry, 'Un cas d'anorexie mentale', *Algeria méd.*, 39, 715 (1935).
Augier, P. and Cossa, P., 'Anorexie mentale et antéhypophyse', *J. méd. franc.*, 25, 356 (1936).
Aurimond, R., 'Contribution à l'étude de l'anorexia psychopathique', thesis (Toulouse, 1930).
Axenfeld, A. and Huchard, H., *Traité des névroses* (Paris: Baillière 1883), p. 1018.

Baeyer, W. v. '"Metabletica", Bemerkungen zum gleichnamigen, Werke von J. H. van den Berg, zugleich zum Problem der Pubertätsmagersucht', *Nervenarzt*, 30, 81 (1959).
Baher, F., 'Fettsucht und Magersucht', in *Handbuch der Inneren Medizin*, 4, VII/I (Berlin: Springer 1954).
Balen, G. F. van, 'Anorexia nervosa und hypophysäre Magerkeit', *Acta med. scand.*, 101, 433 (1939).
Balestre, A., *Du rôle de l'inanition dans la pathologie*, thesis (Paris, 1875).
Balikov, H., 'Functional impairment of the Sensorium as a result of normal adaptive process', *Psychoanal. Study of the Child*, 15, 235 (1960).
Ballet, G., 'L'anorexie mentale', *Méd. moderne*, 18, 255 (1907).
— 'L'anorexie mentale', *Rev. gén. clin. et thér.*, 21, 293 (1907).
Bonsi, H. W., 'Zur Klinik und Pathogenese der Fettsucht', *Med. Welt.*, 162 (1940).
— *Das Hungerödem und andere alimentare Mangelerkrankungen* (Stuttgart: Enke 1949).
— 'Magerkeit als ganzheitsmedizinisches Problem', *Med. Klin.*, 50, 49 (1955).
Baraldi, M., 'Contributo allo studio della anoressia mentale', *Riv. sper. fren.* 76, 381 (1952).

Barber, H., 'Cases of long continued abstinence from food', *Brit. Med. J.*, 1, 544 (1870).

Barcai, A., 'Family therapy in the treatment of anorexia nervosa', *American Journal of Psychiatry.*, 3, 286–90 (1971).

Bargues, R. and Neuvelglise, D., 'À propos d'un cas d'anorexie mentale', *Evolution psychiatrique*, 2, 293 (1950).

Bartels, E. D., 'Studies on hypometabolism; I. Anorexia nervosa', *Acta med. scand.*, 124, 185 (1946).

Bartlett, W. M., 'An analysis of anorexia', *Am. J. Dis. Child.*, 35, 26 (1928).

Bartstra, H. K. G., 'Een geval van anorexia nervosa', *Nederl. tijdschr. geneesk.*, 92, 750 (1948).

Baruk, H. and Corum, R., 'Un cas de nevrose dysphagique. Analyse psychologique et physiologique. Action thérapeutique du scopo-chloralose', *Ann. méd. psychol.*, 93, 271 (1935).

Basaglia, F., 'L'anoressia mentale è una nevrosi o una psicopatia?', *Med. psicosom.*, 4, 263 (1959).

Bass, F., 'L'amenhorrhée au camp de concentration de Térézin (Theresienstadt)', *Gynaecologia*, 123, 211 (1947).

Bateson, G., *Steps to an ecology of mind* (San Francisco: Chandler 1972).

Bauer, B. and Pohl, W., 'Zur Therapie der Anorexia Nervosa', *Ugeskr. laeger*, 118, 1368 (1956).

Bauer, J., 'Endocrine aspects of sprue: relation to pituitary syndrome in anorexia nervosa', *J. Trop. Med.*, 42, 245 (1939).

Beamelon, J., 'Contribution à l'étude clinique et thérapeutique du syndrome anorexie mentale', thesis (Montpellier 1914).

Beck, J. C., and Brochner-Mortensen, 'Observations on the prognosis in anorexia nervosa', *Acta med. scand.*, 149, 409 (1954).

Beeck, H. R., 'An experimental investigation of sexual symbolism in anorexia nervosa employing a subliminal stimulation technique. Prelimary report', *Psychosom. Med.*, 21, 277 (1959).

Benedek, T., 'Dominant ideas and their relation to morbid cravings', *Int. J. Psycho-Anal.* 17, 40 (1936).

Benedetti, G., 'Zur Kenntnis der Fett-und Magersucht', *Schweiz. med. Wschr.*, 80, 1129 (1950).

— 'Diagnostica e terapia delle cosiddette cachessie psicoendocrine', *La Clin. terapeut.*, 8, 457 (1955).

— *Neuropsicologia* (Milan: Feltrinelli 1969).

Bennet, H., 'Hysterical vomiting', *Lancet*, 2, 295 (1868).

Bergmann, G. von, 'Magerkeit und Magersucht', *Dtsch. med. Wschr.*, 60, 123 and 159 (1934).

— 'Das Streben nach Synthese: wissenschaftliche Medizin und

256 SELF-STARVATION

natürliche Heilweisen', *Dtsch. med. Wschr.*, 64, 455 (1938).
Bergmann, G. von, 'Sheehan's disease', *Postgrad. Med. J.*, 3, 237 (1948).
— 'Die psychogene Magersucht', *Med. Z.*, 1, 41, (1944).
Berkman, J. M., 'Anorexia nervosa, inanition and low basal metabolic rate', thesis (Rochester: Minn. Mayo Foundation March 1930).
— 'Anorexia nervosa, anorexia, inanition and low basal metabolic rate', *Am. J. Sc.*, 180, 411 (1930).
— 'Functional anorexia and functional vomiting: their relation to anorexia nervosa', *M. Clin. North American*, 23, 901 (1939).
— 'Some clinical observations in cases of anorexia nervosa', *Proc. Staff Meet. Mayo Clin.*, 18, 81 (1943).
— 'Anorexia nervosa: the diagnosis and treatment of inanition resulting from functional disorders', *Ann. Int. Med.*, 22, 679 (1945).
— 'Anorexia nervosa, anterior pituitary insufficiency, Simmonds' cachexia and Sheehan's disease', *Postgrad. Med.*, 3, 237 (1948).
— 'A concept of starvation oedema', *Proc. Staff Meet. Mayo Clin.*, 25, 265 (1950).
Berkman, J. M., Owen, C. A. and Magath, T. B., 'Physiological aspects of anorexia nervosa', *Postgrad. Med.*, 12, 407 (1952).
Berkman, J. M., Weir, J. F. and Kepler, E. J., 'Clinical observations on starvation oedema, serum protein and the effect of forced feeding in anorexia nervosa', *Gastroenterology*, 9, 357 (1947).
Berlin, I. N., Boatman, M. J., Sheimo, S. L. and Szurek, S. A., 'Adolescent alternation of anorexia and obesity', *Am. J. Orthopsychiat.*, 21, 387 (1951).
Berman, L., 'The treatment of a type of malnutrition (Simmonds' disease-like) with prepituitary growth hormone', *New York Med. J.*, 35, 916 (1935).
Bernstein, I. C., 'Anorexia nervosa treated successfully with electroshock therapy and subsequently followed by pregnancy', *Am. J. Psychiat.*, 120, 1023 (1964).
Bernstein, L. M. and Grossman, M. I., 'Medical nutrition laboratory', *U.S. Army*, Report no. 165 (1955).
Bertalanffy, L. von, *General System Theory* (New York: Braziller 1968).
Bhattacharya, S. and Sen, P. C., 'Post-mortem studies of starvation cases', *Ann. Med.*, 5, 117 (1945).
Bibring, E., 'The mechanism of depression', in *Affective Disorders*, ed. P. Greenacre (New York: International Universities Press 1953).
Bickel, G., 'La maigreur d'origine hypophysaire', *Gaz. méd France*, 15, 535 (1934).
— 'L'insuffisance antéhypophysaire', *Presse méd.*, 44, 1204 (1936).

Biema, H. R. van, Koek, H. C. and Schreuder, J. T. R., 'Hysteric anorexia resembling Simmonds' disease: case', *Nederl. tijschr. geneesk.*, 85, 58 (1941).

Billiottet, J. and Goasguen, P., 'Guérison rapide d'une anorexie mentale par la déconnexion', *Bull. et mém. soc. méd. hôp.* 70, 571 (1954).

Binswanger, H., 'Psychiatrische Aspekte zur Anorexie mentale (Pubertätsmagersucht)', *Z. Kinderpsychiat.*, 19, 141 and 173 (1952).

— 'The case of Ellen West', in *Existence*, R. May *et al.* (New York: Basic Books 1959).

Birley, J. L., 'Anorexia nervosa: a clinical lecture', *St Thomas's Rep.*, 34, 204 (1933).

Birnie, C. R., 'Anorexia nervosa treated by hypnosis in outpatient practice', *Lancet*, 2, 1331 (1936).

— 'Anorexia nervosa and its treatment', *Med. Press Circular*, 207, 360 (1942).

Bittorf, A. von, 'Die Beziehungen schwerer nervöser Dyspepien zur Tuberkulose', *München med. Wschr.*, 790 (1929).

Bleuler, M., *Endokrinologische Psychiatrie* (Stuttgart: Thieme 1954).

Blinder, B. J., Stunkard, A. J. *et al.*, 'Behaviour therapy of anorexia nervosa: effectiveness of activity as a reinforcer of weight gain', paper presented at the 124th Annual Meeting of the American Psychiatric Association (Boston May 1968).

Bliss, E. L., and Migeon, C., 'Endocrinology of anorexia nervosa', *J. Clin. Endocrinol.*, 17, 766 (1957).

Bliss, E. L. and Branch, C. H., 'Anorexia nervosa', *Monograph.* (New York: Hoeber 1960).

Blitzer, J. R., Rollins, N. and Blackwell, A., 'Psychosomatic medicine', 23, 369 (1961).

Boenheim, F. and Heymann, F., 'Beitrag zur Klinik der hypophysären Kachexie', *Dtsch. med. Wschr.*, 56, 18 (1930).

Bom, F., 'Simmonssche Krankheit (endogene Magersucht) bei einem Paar eineiiger Zwillinge', *Nord. med.*, 8, 2506 (1940).

Bond, D. D., 'Anorexia nervosa', *Rocky Mountain Med. J.*, 46, 1012 (1949).

Boss, M., *Introduction à la médicine psychosomatique* (Paris: PUF 1955).

Boutonnier, J. and Lebovici, S., 'Le facteur psychique dans l'anorexie mentale', *Ann. méd. psychol.*, 56, 91 (1938).

— 'Rôle de la mère dans la génèse de l'anorexie mentale', *Cah. psychiat.*, 3 (1948).

Bowlby, J., 'Soins maternels et santé mentale', *Organ. Mond Santé*, (Geneva 1951).

Bouveret, L., *Traité des maladies de l'éstomac* (Paris: Ballière 1893). p. 655.

Brissaud, E. and Souques, A., 'Délire de maigreur chez une hystérique', *Nouvelle Iconographie de la Salpêtrière*, 7, 327 (1894).

Brody, S., *Passivity* (New York: International Universities Press 1964).

Broser, F. and Gottwald, W., 'Symptomatische Psychosen bei Magersucht', *Nervenarzt*, 25, 10 (1955).

Brosin, H. W., 'Anorexia nervosa; case report', *J, Clin. Endocrinol.*, 1, 269 (1941).

— 'Symposium of obesity: psychology of overeating including reference to case of alternating anorexia and obesity', *New England J. Med.*, 248, 974 (1953).

Brosin, H. W., and Appleback C. 'Anorexia nervosa; case report with autopsy findings', *J. Clin. Endocrinol.*, 1, 272 (1941).

Brougher, J. C., 'Pituitary cachexia – report of a patient treated with anterior pituitary extract', *Endocrinology*, 17, 128 (1933).

Brown, W. L., 'Anorexia nervosa', *Lancet*, 1, 864 (1931).

Brown, W. L. and Crookshank, F. G., 'Anorexia nervosa', *Med. Press Circular*, 131, 308 (1931).

Brown, W. L., Crookshank, F. G., Young, J. C., Gordon, G. and Bevan-Brown, C. M., 'Anorexia nervosa', in *Individual Psychological Publications* (London: C. W. Daniel 1931).

Brozek, J., Wells, S. and Keys, A., 'Medical aspects of semistarvation in Leningrad (*Siege 1941–42*)', *Am. Rev. Soviet Med.*, 4, 70 (1946).

Bruch, H., 'Psychological aspects of reducing', *Psychosom. Med.* 14, 337 (1952).

— 'Role of the emotions in hunger and appetite', *Ann. New York Acad. Sc.*, ed. Roy Woldo Miner, 'The regulation of hunger and appetite', 63, 68 (1955).

— 'Weight disturbances and schizophrenic development', *Congress report of II International Congress for Psychiatry* vol II (Zurich 1957)

— 'Conceptual confusion in eating disorders', *J. Nerv. & Ment. Dis.*, 133, 46 (1961).

— 'Transformation of oral impulses in eating disorders', *Psychiat. Quart.*, 35, 458 (1961).

— 'Perceptual and conceptual disturbances in Anorexia nervosa', *Psych. Med.*, 24, 187 (1962).

— 'Treatment of Anorexia Nervosa', in *Current Psychiatric Therapy* (New York: Grune and Stratton 1962).

— 'Effectiveness in psychotherapy of the constructive use of ignorance', *Psychiat. Quart.*, 37, 322 (1963).

Bruch, H., 'The psychiatric differential diagnosis of Anorexia nervosa', in *Anorexia Nervosa*, eds. J. E. Meyer and H. Feldman (Stuttgart: Thieme 1965).
— 'Hunger and instinct', *J. Nerv. & Ment. Dis.*, 149, 91 (1969).
— 'The insignificant difference: discordant incidence of anorexia nervosa in monozygotic twins', *Am. J. Psychiat.*, 126, 85 (1969).
— 'Family background in eating disorders', in *The Child in his Family*, eds E. J. Anthony and C. Koupernik (New York: John Wiley & Sons 1970).
— 'Anorexia nervosa in the male', *Psychosom. Med.*, 33, 31–47 (1971).
— *Activity in the psychotherapeutic process* (printing).
Bruckner, W. L., Wiess, C. H. and Lavietes, P. H., 'Anorexia nervosa and pituitary cachexia', *Am. J. Med. Sc.*, 196, 663 (1938).
Brügger, M., 'Fresstrieb als hypothalamisches Symptom', *Helv. physiol. Pharmacol. Acta*, 1, 183 (1943).
Brull, L., 'Syndromes pseudo-hypophysaires', *Rev. méd.*, 5, 433 (1950).
Brull, L. and Divry, A., *Dénutrition, Tyroide et Metabolism – les États de Carence en Belgique pendant l'occupation allemande, 1940–1944* (Paris: Hermann 1945), pp. 107–9.
Buber, M., *Between Man and Man* (London: Routledge and Kegan Paul 1947).
Budge, E. A. W. (ed.), 'The Paradise or Garden of the Holy Fathers, Being Histories of the Anchorites, Recluses, Monks, Coenobites and Ascetic Fathers of the Deserts of Egypt Between A.D. CCL and CCCC Circiter, Compiled by Athanasius Archbishop of Alexandria', in *Palladius Bishop of Helenopolis, Saint Jerome and Others* (London: Chatto & Windus 1907).
Burger, G. C. E., Drummond, J. C. and Sandstead, H. R., *Malnutrition and Starvation in Western Netherlands* (The Hague: General State Printing Office 1948).
Buvat, J. B., 'L'anorexie psychasthénique', *Gaz. hôp.*, 78, 639 (1905).
Byrne, C. H. C., 'Enlargement of the adrenal in starvation', *Brit. Med. J.*, 2, 135 (1919).

Cade, A. and Ravault, P., 'Anorexie mentale simulant un cancer et terminée par la morte', *J. méd. Lyon*, 134, 43 (1924).
Cahane, M., 'Le rôle du metabolisme du chlore dans l'anorexie et la sitiophobie de certains malades', *Ann. méd. psychol.*, 2, 798 (1936).
Calder, R. M., 'Anterior pituitary insufficiency (Simmonds' disease),' *Bull. Johns Hopk. Hosp.*, 50, 87 (1932).
Cameron, A. T. and Carmichael, J., 'The effect of acute starvation on the body organs of the adult white rat, with special reference to the adrenal glands', *Canad. J. Res. Sect. E.*, 24, 37 (1946).

Cannon, W. B., 'The movements of the stomach studied by means of the Röntgen rays', *Am. J. Physiol.*, 1, 38 (1898).
— *The wisdom of the body* (New York: Norton 1932).
Cannon, W. B. and Washburn, 'Alimentary peristalsis', *Am. J. Physiol.*, 29, 144 (1902).
— *Bodily Changes in Pain, Hunger, Fear and Rage* (Boston: Branford 1929).
Cany, 'Note sur un cas grave d'anorexie mentale amélioré à La Bourboule. Gain de 30 kilos en six mois', *J. méd. Bordeaax*, 109, 524 (1932).
Carmody, J. T. B. and Vibber, F. L., 'Anorexia nervosa treated by prefrontal lobotomy', *Ann. Int. Med.*, 36, 647 (1952).
Cargnello, D., 'Fenomenologia del corpo', *Ann. di fren. e Sc. aff.*, 77, 4 (1964).
Carnot, P. and Libert, E., 'Le goute à goute duodénal dans l'anorexie mentale et les vomissements incoercibles', *Paris méd.*, 43, 276 (1922).
Carr, J. W., 'Case of anorexia nervosa', *Mag. London Royal Free Hosp. Sch. Med. Women*, 14, 153 (1919).
Carrier, J., 'L'anorexie mentale – Trouble instinctivo-affectif', thesis (Lyon 1939).
Carophylis, G., 'Complexus symptomatique constitué par de l'aphagie (refus de manger), alalie (refus de parler) et astasie-abasie, guéri par la suggestion forcée', *Progr. méd.*, 16, 241 (1892).
Catel, W., 'Das Simmondssche Syndrom in Kindesalter', *Mschr. Kinderheilk*, 84, 36 (1940).
Cathala, J., 'Anorexia of young children', *Nourrison*, 37, 65 (1949).
Caujolle, F., Mans, J. and Meynier, D., 'Le molybdate de magnésium dans les anorexies psychiques', *Toulouse méd.*, 53, 341 (1952).
Cervera, L., Folch, A. and Begnaignes, B., 'Considerations sur un cas de maladie de Simmonds', *Rev. franc. d'endocrinol.*, 1, 15 (1934).
— 'Cachexie hypophysaire et anorexie mentale', *Rev. franc. d'endocrinol.*, 15, 291 (1937).
Chaffey, 'A case of anorexia nervosa', *Soc. Study Dis. Child.*, 3, 257 (1902).
Chaptal, J. and Loubatières, 'Anorexie mentale passagèrement améliorée par un extrait frais de lobe antérieure d'hypophyse', *Ann. med. psychol.*, 51, 479 (1943).
Charcot, J. M., 'De l'isolement dans le traitement de l'hystérie', *Progr. méd.*, 1, 161 (1885).
Chatagnon, P. and Scherrer, P., 'L'anorexie mentale et son traitment d'urgence', *Presse méd.*, 47, 1277 (1939).

Christy, N. P., Wallace, E. Z. and Jailer, J. W., 'The effect of intra-venously-administered ACTH on plasma 17, 21-dihydroxy-20-ketosteroids in normal individuals and in patients with disorders of the adrenal cortex', *J. Clin. Invest.*, 34, 899 (1955).

Cioffri, A., 'Contributi recenti in tema de anoressia mentale', *La Medic. internaz.*, 9, 241 (1957).

Cioffari, A. and Ninni, M., 'L'anoressia mentale', *Minerva Medica* (1951).

Clancy, J. and Norris, A., 'Differentiating variables: obsessive compulsive neurosis and anorexia nervosa', *Am. J. Psychiat.*, 118, 58 (1961).

Clow, F. E. 'Anorexia nervosa', *New England J. Med.*, 207, 613 (1932).

Cobb, S., *Emotions and Clinical Medicine* (New York: Norton 1950).

Codet, O., 'À propos de trois cas d'anorexie mentale', *Rev. franc. psychoanal.*, 12, 81 (1948).

Collins, W. J., 'Anorexia nervosa', *Lancet*, 1, 202 (1894).

Cololian, P., 'L'anorexie soi-disant mentale', *Paris méd.*, 39, 389 (1949).

Comby, J., 'Anorexie nerveuse', *Arch. méd. enf.*, 11, 562 (1908).

— 'Anorexie nerveuse', *Arch. méd. enf.*, 12, 926 (1909).

— 'Anorexie nerveuse chez les nourrisons', *Arch. méd. enf.*, 15, 697 (1912).

— 'Anorexie enfantile et juvenile', *Presse méd.*, 1, 40 (1927).

— 'L'anorexie mentale chez les enfants et les adolescents', *Bull. et mém. soc. méd. hôp.*, 62, 1754 (1938).

— 'Maladie de Simmonds et anorexie mentale', *Arch. méd. enf.*, 41, 638 (1938).

Conrad, A., 'The attitude toward food', *Am. J. Orthopsychiat.*, 7, 360 (1937).

Conybeare, J. J., 'A fatal case of anorexia nervosa', *Guy's Hosp. Rep.*, 80, 30 (1930).

Cornil, P. and Schachter, 'La querelle de l'anorexie mentale', *Encéphale*, 2, 371 (1939).

Coulonjou and Hecaen, 'Anorexie mentale. Guérison. Influence incontestable des extraits de lobe antérieur d'hypophyse', *Encéphale*, 34, 46 (1939).

Courbon, P. and Rodepierre, 'Anorexie émotionnelle révélatrice de démence précoce en régression', *Bull. soc. clin. méd. ment.*, 17, 12 (1929).

Courchier, J. L., 'Étude analytique d'un cas d'anorexie mentale grave', *Evolution psychiatrique*, 1, 43 (1947).

Covan, M. R., 'Physiology of appetite', *Rivista de l'Asociation medica argentina*, 66, 335 (1952).

Cremerius, J., 'Zur Prognose der Anorexie Nervosa (13 fünfzehn bis achtzehäjnhrige Katamnesen psychotherapeutisch unbehandelter Fälle)' *Archiv für Psychiatric und Zeitschrift für das gesamte. Neurologie,* 207, 378, 393 (1965).

Cremieux, A., 'Les anorexies mentales', *Compte-rendus du Congrès des Aliénistes et Neurologistes de langue française Montpellier, 1942* (Paris: Masson 1942).

Cremieux A. and Dongier, M., 'Observations statistiques sur les familles où survient une anorexie mentale', *Ann. méd. psychol.,* 1, 639 (1956).

Crespi, F., 'Evoluzione della famiglia ed etica sessuale nella società di domani', *Futuribili,* 20–1, 107–15 (1970).

Crisp, A. H. and Toms, D., 'Primary anorexia nervosa, or a weight phobia in the male: report of 13 cases', *Brit. Med. J.,* 1, 334–7 (1972).

Crisp, A. H., 'Clinical and therapeutic aspects of anorexia nervosa. A study of thirty cases', *J. Psychom. Res.,* 9, 67 (1965).

— 'Some aspects of the evolution, presentation and follow-up of Anorexia Nervosa', *Proc. Roy. Soc. Med.,* 58, 814 (1965).

— 'Anorexia Nervosa in an identical twin', *Postgrad. Med. J.,* 42, 86 (1966).

— 'A treatment regime for Anorexia Nervosa', *Brit. J. Psychiat.,* 112, 505 (1966).

— 'Anorexia Nervosa', *Hospital Medicine* 713 (May 1967).

Cross, E. S., 'Diagnosis and treatment of anorexia nervosa', *M. Clin. North Am.,* 23, 541 (1939).

Curschmann, H., 'Über postpartuale Magersucht', *Mschr. Geburtsh. Gynäk.,* 86, 252 (1930).

— 'Über hypophysäre Kachexie', *München med. Wschr.,* 86, 317 (1939).

— in Matthes and Curschmann, H. *Differentialdiagnose innerer Krankheiten,* 13th edition (Berlin, Göttingen and Heidelberg: Springer 1950). p. 684.

Dalla Volta, *et al.,* 'Precoce sviluppo mammario pilifero associato a disturbi psicogeni in un caso di anoressia', *Minerva pediatrica* (1953).

Dally, P., 'Anorexia nervosa: treatment and follow up', Lecture at Third World Congress of Psychiatry (Montreal 1961).

— *Anorexia Nervosa* (London: W. Heinemann Med. Books 1969).

Dally, P. and Sargant, W., 'A new treatment of anorexia nervosa', *Brit. Med. J.,* 1, 1770–3 (1960).

Damm, G. and Horst-Meyer, H. zur, 'Über die Behandlung mit

Hypophysentransplantation', *Dtsch. med. Wschr.*, 76, 267 (1950).

D'Angelo, S. A., 'The effect of acute starvation on the thyrotrophic hormone level in the blood of rat and mouse', *Endocrinology*, 48, 341 (1951).

D'Angelo, S. A., Gordon, A. S. and Charipper, H. A., 'The effect of inanition on the anterior pituitary-adrenocortical interrelationship in the guinea pig', *Endocrinology*, 42, 399 (1948).

Davis, H. P., 'Anorexia nervosa', *Endocrinology*, 25, 991 (1939).

De Beauvoir, S., *Mémoires d'une jeune fille rangée* (Paris: Gallimard 1958); English translation: *Memoirs of a dutiful daughter*, (London: Penguin Books, 1963).

Debré, R., Mozziconacci, P. and Doumic, A., 'Étude psycho-somatique de l'anorexie nerveuse', *Semaine hôp.*, 26, 455 (1950).

Decandia, S., *Magrezze e adiposità patologiche e loro cura* (Florence: Vallecchi 1946).

De Caro, 'Sindrome diencefalo ipofisaria grave in due cugine: una affetta da schizofrenia con anoressia e fobia, l'altra da psiconevrosi ossessiva', *Attualità medica* (1953).

Declos, 'Anorexia mentale', *Arch. Pediat.* (1953).

Decourt, J., 'À propos des aménorrhées d'origine psychique – les aménorrhées pithiatiques, curables par la persuasion', *Presse méd.*, 52, 116 (1944).

— 'Anorexie mentale et cachexie dite hypophysaire (reflexion tirées de 13 observations)', *Paris méd.*, 23, 249 (1946).

— 'Nosologie de l'anorexie mentale', *Presse méd.*, 59, 797 (1951).

— 'L'anorexie mentale-cachexie psycho-endocrinienne de l'adolescence', Strasbourg médical (1954). p. 233.

— 'L'anorexie mentale au temps de Laségue et de Gull', *Presse Méd.* (1954) p. 355.

— 'La anorexia nervosa', *Rev. méd. cubana*, 67, 165 (1956).

Decourt, J., Grullaumin, C. O., Brault, A. and Verliac, F., 'Étude biologique de trois cas d'annorexie mentale (à propos de cette affection avec la cachexie dite hypophysaire)', *Ann. endocrinol.*, 5, 69 (1944).

Decourt, J., Jayle, M. F., Lavergne, G. H. and Michard, J. P., 'L'aménorrhée des anorexies mentales, notions clinques; étude biologique et biochimique', *Ann. endocrinol.*, 11, 571 (1950).

Decourt, J. and Michard, J., 'Les aménorrhées psychogènes', *Semaine hôp.*, 25, 3352 (1949).

— 'Les rapports de l'annorexie mentale et de la maladie de Simmonds: aperçu historique et position actuelle du problème', *Semaine hôp.*, 25, 3343 (1949).

— 'L'aménorrhée des anorexies mentales. Étude de 32 observations.

Données cliniques, biologiques et biochimiques', *Bull. et mém. Soc. med. hôp.*, 66, 1608 (1950).

Déjérine, J., *Séméiologie des affections du système nerveux* (Paris, 1921), p. 140.

Déjérine, J. and Gauckler, E., 'La réeducation des faux gastropathies', *Presse méd.*, 16, 225 (1908).

— *Les manifestations fonctionnelles des psychonévroses, leur traitement par la psychothérapie* (Paris: Masson 1911).

— *The Psychoneuroses and Their Treatment by Psychotherapy* (Philadelphia: J. B. Lippincott Co. 1913). p. 2.

Delay, J., 'La narco-analyse d'une anorexie mentale', *Presse méd.*, 57, 577 (1949).

Deniau, L., 'De l'hystérie gastrique', thesis (Paris 1883).

Destruelles, Masson-Chiarli, A., Gardien-Jourd'heuil, P. and Gardien, P., 'Le chlorure de sodium en solution hypertonique par voie veineuse dans les anorexies des aliénés', *Ann. méd. psychol.* 93, 446 (1936).

Deutsch, F., 'The associative anamnesis', *Psychoanal. Quart.*, 8, 354 (1939).

— 'The choice of organ in organ neuroses', Int. J. Psycho-Anal. 20, 252 (1939).

— 'Discussão de casos clinicos. Caso n. 20. Anorexia mental e diabete', *Arq. bras. med.*, (1953), 12, p. 384.

Donnadieu, M. J. A., 'L'anorexie mentale', thesis (Bordeaux 1932.)

Dotti, F.,'Il problema diagnostico e terapeutico dell' anoressia nervosa e della malattia di Simmonds', *Gior. clin. med.*, 31, 1431 (1950).

Doumic, A., 'Psychosomatic study of nervous anorexia', *Semaine hôp.*, 26, 455 (1950).

— 'Therapy of nervous anorexia of children', *Semaine hôp.*, 26, 454 (1950).

Dowse, T. S., 'Anorexia nervosa', *Med. Press & Circulation*, 32, 95, 147 (1881).

— 'Anorexia nervosa', *Lancet*, 1, 827 (1881).

Drill, V. A. and Burrill, M. W., 'Effect of thiamine deficiency and controlled inanition on ovarian function', *Endocrinology*, 35, 187 (1944).

Drummond, D., 'Abstract', *Lancet*, 2, 987 (1895).

— 'A case of anorexia nervosa, Northumberland and Durham', *Med. J. Newcastle-upon-Tyne*, 4, 7 (1896).

Dupois, F. A., 'Compulsion neuroses with cachexia (Anorexia nervosa)', *Am. J. Psychiat.*, 106, 107 (1949).

Dupois, F. S. 'Anorexia nervosa. A re-evaluation of the problem', *J. Insurance Med.*, 5, 1 (1950).

Dubois, P., *The Psychic Treatment of Nervous Disorders* (New York: Funk & Wagnall 1907). p. 251.

Dupois, R., 'De l'anorexie mentale comme prodrome de la démence précoce', *Ann. méd. psychol.*, 10, 431 (1913).

Dührssen, A., 'Zum Problem der psychogenen Esstörung', *Psyche*, 4, 56 (1950).

Dunn, C. W., 'Report of a case of "Simmonds' disease" with recovery', *J. Nerv. & Ment. Dis.*, 83, 166 (1936).

— 'Anorexia nervosa', *Lancet*, 1, 723 (1937).

Durand, Ch., 'Psychogénèse et traitement de l'anorexie mentale', *Helv. med. Acta*, 22, 368 (1955).

Eaton, L and Meeks, L., 'Case reports. Simmonds' disease or anorexia nervosa', *Quart. Bull. Indiana M. Center*, 9, 60 (1947).

Ebbecke, U., 'Hunger, Durst Sättigung, Übelkeit, Ekel von der physischen und psychischen Seite betrachtet', *Acta neuroveg*, 10, 409 (1955).

Edge, A. M., 'A case of anorexia nervosa', *Lancet*, 1, 818 (1888).

Ehresing, R. H. and Weitzman, E. L., 'The mother–daughter relationship in anorexia nervosa', *Psychosom. Med.*, 32, 201 (1970).

Eissler, K. R., 'Some psychiatric aspects of anorexia nervosa', *Psycho. Rev.*, 30, 121 (1943).

Eitinger, L., 'Anorexia nervosa', *Nord. med.*, 45, 915 (1951).

Ehrhardt, K. and Kittel, Ch., 'Zur Behandlung hypophysärer Störungen durch Hypophysenimplantation', *Z. Klin. Med.*, 132, 245 (1937).

Elst, R. van der, 'L'anorexie nerveuse', *Presse méd.*, 1, 40 (1927).

Emanuel, R. W., 'Endocrine activity in anorexia nervosa', *J. Clin. Endocrinol.*, 16, 801 (1956).

Enright, J. I., 'War edema in Turkish prisoners of war', *Lancet*, 1, 314 (1920).

Escamilla, R. F., 'Anorexia nervosa or Simmonds' disease', *J. Nerv. & Ment. Dis.*, 99, 583 (1944).

— 'Pituitary insufficiency – characteristic clinical and autopsy findings in a patient with pituitary myxedema', *J. Clin. Endocrinol.*, 15, 492 (1955).

Escamilla, R. F. and Lisser, H., 'Simmonds' disease (hypophysial cachexia)', *Calif. & West. Med.*, 48, 343 (1938).

— 'Simmonds' disease. A clinical study with review of the literature; differentiation from anorexia nervosa by statistical analysis of 595 cases, 101 of which were proved pathologically', *J. Clin. Endocrinol.*, 2, 65 (1942).

Evans, J. C. G., 'Anorexia nervosa', *Lancet*, 1, 268 (1939).

Faber, K., 'Nervos anorexia', *Arch. Verdauungskr.*, 37, 17 (1926).

Fairbairn, W. R. D., *An object relation theory of the personality* (New York: Basic Books 1962).

Falta, W., *The Ductless Glandular Diseases* (Philadelphia: P. Blakistons 1915), p. 440.

— 'Die endogene Magerkeit (Magersucht)', in *Handbuch der Inneren Medizin*, 2nd edit., IV, 2 (Berlin: Springer 1927).

— 'Hypophysäre Krankheitsbilder', *Arch. inn. Med.*, 33, 277 (1940).

Farquharson, R. F., 'Anorexia nervosa', *Illinois Med. J.*, 80, 193 (1941).

— *Simmonds' Disease – Extreme Insufficiency of the Adrenohypophysis* (Springfield, Ill.: Charles C. Thomas 1950).

Farquharson, R. F., and Hyland, H., 'Anorexia nervosa: metabolic disorder of psychologic origin', *JAMA*, 111, 1085 (1938).

— 'Anorexia nervosa: the course of 15 patients treated from 20 to 30 years previously', *Canad. Med. Ass. J.*, 94, 411 (1966).

Federn, P., *Ich-psychologie und die Psychosen* (Bern: Huber 1956).

Fenichel, O., *Anorexia (1945). Collected Papers of O. Fenichel*, II (London: Routledge and Kegan Paul 1955).

Fère, M. D. and Girou, M., 'A propos du rôle pathogène de la stimulation, anorexic suite d'ârret volontaire de l'alimentation', *Rev. neurol.*, 13, 144 (1905).

Feuchtinger, O., 'Die diencephal-hypophysäre Fett-und-Magersucht', *Dtsch. Arch. klin. Med.*, 180, 377 (1942).

— 'Hypothalamus, vegetatives Nervensystem und innere Sekretion', *Arch. inn. Med.*, 36, 248 (1942).

— 'Konträre und paradoxe Reaktionen als Folge diencephal-hypophysärer Regulationsstörungen', *Nervenarzt*, 16, 428 (1943).

— *Fettsucht und Magersucht* (Stuttgart: Enke 1946).

Forchheimer, F., 'Anorexia nervosa in children', *Arch. Pediat.*, 24, 801 (1907).

Fornari, F., 'Problemi del primo sviluppo psichico', *Riv. di psicol.*, 54, 201 (1960).

Fowler, R., *The Case of the Welsh Fasting-Girl (Sarah Jacob)* (London: H. Renshaw 1871).

Franklin, J. C., Schiele, B. C., Brozek, J. and Keys, A., 'Observations on human behaviour in experimental semi-starvation and rehabilitation', *J. Clin. Psychol.*, 4, 28 (1948).

Frazier, S. H., Faubion, M. H., Griffin, M. E. and Johnson, A. M., 'A specific factor in symptom choice', *Proc. Staff Meet. Mayo Clin.* 30, 227 (1955).

Freud, A., *The Psychoanalytic Study of Infantile Feeding Distur-bances. The Psychoanalytic Study of the Child*, II (London: Imago 1946).

— *Adolescence. The Psychoanalytic Study of the Child*, XIII (London, Imago 1958).

— *Normality and Pathology in Childhood*, (New York: International Universities Press 1965).

Freud, S., *Collected Works*, I–XVII (London: Imago 1940, 1941, 1942, 1943, 1946, 1947, 1952).

— *An Autobiographical Study* (New York: Norton 1952).

— *Introductory Lectures on Psychoanalysis* (London: Hogarth Press 1963).

Friedlander, A., 'A case of anorexia nervosa in an infant', *Med. J. (St Louis)*, 13, 446 (1906).

Frisk, M. and Backstrom-Jarrinen, L., 'Anorexia Nervosa: a study on a boy', *Ann. Paediat*, 2, 98 (1965).

Frugoni, C., 'Sindrome cachettico-edemica da anoressia psichica', *Rassegna clin. scientifica*, 27, 259 (1951).

Fuchs, E., 'Verweigerte Nahrungsaufnahme', *Z. psychanal. Pädiat.*, 4, 128 (1930).

Galetti, P. M., and Labhart, A., 'Étude de la fonction thyroïdienne dans l'anorexia mentale', *Helv. med. Acta.*, 22, 536 (1955).

Gallavan, M. and Steegmann, A. T., 'Simmonds' disease (Anterior hypophysial insufficiency). Report of 2 cases with autopsy', *Arch. inn. Med.*, 59, 865 (1937).

Galván, J. M. G., 'Valoración sindrómica de la anorexia', *Rev. méd. latinoam.*, 15, 1576 (1930).

Gasne, G., 'Un cas d'anorexie hystérique', *Rev. neurol.*, 8, 574 (1900).

Gebsattel, V., 'Prolegomena einer medizinischen Anthropologie', *Jb. Psychol. Psychother. med. Anthropol.*, 7, 193 (1960).

Geldrich, I., 'Simmondssche Krankheit im Kindesalter', *Mschr. Kinderheilk.*, 80, 103 (1939).

Gendre, B., 'Les anorexies et leur traitement', *J. méd. int.*, 7, 12 (1903).

Gennes, L. de, 'Cachexie hypophysaire', *Bull. et mém. soc. méd. hôp.*, 60, 1519 (1936).

— 'Les anorexies mentales', *Gaz. méd. France*, 62, 1705 (1955).

Gennes, L. de, Delarue, G. and Rogé, E., 'Maladie de Simmonds. Étude anato-clinique', *Bull. et mém. soc. méd. hôp.*, 60, 387 (1936).

Georgi, F. and Levi, R., 'Pathophysiology and therapy of so-called pubertal thinness (Mental anorexia): problem of psychophysical correlations', *Nervenarzt*, 22, 365 (1951).

Gerö, G., 'An equivalent of depression: anorexia', in *Affective*

Disorders, ed. P. Greenacre (New York: International Universities Press 1953).

Giffin, M. E., Frazier, S. H., Robinson, D. B. and Johnson, A. M., 'The internist's role in successful treatment of anorexia nervosa', *Proc. Staff Meet. Mayo Clin.*, 32, 171 (1957).

Gilabert, F. Z., 'Anorexia mental', *Sem. Med. Española*, 751 (1941).

Gilles de la Tourette, *Traité clinique et thérapeutique de l'hystérie* 3 (Paris: Plon 1895) p. 246.

Gilles de la Tourette and Chatelineau, H., 'La nutrition dans l'hystérie', *Progr. méd.* (1890), p. 89.

Gillespie, R. D., 'Treatment of functional anorexia', *Lancet*, 1, 995 (1931).

Girou, J., 'Anorexie, suite d'arrêt volontaire de l'alimentation', *Rev. neurol.*, 13, 145 (1905).

Glado, J. B., *De Anorexia* (Lipsiae 1696).

Glatzel, H., 'Ernährungskrankheiten', in *Handbuch der Inneren Medizin*, VI/2 (Berlin, Göttingen, Heidelberg: Springer 1954).

— 'Ernährungs-Therapie', in *Handbuch der Inneren Medizin*, VI/2 Berlin, Hiedelberg, Göttingen: Springer 1954).

Glazebrook, A. J., Matas, J. and Prosen, H., 'Compulsive neuroses with cachexia', *Canad. Med. Ass. J.*, 75, 40 (1965).

Godard, P., 'Les diverses formes d'anorexie', *Schwiez. med. Wschr.*, 18, 1233 (1937).

Goiten, P. L., 'Potential prostitute: the role of anorexia in the defense against prostitution desires', *J. Crim. Psychopath.*, 3, 359 (1942).

Gomes, F. M., 'Constitutional factor in essential anorexia', *Pediatria e puericultura*, 19, 154 (1949).

Gordon, D., Horwitt, B. N. and Segaloff, A., 'Adrenal response to ACTH in various clinical conditions', *J. Clin. Endocrinol.*, 14, 297 (1954).

Gottesfeld, B. H. and Novaes, A. C., 'Narcoanalysis and subshock insulin in treatment of anorexia nervosa', *Digest Neurol. & Psychiat.* (Institute of Living), 13, 486 (1945).

Green, H. H., 'Perverted appetites', *Physiol Rev.*, 5, 336 (1925).

Greenblatt, R. B., Barfield, W. E. and Clark, S. L., 'The use of ACTH and cortisone in the treatment of anorexia nervosa', *JMA*, 40, 299 (1951).

Greenhow, 'Discussion', *Brit. Med. J.*, 2, 527 (1873).

Greenwald, H. M., 'Anorexia nervosa', *Am. Med.*, 23, 875 (1828).

Groen, J. J. and Feldman-Toledano, Z., 'Educative treatment of patients and parents in Anorexia Nervosa', *Brit. J. Psychiat.*, 112, 671 (1966).

Grossman, M. I., 'Integration of current views on the regulation of hunger and appetite', *Ann. New York Acad. Sc.*, ed. Roy Waldo Miner, 'The regulation of hunger and appetite', 63, 76 (1955).

Grote, L. R. and Meng, H., 'Über interne und psychotherapeutische Behandlung der endogenen Magersucht', *Schwiez. med. Wschr.*, 64, 137 (1934).

Guiora, A., 'Dysorexia, a psychopathological study of anorexia and bulimia', *Am. J., Psychiat.*, 124, 391 (1967).

Gull, W. W., 'The address in medicine delivered before the Annual Meeting of the British Medical Association at Oxford', *Lancet*, 2, 171 (1868).

— 'Anorexia hysterica (aspepsia hysterica)', *Brit. Med. J.*, 2, 527 (1873).

— 'Meeting of the Clinical Society', *M. Times &. Gaz.*, 2, 534 (1873).

— 'Anorexia nervosa (aspepsia hysterica, anorexia hysterica)', *Tr. Clin. Soc.*, 7, 22 (1874).

Guntrip, H., *Personality structure and human interaction* (New York: International Universities Press 1961).

Hagerdorn, H. C., 'Anorexia nervosa', *Acta med. scand.*, 151, 201 (1955).

Haley, J., 'The family of the schizophrenic: a model system', *J. Nerv. & Ment. Dis.*, 129, 357–74 (1959).

— *Strategies of psychotherapy* (New York: Grune & Stratton 1963).

— 'Toward a theory of pathological systems', in *Family Therapy and disturbed families* G. Zuk, and B. Nagy, J. Ed. Science and Behav. Books, Palo Alto, California (1967).

Haley, J., (ed.), *Changing family. A family therapy reader* (New York: Grune & Stratton 1971).

Halmi, K. A. and Rigas, C., 'Urinogenital malformations associated with anorexia nervosa', *Brit. J. Psychiat.*, 122, 79–81 (1973).

Hamburger, W. W., 'The occurrence and meaning of dreams of food and eating', *Psychosom. Med.*, 20, 1 (1958)

— 'Discussion of Dr Stunkard's Paper. Obesity and the denial of hunger', *Psychosom. Med.*, 21, 290 (1959).

Hammond, W. A., *Fasting Girls: Their Physiology and Pathology* (New York: Putnam 1879).

Hanot, V., 'Notice sur le professeur Lasèrgue', *Arch. gén. méd.* 2, 5 (1883)

Hansen, O. E., 'Behandling of anorexia nervosa', *Ugeskr. laeger.*, 118, 1368 (1956).

Harderus, J. R., *De anorexia* (Basillae 1703).

Harnick, J., 'The various developments undergone by narcissism in men and in women', *Int. J. Psychaonal.*, 5, 66 (1924).

Harris, G. W., 'Neutral Control of the pituitary gland', *Physiol. Rev.*, 28, 129 (1948).

Harris, I. D., 'Relation of resentment and anger to functional gastric complaints', *Psychosom. Med.*, 8, 211 (1946).

Hawkinson, J. F., 'Simmonds' disease (*pituitary cachexia*)', *JAMA*, 105, 20 (1935).

Hebb, D. C., *Organization of behaviour* (New York: Wiley 1949).

Heilmeyer, L., 'Hungerschäden', *Med. Klin.*, 41, 243 (1946).

Helwig-Larsen, P., Hoffmeyer, H., Keeler, J., Thaysen, E. H., Thaysen, J. H., Thygensen, P. and Wulff, M. H., 'Famine disease in German concentration camps, complications and sequels', *Acta. med. scand.*, 274 (1952).

Heni, F., 'Primary psychogenic thinness (anorexia nervosa) and its therapy', *Endocrinology*, 28 (1951).

Hermann, K., 'Neuere Erfahrungen mit der Simmondsschen Krankheit', *München med. Wschr.*, 81–2, 1460 (1934).

Hertz, H., 'Nervous anorexia', *Acta med. scand.*, 266, 523 (1952).

Heydt-Gutscher, D., 'Psychotherapie einer Magersuchtigen', *Z. Psychosom. Med.*, 6, 77, 185 (1960).

Hiltmann, H. and Clauser, G., 'Psychodiagnostik und aktivanalytische Psychotherapie', *Praxis der Psychoth.*, 6, 168 (1961).

Hirschmann, I., 'Indistinktmechanismen im menschlichen Nahrungsverhalten', *Stud. Generale*, 7, 285 (1954).

Hirschmann, Y., 'Pathologischer Appetenzwandel', *Arch. für Psych. und Nervenkrankheiten* (1924), p. 369.

Hofe, F. H., von, 'Diet in the treatment of anorexia', *J. Med. Soc.*, 34, 87 (1937).

Hollander, F. *et al.*, 'The regulation of hunger and appetite', *Ann. New York Acad. Sc.*, 63, 1 (1955).

Horney, K., *La personalité névrotique de notre temps* (Paris: L'Arche 1953).

Hultgren, H. N., 'Clinical and laboratory observations in severe starvation', *Stanford Med. Bull.* 9, 175 (1951).

Hutinel, P., 'L'anorexie mentale', *Rev. gén. clin. et thér.*, 23, 358 (1909).

Inches, R. R. 'Anorexia Nervosa', *Maritime Med. News*, 7, 73, (1895).

Janet, P., *Les obsessions et la psychasthénie*, 2nd edit. (Paris: Alcan 1908).

Jaspers, K., *Wesen und Kritik der Psychotherapie* (Munich: Piper 1955).
Jersild, T., 'Simmonds' syndrome', *Nord. med.*, 20, 1789 (1943).
Jochmus, I., 'Anorexia Nervosa in two male adolescents', *Prax Kinderpsychol.*, 16, 1 (1967).
Jores, A., 'Die Anorexia nervosa als endokrinologisches Problem', *Biblioteca pediatrica supplementa ad annales pediatrici*, 58, 206 (1954).
— 'Krankheiten der Hypophyse und des Hypophysenzwischenhirn-systems', in *Handbuch der Inneren Medizin*, VII/1 (Berlin, Göttingen, Heidelberg: Springer 1955).
Jourdan, H. A., Wieland, W. F., Zelbley, S. P., Steller, E. and Stunkard, A., 'Direct Measurement of food intake in man: a method for the objective study of eating behaviour', *Psychosom. Med.*, 28, 836 (1966).

Kamal, S., 'L'Anorexie mentale', thesis (Lyon 1911).
Katz, D., *Hunger und Appetite* (Leipzig: Barth 1932).
— 'Zur Grundlegung einer Bedürfnispsychologie', *Acta Psychol.*, 1, 122 (1935).
Katzenstein-Sutro, E., 'Über einem Fall von Pubertätsmagersucht', *Schweiz. med. Wschr.*, 83, 1526 (1953).
Kaufman, M. R. and Heiman, M. E., *Evolution of psychosomatic concepts. Anorexia Nervosa: a paradigm*. International Universities Press (New York: 1964).
Kay, D. W. K., 'Anorexia nervosa: A study in prognosis', *Proc. Roy. Soc. Med.*, 46, 669 (1953).
Kay, D. W. K., and Leigh, D., 'The natural history, treatment and prognosis of anorexia nervosa based on a study of 38 patients', *J. Ment. Sc.*, 100, 411 (1954).
Kay, D. W. K., Shapira, K. and Brandon, S., 'Early factors in anorexia nervosa compared with non-anorexia groups', *J. Psychosom. Res.*, 11, 133 (1967).
Kelley, K., Daniels, G. E., Poe, J., Easser, R. and Monroe, R., 'Psychological correlations with secondary amenorrhea', *Psychosom. Med.*, 16, 129 (1954).
Keys, A., Brosek, J., Henschel, A., Mickelsen, A. and Taylor, H. L., *The Biology of Human Starvation* (Minneapolis: University of Minnesota Press 1950).
Kind, H., 'Psicopatologia dell'insufficienza del lobo anteriore', *Rec. Progr. in Medicina*, 24, 443 (1958).
King, A., 'Primary and Secondary Anorexia Nervosa Syndromes', *Brit. J. Psychiat.*, 109, 470 (1963).

Kissel, M., 'Cas d'anorexie hystérique grave chez une fille de 11 ans', *Rev. neurol.*, 2, 575 (1894).

Klein, M., 'A contribution to the Psychogenesis of Maniac-depressive States', I (1934), in *Contributions to Psychoanalysis 1921–1945* (London: Hogarth 1950).

Klotz, H. P., Baller, C. and Laval, I., 'Un cas d'anorexie mentale chez une jumelle homozygote', *Acta Psychother. et Psychosom.*, 10, 76 (1962).

Klotz, H. P. and Lumbroso, P., 'Remarques cliniques pathogéniques et thérapeutiques sur l'anorexie mentale: la notion d'abiorexie', *Semaine hôp.*, 31, 440 (1955).

Knipping, H. W., 'Über die Entstehung der Magersucht', *Dtsch. med. Wschr.*, 61, 1075 (1935).

Koehler, H., 'Über Kriegsamenorrhoe', *Zentralbl. Gynäk.*, 43, 359 (1919).

Köhler, A., 'Psychische Faktoren bei Gewichtsverschiebungen', *Z. Psychosom. Med.*, 3, 109 (1957).

Koller, Th., 'Pübertätsmagersucht', *Geburtsh. u. Frauenheilk.*, 14, 668 (1954).

Korbsch, R., 'Zum Krankheitsbild der Magenschleimhautatrophie', *Dtsch. med. Wschr.*, 60–1, 356 (1934).

— 'Die Magersucht im Gefolge der akuten Magenschleimhautatrophie junger Mädchen, als eigenes Krankheitsbild', *Dtsch. med. Wschr.*, 62, 1948 (1937).

Kornmannus, J. J., *De Anorexia* (Altorfii 1685).

Krauel, G., 'Zur Behandlung der Simmonsschen Kachexie mit Transplantation von Kalbshypophysen', *Med. Welt.*, 16, 999 (1942).

Krause, F, and Müller, O. H., 'Über schwere Hypophysenvorderlappen-Insuffizienz und ihre Behandlung', *Klin. Wschr.*, 16, 118 (1937).

Kubie, L. S., 'The central representation of the symbolic process in psychosomatic disorders', *Psychosom. Med.*, 15, 1 (1953).

Kuhn, R., 'Zur Daseinsanalyse der Anorexia mentalis', *Nervenarzt*, 22, 11 (1951).

— 'Zur Daseinsanalyse der Anorexia mentalis II. Studie', *Nervenarzt*, 24 191 (1953).

Kundstadter, R. H., 'Pituitary emaciation (von Bergmann)', *Endocrinology*, 22, 605 (1938).

Kunz, H., *Die Bedeutung der Daseinsanalytik Martin Heideggers für die Psychologie und philosophische Anthropologie. Martin Heideggers Einfluss auf die Wissenschaft* (Bern: Francke 1949).

Kylin, E., 'Die Simmondssche Krankheit', *Ergn. inn Med.*, 49, 1 (1935).

Kylin, E., 'Magersucht in der weiblichen Spätpubertät', *Dtsch. klin. Med.*, (1937), pp. 115–80.
— *Die Klinik der hypophysären Erkrankungen* (Leipzig: Barth 1943).

Labbe, L. A., 'L'anorexie: données récentes sur sa pathologie', *Acta neurol. et psychiatr. belg.*, 52, 165 (1952).
Labbe, L. A. and Stevenin, H., 'Le metabolisme basal dans l'alimentation insuffisante', *Presse méd.*, 1, 401 (1925).
Labiche, A., 'Contribution à l'étude de l'anorexie mentale', thesis (Paris 1934).
Laboucarié, J. and Barres, P., 'Les aspects cliniques, pathogéniques et thérapeutiques de l'anorexie mentale', *Evolut. psychiat.*, 1, 119 (1954).
Lafon, R., Billet, M. and Billet, B., 'Anorexie essentielle des jeunes filles et encephalophatie atrophiante', *Ann. méd. psychol.*, 108, 248 (1950).
Lafora, G. R., 'La anorexie psicogenética de las mujeres adolescentes', *Neurobiol.*, 7, 121 (1927).
Laing, R. D. and Esterson, A., *Sanity, madness and the family* (New York: Basic Books 1964).
Lakin, C. E., 'Anorexia', *Transaction of the Medical Society of London*, 66, 213 (1951).
Langdon-Brown, W., 'Anorexia nervosa', *Lancet*, 1, 473 (1937).
Lasègue, E. C., 'On hysterical anorexia', *Med. Tms. Gaz.*, 2, 265 (1873).
— 'De l'anorexie hystérique', *Arch. gén. méd.*, 21, 385 (1873).
Launay, C., 'Anorexie mentale des grandes enfants et des adolescents', *Gaz. Méd. France*, 62, 177 (1955).
Lebond, S. and Butas, N., 'Maigreur neurohypophysaire', *Laval méd.*, 18, 1360 (1953).
Leede, S., 'Anorexie nervosa: hypoglycemia or hypodrenia', *Northwest Med.*, 27, 233 (1928).
Lehmann, E., 'Feeding Problems of Psychogenic Origin: A Survey of the Literature', in *The Psychoanalytic Study of the Child*, 3–4 (New York: International Universities Press).
Lehmann, C. E., *De Anorexia* (Ludg. Bat. 1710).
Leichtentritt, B., 'Pubertätsneurose, Hungerzustand und Niereninsuffizienz', *Med. Klin.*, 11, 355 (1932).
Lemieux, R. and Martel, A., 'Maigreur par anorexie mentale', *Laval méd.*, 11, 471 (1946).
Leonard, C. E., 'Analysis of a case of functional vomiting and bulimia', *Psychoanal. Rev.*, 31, 1 (1944).

Lerman, J. and Stebbins, H. D., 'The pituitary type of myxedema', *JAMA*, 119, 391 (1942).

Lesser, L. C. *et al.*, 'Anorexia nervosa in children', *Am. J. Orthopsychiat.*, 30, 572 (1960).

Lévi, L., 'Anorexie mentale et corps tyroide', *Encéphale*, 17, 507 (1922).

Lévi, M., 'Contributo all conoscenza dell'anoressia', *Riv. pat. e nerv.*, 70, 292 (1949).

— 'Mental anorexia', *Riv. di pat. nerv. e ment.*, 62, 297 (1949).

Lexton, D. L., 'Diagnosis and treatment of anorexia nervosa', *Ann. West. Med. and Surg.*, 397 (1950).

Leyton, G. B., 'Effects of slow starvation', *Lancet* 2, 73 (1946).

Lidz, T., *The Family and Human Adaptation* (New York: International Universities Press 1963).

Lingen, C., 'Case of voluntary starvation: death on the tenth day', *Brit. Med. J.*, 1, 384 (1870).

Linn, L., 'Psychoanalytic contribution to psychosomatic research', *Psychosom. Med.*, 20, 88 (1958).

Lipscombe, F. M., 'Medical aspects of Belsen concentration camp', *Lancet*, 2, 312 (1945).

Lloyd, J. H., 'Hysterical tremor and hysterical anorexia (anorexia nervosa) of a severe type', *Am. J. Med. Sc.*, 106, 264 (1893).

Loeb, L., 'The clinical course of Anorexia Nervosa', *Psychosom. Med.*, 5, 345 (1964).

Loeper, M. and Fau, R., 'Cachexie hypophysaire et anorexie mentale', *Monde méd.*, 46, 921 (1936).

Loeper, M. and Sainton, J. B., 'Le diagnostic de la cachexie hypophysaire. Anorexie mentale et insuffisance gladulaire par inanition', *Progr. méd.*, 1409 (1937).

Loeser, A. A., 'Emotional shock on hormone release and endometrial development', *Lancet*, 1, 518 (1943).

Löffler W., 'Die anorexia nervosa', *Helv. med. Acta*, 22, 351, (1955).

Loo, P., 'L'anorexia mentale', *Ann. méd. psychol.*, 116, II, 734 (1958).

Lopfen, M. W., 'L'anorexie mentale', *Ann. méd. psychol.*, 2, 2 (1955).

Lorand, S., 'Anorexia nervosa. Report of a case', *Psychosom. Med.*, 5, 282 (1943).

Lövey, E. and Bona, E., 'Anorexia nervosa', *Ztschr. ges. inn. med.*, 12, 749 (1957).

Low, M. B., 'Anorexia in children', *New England J. Med.*, 214, 834 (1936).

Lublin, A., 'Lipogene und antilipogene Hormonwirkungen als Ursache endogener Fettsucht und Magersucht', *Klin. Wschr.*, 2276 (1929).

Lucke, H., 'Hypophysäre Magersucht und Insulin', *Klin Wschr.*, 1988 (1932).

Luft, R. and Spogren, B., 'Disturbed electrolyte metabolism in two cases of nervous anorexia', *Acta endocrinol.*, 17, 264 (1954).

Lukas, H., 'Therapie einer Magersüchtigen', *Z. Psychoter. med. Psychol.*, 6, 159 (1956).

Lurie, O. R., 'Psychological factors associated with eating difficulties in children', *Am. J. Orthopsychiat.*, 11, 452 (1941).

Lurmont, H., 'Les diverses formes de l'anorexie nerveuse: leur diagnostic', *Médecine*, 1, 603 (1920).

Lutz. J., 'Kombination einer Neurose bei Pubertätmagersucht mit katatonieartigem Zustandsbild', *Z. Kinderpsychiat.*, 14, 68 (1947–8).

— 'Die Frage der psychischen Faktorehn bei der Pubertätsmagersucht', *Z. Kinderpsychiat.*, 17, 51 (1950–1).

Lyon, G., 'Les anorexies et leur traitement', *Bull. méd.*, 41, 39, (1927).

Macculloch, J. A., 'Fasting (Introductory and non-Christian)', in *Encyclopedia of Religion and Ethics*, ed. J. Hastings, 5 (New York; Scribner, 1912), p. 759.

Mach, R. S. and Durand, Ch., 'Anorexie mentale, troubles digestifs et Acth', *Praxis*, 41, 1038 (1952).

Maclean, P. D., 'Psychosomatic disease and the visceral brain. Recent development bearing on the Papez theory of emotion', *Psychosom. Med.*, 11, 338 (1949).

Maddock, W. O. and Heller, G. G., 'Dichotomy between hypophysial content and amount of circulating gonadotrophins during starvation', *Proc. Soc. Exper. Biol. & Med.*, 66, 595 (1947).

Magendatz, H. and Proger, S., 'Anorexia nervosa or hypopituitarism', *JAMA*, 114, 1973 (1940).

Malmstrom, G., 'Anorexia nervosa', *Excerpta Med. Neurol. & Psychiat.*, 2, 469 (1949).

Mamou, H., 'La maigreur d'origine cérébro-hypophysaire', *J. méd. chir. prat.*, 105, 26 (1934).

Marshall, C. F., 'A fatal case of anorexia nervosa', *Lancet*, 1, 149 (1895).

Mark, H., 'Die hypophysäre Kachexie (Morbus Simmonds)' in *Handbuch der Inneren Medizin*, Vol VI/1 (Berlin, Göttingen, Heidelberg: Springer 1941).

Masserman, J. H., 'Psychodynamisms in anorexia nervosa and neurotic vomiting', *Psychoanal. Quart.*, 10, 211 (1941).

Matthews, R. A. and O'Brien, W. R., 'Psychosomatic approach to gynecological problems', *M. Clin. North America*, 32, 1583 (1948).

May, E. and Robert, P., 'La cachexie hypophysaire ou syndrome de Simmonds', *Ann. Med.*, 38, 317 (1935).

May, R., Angel, E. and Ellenbergen, H. F., *Existence* (New York: Basic Books 1959).

Mayer, A., 'Zur Psychologie der weiblichen Pubertätsmagersucht: die Pubertätsmagersucht als "Schicksalskrankheit"', *Med. Klin.*, 52, 2185 (1957).

Mayer, J., 'Overweight and obesity', *Atlantic Monthly*, 196, 69 (1955).

Mccullagh, E. P. and Tupper, W. R., 'Anorexia nervosa', *Ann. Int. Med.*, 14, 817 (1940).

Mead, M., *Male and Female*, (London: Gollancz 1950).

Means, J. H., Hertz, S. and Lerman, J., 'The pituitary type of myxedema or Simmonds' disease masquerading as myxedema', *Tr. A. Am. Physicians*, 55, 32 (1940).

Meignant, P., 'Anorexie mentale guérie par narcoanalyse', *Rev. méd. Nancy*, 73, 180 (1948).

Membrives, J. R., 'Tratamiento de la anorexia mental con corticotrofina', *Prensa med. argent.*, 38, 3407 (1951).

Meng, H., 'Das Problem der Organ-Psychose', *Inter. Z. artzl. Psychoanal.*, 20, 439 (1934).

— 'Organische Erkrankung als Organ-Psychose', *Schweiz Arch. Neurol. Psychiat.*, 26, 271 (1935).

Menninger, K. A., 'Somatic correlations with the unconscious repudiation of femininity in women', *J. Nerv. Ment. Dis.*, 89, 514 (1939).

Meyer, B. C., and Weinroth, L. A., 'Observations on psychological aspects of anorexia nervosa', *Psychosom. Med.*, 19, 389 (1957).

Meyer, H. H., 'Über Magersucht', *Dtsch. med. Wschr.*, 64, 1400 (1938).

Meyer, J. E., *Die Entfremdungserlebnisse* (Stuttgart: Thieme 1959).

— 'Das Syndrom der Anorexia nervosa, Katamnestische Untersuchungen', *Arch. für Psych. und Neur.*, 202, 31–59 (1961).

— 'Anorexia nervosa of adolescence. The central syndrome of the Anorexia nervosa group', *Brit. J. Psychiat.*, 118, 539 (1971).

Meyer, J. E., Feldmann, H. (eds.) *Anorexia nervosa. Symposium on 21–5 April 1965 in Göttingen* (Stuttgart: Thieme 1965).

Meyer, W. C., 'Untersuchungen und Beobachtungen an Fällen von hypophysärer Magersucht (Simmonds) und deren Behandlung, insbesondere durch Hypophysenimplantation', *Dtsch. Arch. klin. Med.*, 182, 351 (1938).

Meyler, L., 'Simmonds' disease (Hypophysary Emaciation)', *Acta med. scand.*, 96, 157 (1938).

Meyres, A. W., 'Some morphological effects of prolonged inanition', *J. Med. Res.*, 36, 51 (1917).

Michaux, L. and Georges-Janet, L., 'Un facteur d'anorexie mentale des adolescents, la répudiation des soucis matériels, affermation d'intellectualisme pur', *Presse méd.*, 64, 181 (1956).

M'Ilvaine, G., *De Anorexia* (Edinburgh 1770).

Miner, R. W., ed., 'The regulation of hunger and appetite', *Ann. New York Acad. Sc.*, 63, 1 (1955).

Minuchin, S., 'The use of an ecological framework in the treatment of a child', in *The Child in his Family*, eds. J. Anthony and C. Koupernik (New York: Wiley 1970).

— 'Treatment of a case of Anorexia nervosa', *IV Int. Congress of Child Psych.* (Jerusalem 3–7 August 1970).

Mollaret, P. and Péron, N., 'Anorexia mentale à forme grave. Nécessité vitale de la cure d'alimentation', *Bull. et mém. soc. méd. hôp.*, 62, 1716 (1938).

Möller, E., 'Quantitative Verhältnisse des Stoffwechsels bei Unternährung, illustriert durch 4 Fälle von nervoser Anorexia', *Klin. Wschr.*, 3, 1575 (1924).

Morgulis, S., *Fasting and Undernutrition: A Biological and Sociological Study of Inanition* (New York: Dutton 1932).

Morlock, C. G., 'Anorexia nervosa', *Proc. Staff Meet. Mayo Clin.*, 14, 24, (1939).

Morton, R., *Phthisiologia – or a Treatise of Consumptions* (London; Smith & Walford 1694).

Moschowitz, E., 'Anorexia Nervosa', in *Robert T. Frank Annual Volume* (St Louis: 1937), p. 359.

Moura, C. de, 'Anorexia hysterica', *Rev. med. Saõ Paulo*, 7, 513 (1904).

Mullahy, P., in Sullivan, H. S., *Conception of Modern Psychiatry* (New York: Norton 1953), pp. 242–3.

Müller, H., 'Pubertätsmagersucht der jungen Mädchen', *Med. Klin.*, 51, 209 (1956).

Myers, J. M., 'Mental anorexia simulating pituitary cachexia', *Southwestern Med.*, 23, 367 (1939).

Nathan, M., 'Les anorexies mentales de l'adolescence et de l'âge adulte', *Presse méd.*, 34, 390 (1926).

— 'Une forme tardive d'anorexie mentale', *Presse méd.*, 36, 1603 (1928).

— 'Quelques considérations sur l'anorexie mentale', *Rev. gén. clin. et thér.*, 45, 838 (1931).

Naudeau, J., 'Observations sur une maladie nerveuse accompagnée d'un degoût extraordinaire pour les aliments', *J. méd. chir. et pharmacol.*, 80, 197 (1789).

Nemiah, J. C., 'Anorexia nervosa', a clinical psychiatric study, *Medicine*, 29, 225 (1950).

— 'Anorexia nervosa: Fact and theory', *Am. J. Digest Dis.*, 3, 249 (1958).

Neyroud, M., 'L'anorexie de l' enfant et la médicine psychoso-matique', *Praxis*, 43, 47, 1954; *Z. Kinderpsychiat.*, 23, 158 (1956).

Nicole, G., 'A prepsychotic anorexia', *Lancet*, 2, 1173 (1938).

Nicholson, R., 'Simmonds' disease', *Lancet*, 1, 951 (1936).

Niles, G. M., 'Anorexia', *Southern Med. J.*, *, 376 (1908).

Nobêcourt, P., 'L'anorexie mentale ou psychique', *Pediat. prat.*, 33, 11 (1935).

Nogues, G., 'L'anorexie mentale: ses rapports avec la psycho-physiologie de la faim', thesis (Toulouse 1913).

Novelianskaya, K. A., 'A form of prolonged pathological reaction in puberty (anorexia nervosa in adolescents)', *Zh. Nevropat., I. Psikkiat.*, 18, 861 (1958).

Oberdisse, K., 'Die Fettsucht und die Magersucht', *Medizinische Kongressberichte*, 1959 (1835).

Odlum, D., 'Discussion', *Lancet*, 2, 1173 (1938).

Ogle, J. W., 'A case of hysteria: "Temper-Disease', hysterical (?) congestion of the lungs and persistent vomiting', *Brit. Med. J.*, 2, 57 (1870).

Oppenheimer, B. S., 'Simmonds' disease versus anorexia nervosa: a report of a case with necropsy findings', *J. Mt Sinai Hosp.*, 10, 640 (1944).

Osgood, E. E., 'Pituitary cachexia', *Endocrinology*, 23, 656 (1938).

Osler, W., *Practice of Medicine* (New York: Appleton 1893), p. 973.

— 'The phthisiologia of Richard Morton', *Med. Lib. & Hist. J.*, 2, 1 (1904).

— *The Evolution of Modern Medicine* (New Haven: Yale University Press 1921).

Ottonello, P., 'Contributo alla delimitazione clinica della anoressia mentale', *Riv. pat. nerv.*, 50, 353 (1937).

Pagniez, P., 'Anorexie mentale et hypophyse', *Presse méd.*, 47, 668 (1939).

Paingault, M., 'Maladie de Simmonds (Discussion des Rapports entre la Cachexie hypophysaire et l'Anorexie mentale)', thesis (Paris 1937).

Palmer, G. B., 'Three cases of so-called anorexia nervosa', *New Zealand Med. J.*, 50, 57 (1951)

Palmer, H. A., 'Beriberi complicating anorexia nervosa', *Lancet*, 1, 269 (1939).

Palmer, H. D. and Jones, M. S., 'Anorexia nervosa as a manifestation of compulsion neurosis: a study of psychogenic factors', *Arch. Neurol. & Psychiat.*, 41, 856 (1939).

Palmer, J. O., Mensh, I. O. and Matarazzo, J. S., 'Anorexia nervosa: Case history and psychological examination data with implications for test validity', *J. Clin. Psychol*, 8, 168, (1952).

Pardee, I. H., 'Cachexia nervosa: A psychoneurotic Simmonds' syndrome', *Arch. Neurol. & Psychiat'*, 41, 841 (1939).

— 'Cachexia (anorexia) nervosa', *M. Clin. North Am.*, 25, 755 (1941).

Parker, H. L., 'Anorexia nervosa', *Irish J. Med. Sc.*, 175, 289 (1940).

Patterson, S. W., 'Anorexia Nervosa', *Lancet*, 1, 1009 (1940).

Peltz, H. D., 'Kritisches zur Pubertätsmagersucht', *Ärtzle, Wschr.*, 11, 781 (1956)

Pernet, J., 'Anorexie mentale', *Rev. méd.*, 43, 412 (1926).

Péron, N., 'Quelques considérations sur le traitement des anorexies mentales', *Bull, gén. thér.*, 187, 390 (1936).

— 'Defense de l'anorexie mentale', *Paris méd.*, 2, 65 (1938).

Pflanz, M., 'Soziolanthropologische Aspekte der Anorexia nervosa', in *Anorexia Nervosa*, eds. J. E. Meyer and H. Feldman (*op,cit.*).

Pinna, L., *La Famiglia Esclusiva* (Bari: Laterza 1971).

Playfair, W. S., 'Note on the so-called anorexia nervosa', *Lancet*, 1, 817 (1888).

Plumier, L., 'Un cas d'anorexia mentale', *Rev. méd.*, 3, 73 (1948).

Poix, G., 'Anorexie mentale', *Rev. neurol.*, 23, 515 (1912).

Pope, C., 'Discussion', *West Lond. Med. J.*, 9, 204 (1904).

Porot, A., *Manuel alphabétique de psychiatrie clinique, thérapeutique et médicolégale*, (Paris: PUF 1952).

Porot, M., 'Le test de Rorschach dans l'anorexie mentale', *Algérie-méd.*, 50, 60 (1947).

Puech, A., Combier, C., Pages, A. and Mimran, R., 'Cachexie psychogéne avec pseudo-alteration du champ visuel: échec du traitement par l'ACHT – effet remarquable de l'insulina-therapie', *Montpellier Médical*, 44, 130 (1953).

Querido, A., 'De pathophysiologie van anorexia nervosa', *Nederl. tijdschr. geneesk.*, 92, 660 (1948).

Rahman, L., Richardson, H. B. and Ripley, H. S., 'Anorexia

nervosa with psychiatric observations', *Psychosom. Med.*, 1, 335 (1939).

Raimbault, A., 'Le syndrome anorexie mentale: Ètude sémiologique et prognostique', thesis (Paris 1914).

Rank, B., Putnam, M. C. and Rochlin, G., 'The significance of the "Emotional Climate" in early feeding difficulties', *Psychosom. Med.*, 10, 279 (1948).

Raymond, F., 'Anorexie hystérique', *J. méd. interne*, 6, 194 (1902).

— 'Anorexie hystérique et anorexie mentale', *J. méd. interne*. 6, 166 (1902).

— 'Anorexie hystèrique', *J. méd. chir. prat.*, 76, 646 (1905).

Raymond, F. and Rougean, M., 'Anorexie mentale et hypophyse', *Ann. méd. psychol.*, 95, 634 (1937).

Reforzo Membrives, J., 'Therapy of mental anorexia by means of adrenocorticotropic hormone', *Prensa med. argent.*, 38, 3407 (1951).

Regester, R. P. and Cuttle, T. D., 'Cachexia hypophyseopriva (Simmonds' disease)', *Endocrinology*, 21, 558 (1937).

Reifenstein, E. C., Jr., 'Psychogenic or "hypothalamic" amenorrhea', *M. Clin. North Am.*, 30, 1103 (1946).

Reiss, M., 'Unusual pituitary activity in case of anorexia nervosa', *J. Ment. Sc.*, 89, 270 (1943).

Repetto, R., Ianni, J. and Benzecry, I., 'Caquexia nervioso y enfermedad de Simmonds', *Arq. Clin.*, 2, 267 (1946).

Reye, E., 'Das klinische Bild der Simmondsschen Krankheit (Hypophysäre Kachexie) in ihrem Anfangsstadium und ihre Behandlung', *München med. Wschr.*, 73, 902 (1926).

— 'Die ersten klinischen Symptome bei Schwund des Hypophysenvorderlappens (Simmondsschen Krankheit) und ihre erfolgreiche Behandlung', *Dtsch. med. Wschr.*, 54, 696 (1928).

Richardson, H. B., 'Simmonds' disease and anorexia nervosa', *Tr. A. Am. Physicians*, 52, 141 (1937).

Richet, C., 'Jusqu'où, dans l'état nerveux hystérique, peut aller la privation d'aliments', *Rev. neurol.*, 5, 613 (1897).

Rist, 'Observation d'anorexie idiopathique', *Bull. Soc. méd. Suisse Rom.*, 12, 59 (1878).

Robinson, T., 'Sudden death in a case of hysterical vomiting', *Lancet*, 1, 1380 (1893).

Roch, M. and Monnier, M., 'Anorexie mentale', *Rev. méd. Suisse Rom.*, 61, 321 (1941).

— 'Anorexia mentalis und Simmondssche Krankheit', *Schweiz. med. Wschr.*, 71 1009 (1941).

Rohmer, M. P. and Jung, F., 'Un cas d'anorexie mentale, simulant la maladie de Simmonds', *Bull. Soc. ped.*, 36, 524 (1938).

Roith, A. I., 'Extreme sensitivity to insulin', *Brit. Med. J.*, 1, 1306 (1954).

Rolla, E. H. and Grinberg, L., 'Anorexia nervosa y claustrofobia', *Rev. Psicoanal.*, 13, 468 (1956).

Rolland, C. F., 'Anorexia nervosa', *Proc. Nutrition Soc.*, 12, 153 (1953).

Rosair, H. B., 'A case of prolonged hunger strike', *Indian M. Gaz.*, 71, 529 (1936).

Rose, J. A., 'Eating inhibitions in children in relation to anorexia nervosa', *Psychosom. Med.*, 5, 117 (1943).

Rosencher, H., 'Medicine in Dachau', *Brit. Med. J.*, 2, 953 (1946).

Ross, C. W., 'Anorexia nervosa with special reference to the carbohydrate metabolism', *Lancet*, 1, 1041 (1938).

Rossier, P. H., Staehelin, D., Bühlmann, A. and Labhart, A., 'Alkalose und Hypokaliämie bei Anorexia nervosa ("Hunger-Alkalose")', *Schweiz. med. Wschr.*, 85, 456 (1955).

Rossini, R., 'Brevi considerazioni in tema di patogenesi e di inquadramento nosografico dell'anoressia mentale', *Riv. per. fren.*, 83, 1 (1959).

Roudepierre, M., 'Anorexia mentale grave – guérison clinique par un coma insulinique accidental', *Ann. med. psychol.*, 99, 313 (1941).

Rougean, R., and Rougean, M., 'Anorexia mentale et hypophyse', *Ann. méd. psychol.*, 95, 634 (1937).

Rouquier, A. and Michel, J., 'Anorexia pithiatique élective', *Encéphale*, 29, 277 (1934).

Rubbens, T. and Wallez, F., 'Le traitement de la sitiophobia par la Nc-Cl hypertonique et le scopochloralose', *J. belg. neurol. et psychiat.*, 38, 39 (1938).

Rudolfer, N., 'Un caso de anorexia nerviosa', *Rev. psicoanal.*, 13, 491 (1956).

Rüegg, M., 'Zum psychischen Bild der Pubertätsmagersucht', *Diss.*, (1950).

Russell, C. F. M., 'Metabolic aspects of Anorexia nervosa', *Proc. Roy. Soc. Med.*, 58, 811 (1965).

— 'The nutritional disorder in Anorexia nervosa', *J. Psychosom. Res.*, 11, 141 (1967).

Ryle, J. A., 'Anorexia Nervosa', *Lancet*, 2, 893 (1936).

— *The Natural History of Disease* (London: Oxford University Press 1936), p. 127.

— 'Discussion on anorexia nervosa', *Proc. Roy. Soc. Med.*, 32, 735 (1939).

Salter, H., 'Hysterical vomiting', *Lancet*, 2, 1 and 37 (1868).
Sbarigia, C., 'Anoressia mentale e morbo di Simmonds', *Brevia ITR*, 6, 187 (1953).
Schacther, M., 'Une fausse anorexie mentale chez un garçon de onze ans', *Ann. neuropsychiat. et psychoanal.*, 2, 232 (1955).
Schermann, J., 'Anorexia mental e sindrome de Simmonds', *Arq. Clin.*, 4, 99 (1947).
— 'Anorexie mental e diabete', *Arq. brasil. med.*, 43, 384 (1953).
Scheunert, G., 'Zum Problem der Gegenübertragung', *Psyche*, 13, 574 (1959–60).
Schiele, B. C. and Brozk, J., ' "Experimental neuroses" resulting from semistarvation', *Man. Psychosom. Med.*, 10, 33 (1948).
Schilder, P. and Wechsler, D., 'What do children know about the interior of the body?', *Int. J. Psycho-Anal.*, 16, 355 (1935).
— *The Image and Appearance of the Human Body* (New York: International Universities Press 1950).
Schilling, F., *Selbstbeobachtungen im Hungerzustand*, 'Beiträge aus der allgemeinen Medizin', VI (Stuttgart: Enke 1948).
Schneider, R., 'Störungen der Ernährungstriebe', *Schweiz. Arch. Neurol. Psychiat.*, 58, 315 (1947).
— 'Ichstörungen und -entfremdungen', *Fortschr. Neurol. Psychiat.*, 16, 343 (1949).
Schnyder, M. L., 'Les anorexies de la puberté', *Presse méd.*, 1, 282 (1913).
Schreier, K., 'Adipositas in Kindesalter', *Dtsch. med. Wschr.*, 84, 1297 (1959).
Schüpbach, A., 'Zur Hormonbehandlung der Simmondsschen Krankheit und verwandter asthenischer Zustände', *Schweiz. med. Wschr.*, 17, 1245 (1936).
— 'Postpartuales Myödem und Simmonssche Krankheit', *Schweiz. med. Wschr.*, 81, 610 (1951).
Schur, M. and Medvel, C. V., 'Über Hypophysenvorderl appenin-suffizienz', *Arch. inn. Med.*, 31, 67 (1937).
Scott, W. C. M., 'Notes on the psychopathology of mental anorexia nervosa', *Brit. J. med. Psychol.*, 21, 241 (1947–8).
Scouras, P., 'Anorexie mentale d'origine complexuelle. Action combinée de l'électrochoc et de la narcoanalyse', *Encéphale*, 39, 545 (1950).
Seblond, S. and Butos, N., 'Maigreur neurohypophysaire', *Laval Med.*, 18–20, 1360 (1953).
Seemann, W. F., 'Über Hungerreaktionen von Kriegsgefangenen', *Psyche*, 4, 107 (1950–1).
Seligrus, V., *De anorexia* (Vitembergae 1706).

Selling, L. S. and Ferraro, M. A., *The Psychology of Diet and Nutrition* (New York: Norton 1945).

Seltmann, O., 'Anorexia cerebralis und centrale nutritionsheurosen', *Centralblatt*. 16, 227 (1895).

Selvini Palazzoli, M., 'Emaciation as magic means for the removal of anguish in anorexia mentalis', *Acta psychother*., 9, 37 (1961).

— 'Il viraggio degli aspetti contradditori dei fenomeni in psicoterapia', *Arch. psicol. Neur. Psich*., 22, 6 (1961).

— 'The meaning of the body for anorexic patients', 6th Int. Congress of Psychotherapy, London 1964, *Selected Lectures*, 98 (New York, Karger, Basel: 1965).

— 'Contesto e metacontesto nella psicoterapia della famiglia', *Arch. Psicol. Neurol. Psich*., 3, 203–11 (1970).

— 'The families of patients with Anorexia nervosa', in *The Child in his Family* eds. J. Anthony and C. Koupernik (New York: Wiley 1970).

— 'Racialism in the family', *The Human Context*, 3, 624 (1972).

Selvini Palazzoli, M. and Ferraresi, P., 'L'obséde et son conjoint', *Social Psych*., 7, 2 (1972).

Selye, H., *Textbook of Endocrinology*, Acta endocrinol. (University of Montreal 1947).

Sexton, D. L., 'The diagnosis and treatment of anorexia nervosa', *Ann. West. Med. & Surg*., 4, 397 (1950).

Shaw, M., 'Simmonds' disease (pituitary cachexia)', *Proc. Roy. Soc. Med*., 28, 1176 (1935).

Sheehan, H. L., 'Post-partum necrosis of the anterior pituitary', *J. Path & Bact*., 45, 189 (1937).

— 'Simmonds' disease due to post-partum necrosis of the anterior pituitary', *Quart. J. Med*., 8, 277 (1939).

— 'Nutritional state in Simmonds' disease', *Proc. Roy. Soc. Med*., 41, 187 (1948).

— 'Physiopathologie der Hypophyseninsuffizienz', *Helv. med. Acta*. 22, 324 (1955).

Sheehan, H. L. and Murdoch, R., 'Post-partum necrosis of the anterior pituitary: pathological and clinical aspects', *J. Obst. & Gynaec. Brit. Emp*., 54, 456 (1938).

Sheehan, H. L. and Summers, V. K., 'The syndrome of hypopituitarism', *Quart. J. Med*., 18, 319 (1937).

Sheldon, J. H., 'Anorexia nervosa with special reference to the physical constitution', *Lancet*, 1, 369 (1937).

— 'Discussion', *Proc. Roy. Soc. Med*., 32, 738 (1939).

Sheldon, J. H. and Young, F., 'On the carbohydrate metabolism in anorexia nervosa', *Lancet*, 1, 257 (1938).

Siebenmann, R. E., 'Über eine tödlich verlaufende Anorexia nervosa mit Hypokaliämie', *Schweiz. med. Wschr.*, 85, 468 (1955).

— 'Zur pathologischen Anatomie der Anorexia nervosa', *Schweiz. med. Wschr.*, 85, 530 (1955).

Sifneos, P. E., 'A case of anorexia nervosa treated successfully by leucotomy', *Am. J. Psychiat.*, 109, 356 (1952).

Silver, S., 'Simmonds' disease (Cachexia hypophyseopriva). Report of a case with postmortem observations and review of literature', *Arch. Int. Med.*, 51, 175 (1933).

Silverston, K. T. and Russell, C. F. M., 'Gastric hunger contractions in Anorexia nervosa', *Brit. J. Psychiat.*, 113, 257 (1967).

Simmonds, M., 'Über embolische Prozesse in der Hypophysis', *Arch. path. Anat.*, 217, 226 (1914).

— 'Über Hypophysisschwund mit tödlichem Ausgang', *Deuts. med. Wschr.*, 40, 322 (1914).

—'Über Kachexie hypophysären Ursprungs', *Dtsch. med. Wschr.*, 42, 190 (1916).

— 'Atrophie des Hypophysisvorderlappens und hypophysäre Kachexie', *Dtsch. med. Wschr.*, 44, 852 (1918).

Small, S. M. and Milhorat, A. T., 'Anorexia nervosa: Metabolism and its relation to psychopathologic reactions', *Am. J. Psychiat.*, 100, 681 (1944).

Smirnoff, V. N., 'Kritische Bemerkungen zum Problem der Anorexia mentalis', *Psyche*, 12, 430 (1958–9).

Smith, W. J., Powell, E. K. and Ross, S., 'Food aversion: some additional personalty correlates', *J. of Consulting Psychology*, 145 (1955).

Smitt, J. W., 'Anorexia nervosa complicated by beriberi', *Acta psychiat. neurol.*, 21, 887 (1946).

Sollier, P., 'Anorexie hystérique (sithiergie hystérique)', *Rev. méd.*, 11, 625 (1891).

— 'L'anorexie mentale', *J. méd.*, 23, 429 (1895).

— 'L'anorexie mentale', *Proc. Cong. Med. alienistes et Neurol.*, 2, 360 (1896).

— 'Les anorexies nerveuses', *J. belg. neurol.*, 15, 201 (1910).

Soltmann, O., 'Anorexia cerebralis und centrale Nutritionsneurose', *Jb. Kinderheilk.*, 38, 1 (1894).

Sommer, B., 'Übertragungsprobleme in der Behandlung der Pubertätsmagersucht', *Acta psychother.*, 3, 383 (1955).

— 'Die Pubertätsmagersucht als leib-seelische Störung einer Reifungskrise', *Psyche*, 9, 307 (1955–6).

Souques, A., 'Une cause provocatrice de l'anorexie mentale des jeunes filles', *Rev. neurol.*, 2, 562 (1925).

Sours, J. A., 'Clinical studies in anorexia nervosa syndrome', *New York Med. J.*, 68, 1963 (1968).

Spence, A. W., 'Anorexia nervosa', *St Barth. Hosp. J.*, 52, 129 (1948).

Spitz, R., *No and Yes* (International Universities Press 1957).

— *The First Year of Life* (New York: International Universities Press 1965).

Staehelin, D., Reber, K. and Bühlmann, A., 'Das Saure-Basen Gleichgewicht bei Anorexis mentalis und bei akutem Hungerzustand', *Helv. med. Acta*, 22, 530 (1955).

Staehelin, J. E., 'Über präschizophrene Somatosen', *Schweiz. med. Wschr.*, 73, 1213 (1943).

Staff Conference Vanderbilt University Hospital, 'Anorexia nervosa', *J. of the Tennessee State Medical Association*, 46, 330 (1953).

Staübli-Frölich, U. M., 'Probleme der anorexia nervosa', *Schweiz. med. Wschr.*, 83, 811 (1953).

Stefko, W., 'Les modifications des glandes à sécrétion interne à la suite d'une alimentation insuffisante chez l'homme', *Rev. franc. d'endocrin.*, 6, 103 (1928).

— 'Zur Pathologie der Inanition. Der Ernährungsfaktor im Kropfproblem', *Schweiz. med. Wschr.*, 61, 171 (1931).

Stein, J. and Fenigstein, H., 'Anatomie pathologique de la maladie de famine', in *Maladie de famine. Recherches cliniques sur la famine executées dans le Ghetto de Varsovie en 1942*, ed. E. Apfelbaum (Warsaw: Amercian Joint Distribution Committee 1946).

Steinberg, A., Schechter, F. R. and Segal, H. I., 'True pituitary Addison's disease – a pituitary unitropic deficiency (15 year follow-up)', *J. Clin. Endocrinol.*, 14, 1519 (1954).

Stephens, D. J., 'Anorexia nervosa: endocrine factors in undernutrition', *J. Clin. Endocrinol.*, 1, 257 (1941).

Stephens, D. J. and Allen, W. M., 'The effect of refeeding and of the administration of pituitary extract on ovaries of undernourished Guinea pig', *Endocrinology*, 28, 580 (1941).

Stephens, L., 'Case of anorexia nervosa, necropsy', *Lancet*, 1, 31 (1895).

Stevenin, H. and Gaube, R., 'Maladie de Simmonds et anorexie mentale', *Monde méd.*, 48, 489 (1938).

Stock, J. W., 'A case of pituitary cachexia', *Lancet*, 2, 349 (1930).

Stoer, E. E., 'L'anorexie mentale', thesis (Strasbourg 1932).

Stokvis, B. 'Organneurosen und Organpsychosen', *Schweiz. med. Wschr.*, 74, 943 (1944).

— 'Die "Organpsychose" (Meng) in ihrer Bedeutung für die psychosomatische Medizin', *Psyche*, 6, 228 (1952–3).

Straus, E. B., 'Anorexia nervosa', *St Barth. Hosp. J.*, 52, 116 (1948).

Striker, C., 'A case of Simmonds' disease (cachexia hypophyseo-priva) with recovery', *JAMA*, 101, 1994 (1933).

Stroebe, F., 'Die Simmondssche Krankheit', *Med. Klin.*, 32, 859 (1936).

Stunkard, A., 'Untoward reactions to weight reduction among certain obese persons', *Ann. of the New York Acad. Sc.*, ed. Roy Waldo Miner, 'The regulation of hunger and appetite', 63, 4 (1955).

— 'Obesity and the denial of hunger', *Psychosom. Med.*, 21, 281 (1959).

— 'Hunger and satiety', *Am. J. Psychiat.*, 118, 212 (1961).

Sullivan, H. S., *Clinical Studies in Psychiatry* (New York: Norton 1956).

— *The Interpersonal Theory of Psychiatry*, ed. H. S. Perry & M. L. Gawel (London: Tavistock 1956).

Sundermann, F. W. and Rose, E., 'Studies in serum electrolytes. XVI. Changes in the serum and body fluids in anorexia nervosa', *J. Clin. Endocrinol.*, 8, 209 (1948).

Sutherland, H. A., 'A case of chronic vomiting in which no food was taken, except koumiss, for sixteen months', *Tr. Clin. Soc.*, 14, 113 (1881).

Sydenham, A., 'Amenorrhoea at Stanley camp, Hong Kong, during internment', *Brit. Med. J.*, 159 (1946).

Sylvester, E., 'Analysis of psychogenic anorexia in a four year old', in *The Psychoanal. Study of the Child*, I (London: Imago 1945).

Szilasi, W., 'Die Erfahrungsgrundlage der Daseinsanalyse L. Bins-wangers', *Schweiz. Arch. Neurol. Psychiat.*, 67, 74 (1951).

Targowla, R. and Lamache, A., 'Le traitement par l'insuline des états d'anorexie de sitiophobie et de dénutrition dans les troubles psychonévropathiques', *Prat. Méd. France.*, 7, 452 (1926).

Tassart, J. C., 'Anorexia', *Rev. méd. latoniam.*, 13, 1350 (1928).

Taylor, S., 'A case of anorexia nervosa', *West London Med. J.*, 9, 110, 204 (1904).

Thaler Singer, M. and Whynne, L. C., 'Principles for scoring communication defects and deviances in parents of schizophrenics. Rorschach and T.A.T. scoring manuals', *Psychiatry*, 29, 260 (1966).

Thannhauser, S. J., 'Endogene Magerkeit', *Verh. dtsch. Ges. Verdau, u. Stoffwechselkr.*, 9, 96 (1929).

Theander, S., 'Anorexia nervosa', *Acta Psych. Scand. Suppl.*, 214 (1970).

Thiel, M., 'Die Distanzproblematik in der Philosophie', *Stud. Generale*, 4, 271 (1951).

— 'Philosophie und Psychotherapie', *Jb. Psychol. Psychother. med. Anthropol.*, 2, 297 (1954).

Thiemann, E., *Die Pubertätsmagersucht als überwiegend psychisch bedingte Erkrankung* (Stuttgart: Schattauer 1957).

Thomä, H., *Anorexia nervosa* (Stuttgart: Klett 1961).

Thorn, G. W., Forsham, P. H., Frawley, T. F., Hill, R. S., Roche, M., Staehelin, D. and Wilson, D. L., 'The clinical usefulness of ACTH and cortisone', *New England J. Med.*, 242, 783 (1950).

Tiemann, F., 'Das Krankheitsbid der Anorexia nervosa, seine Differentialdiagnose und Behandlung', *Med. Klin.*, 53, 328 (1958).

Titeca, R., 'Deux cas d'anorexie mentale chez des jeunes filles', *Scopel*, 89, 2130 (1936).

Tixier, L., 'L'anorexie des nourissons et son traitement', *Monde méd.*, 38, 769 (1928).

Tournier, C., 'Quelques cas de vomissements névrosiques', *Province méd. Lyon*, 11, 505 (1897).

Trefzer, C., 'Hungerstreik in Kindesalter', *Diss.* (1939).

Tronchetti, F. and Fiaschi, E., 'Dispepsia e anoressia nella magrezza giovanile', *Rass. Neur. veg.*, 3, 5 (1942).

Tucker, W. I., 'Lobotomy case histories: Ulcerative colitis and anorexia nervosa', *Lahey Clin. Bull.*, 7, 239 (1952).

Tyson, R. G., 'Anorexia nervosa – an unusual case study', *Permanent Found. Med. Bull.*, 10, 315 (1952).

Vague, J., Favier, G. and Torresani, J. L., 'Maigreur nerveuse chez le frère et la soeur', *Ann. endocrinol*, 18, 393 (1957).

Valabrègue, C., 'Libérer la femme c'est libérer l'homme', *Planning familial*, 2, 1–3 (1971).

Van Balen, G. F., 'Anorexia nervosa und hypophysäre Magerkeit', *Acta med. scand.*, 101, 433 (1939).

Van Der Vorm, J., *De Anorexia*, (Lugd. Bat. 1762).

Vaudet-Brun, 'Contribution à l'Étude de l'Anorexie nerveuse du Nourrisson', thesis (Paris 1921).

Venables, J. F., 'Anorexia nervosa. A study of the pathogenesis and treatment of nine cases', *Guy's Hosp. Rep.*, 80, 213 (1930).

Venning, E. H. and Browne, J. S. L., 'Excretion of glycogenic corticoids and of 17-ketosteroids in various endocrine and other disorders', *J. Clin. Endocrinol.*, 7, 79 (1947).

Index